The Last Yahi

The Last Yahi

A Novel about Ishi

A novel based on the last Stone Age Yahi who gave himself up
to civilization at a slaughterhouse in Oroville, California, on
August 29, 1911, and became known to the world as Ishi.

L. D. Holcomb

Writers Club Press
San Jose New York Lincoln Shanghai

The Last Yahi
A Novel about Ishi

All Rights Reserved © 2000 by Lawrence Donray Holcomb

Writers Club Press
an imprint of iUniverse.com, Inc.

For information address:
iUniverse.com, Inc.
620 North 48th Street, Suite 201
Lincoln, NE 68504-3467
www.iuniverse.com

Cover Painting by Ken Speer

ISBN: 0-595-12766-5

Printed in the United States of America

For my daughter
Holly Frances Holcomb
The stars sigh for her in their nightly splendor

Foreword

On August 29, 1911, the Stone Age came to a close on the North American continent when the last Stone Age man surrendered at a slaughterhouse in Oroville, California. We never learned his name, for no other member of his tribe was left to introduce him. His strong personal etiquette required that he should never state his name upon direct request. To ask him directly what his name was would have been impolite. However, he became known to the world as Ishi. At least two stories about how he received his name exist: the first being that the Yana word for man is *ishi*, so an anthropologist named him Ishi—and the second being that the sheriff of Oroville, California, upon hearing the clamorous questions of reporters, such as, "Who is he?", simply mimicked the last two words of the question, "…is he?", and, of course, in so replying told the reporters that the Indian's name was Ishi. I tend to believe the second story.

Likewise, we never learned the names of the other Yahi members of his tribe, who had died or had been killed. If Ishi had used their names, he would have been calling them back from their proper places in the spirit world to haunt the living, mainly himself. Furthermore, if Ishi had discussed the exact events of their day to day lives or how they had died, he would have brought back horrible memories. He discussed how the Yahi lived in general, but he discussed little about their deaths or what any individual actually did. The only specific name which Ishi used was Chunoyahi, who was not a Yahi but a displaced Atsugewi Indian living with the Yahi, and perhaps Chunoyahi was not his actual name but a label describing the type of Indian he was. Whatever the case may be, Chunoyahi had a stolen steel ax and consequently was readily able to make bow staves from cedar blocks, which split easily into the raw shapes of bows. He was apparently an excellent hunter and not one to accept the defeat of his entire tribe.

As a result, in my attempt to write a realistic, fictional account of Ishi's life in the wilderness, I used the names the names of Yana mythological First People, the Mapchemaina, as the names of characters. Ishi's new and "realistic" name is Yolaina, which means Bravest Person in Yana mythology. Yolaina's mother's name is Hitchinna, or Wildcat Woman, and Yolaina's father's name is Pul Miauna, or Colored Bow Man (or Rainbow Man). A name chart is included at the end of this introduction.

Ishi and his story offer us one of the last aesthetically pure glimpses of the Stone Age. If one takes the time to learn about his religious mythological views, one takes a large step toward understanding the evolution of ideas from the distant past to the immediate present. When the people of the Gold Rush in California began their war with the Yahi in 1850, they, of course, were after gold and land and new lives, and they, as a whole, were true believers in Manifest Destiny. Many did not care whose land they took, and many did not care whom they killed to get the land. They certainly did not care about what ideas they might learn from the Yahi. They were profoundly ignorant.

The notorious Neanderthal skull would not be discovered in a cave in the Neander Valley of Germany and brought to the attention of the scientific community until 1856. Charles Darwin would not publish *The Origin of the Species by Natural Selection; or, The Preservation of Favored Races in the Struggle for Life* until 1859. The Cro-Magnon site in the Vezere Valley of South Western France would not be discovered until 1868. In short, the concepts that people had inhabited the planet for hundreds of thousands of years; that people had evolved or changed over hundreds of thousands of years; that people had lived in various stages of the Stone Age for hundreds of thousands of years; and that modern ideas about justice, religion, morality, mores, and even science rested solidly on the backs of the Stone Age peoples were unknown to the settlers. They could not have justified their killing and stealing with such concepts; they firmly believed all primitive people were uncivilized savages. To many settlers, Indians deserved to be hated. After all, the settlers had the might that came with metal, with gunpowder, with steam engines, and with scientific and industrial revolutions. They had little understanding of how close many of their ideas and values were to a savage's ideas.

From Ishi's viewpoint, another world filled with innumerable First People, Mapchemaina, previously existed, but he now lived in that world. The First People had human forms and spirits, and they lived in complete harmony for what seemed to be endless time, but a few of them finally fell into conflict. Then a vast majority of them fell into conflict; as a result, most of them turned into various kinds of living creatures—both plants and animals—and into everything that we see on the earth or in the sky, except people. The small number of First People that still lived in harmony sailed westward beyond the line where the sky meets the earth or water. They remain there in the upper regions and will live there in perfect harmony forever. People who died and were properly buried went to live with the First People.

In Ishi's mythology, the resolution between two First People in conflict resulted in one saying to the other, "Here after you will be nothing but a_____," and the other might reply to the first one, "You will be nothing but a_____." On both sides a metamorphosis immediately took place. Thus, the reality of existence is explained in primary creation myths, and all of Ishi's institutions were patterned on the models of the First People, his divinities. Ishi knew how to act on a given occasion because his Gods had acted in certain ways under similar conditions in a previous world, and he felt an important need to communicate with the spirits of his divinities. His stories were extensive, full of interest, and rich in details. We can understand much about Ishi's politics, social life, and medicine by understanding his myths; they represent an unbroken and untainted progression of human thought from the distant past, from hundreds of thousands of years ago, and from the first beginnings of human intelligence. Ishi's myths, and others like them, represent our closest links to how people acted in the primeval world. Primitive people were not, under any circumstance, more brutal or cruel than modern people, and any form of human decency which one can conceive was modeled by the First People. Ishi's myths clearly show "…what took place at certain periods in the world of mind, in the interior of man." (Curtin xxxii) Ishi was not a wild savage; he was a decent human being.

Many people might fairly ask how the views of Ishi can be compared to their own modern religious beliefs. At first such a comparison, to them, seems ludicrous; however, in the beginning nothing existed but a god in human form. In Ishi's view, in the beginning countless gods existed in modern human form, but if one conceives of the angels, demons, and devil as the divinities of lesser importance to a modern religious person, the concepts are quite close. God created man by shaping clay; Jupka created people by placing buckeye sticks upon the ground. God created the heavens and the earth; gods created the heavens and the earth. God taught people the correct way to live; gods taught people the correct way to live. However, modern religions have less respect for nature and for women than Ishi's animism. An animist could not witness the wholesale destruction of forests and not be alarmed. An animist could not justify a child or woman having less than a man. When Ishi killed a deer, he did so with ritualistic reverence, and he did so to share fully with those he loved and knew. He lived according to the maxims of his religion.

I give credit here to Jeremiah Curtin for his book *Creation Myths of Primitive America in Relation to the Religious History and Mental Development of Mankind.* He recorded thirteen Southern Yana myths and interpreted their meanings in his introduction. To write *The Last Yahi,* I borrowed liberally from Curtin's ideas and hard work. I take credit for none of the essential ideas which I used to interpret Ishi's religion. I used several phrases from Curtin's foreword to help write this foreword, and I adapted Curtin's myths for direct use in my novel. To study Ishi's religion or mental state, one should read Jeremiah Curtin's wonderful book.

I must also give credit to Thomas T. Waterman for writing *The Yana Indians.* Mr. Waterman was the anthropologist from Berkeley who met Ishi when he was in the jail at Oroville. Mr. Waterman accurately laid out a chronological history of the conflict between the Yahi and the whites, and because of his work, I was able to structure my novel around real historical events. Since Ishi was not telling us about the specific events in his life, I relied on Waterman. Through Waterman I imagined what Ishi's life must have been like.

I wrote and rewrote *The Last Yahi* over a sixteen year period. I completed the first draft after I quit teaching for American River College and moved to live in the wilderness of upper Mill Creek. I wanted to feel Ishi's loneliness. I wanted to see the natural grandeur of Ishi's wilderness: the snow on the spires of the volcanic basalt, the rainbows arching over the river canyon, and the curious ring-tailed cat scampering away from a dying campfire. I made every attempt to make *The Last Yahi* as geographically accurate as possible—to make the reader aware of Ishi's world. On August 15, 1865, Hi Good, Henry Curtis, W. J. Segraves, and others attacked a group of Yahi at the base of Three Knolls. In the attack, at least according to Theodora Kroeber, Ishi's father was probably killed. I camped at the base of Three Knolls.

I invite the reader to step into my imagination—to imagine the death of the Stone Age.

Name Chart

Ahalamila.............................Gray Wolf Man

Bohkuina ....Silver-Gray Fox Man

Chikpina ....Weasel Woman; grandmother of Halai Auna; mother of Chuhna

Chikpitpa...........................Young Weasel Man

Chuhna...............................Spider Woman; Pul Miauna's second wife; mother of Halai Auna

Chunoyahi..........................Hat Creek Indian Man; displaced Atsugewi Indian who became a member of Yolaina's tribe; master bow maker

Dari Jowa...........................White-headed Eagle Man; Pul Miauna's brother; Igupa Topa's younger son; Yolaina's uncle

Demauna ....Pine Martin Man; displaced member of Black Rock Village; Pahnino's husband

Gowila................................Lizard Man

Halai Auna.........................Morning Star Woman; Chuhna's daughter; Hitchinna's adopted daughter; Yolaina's adopted sister

Hitchinna..........................Wildcat Woman; Pul Miauna's wife; Jupka's daughter; Yolaina's mother

Hwipajusi ....Whistling Swan Man

Ichpul...................................Frog Man; Frog Woman

Igupa Topa..............................Sweatlodge Man, son of Tuina or Sun
                                        Man; chief of Tcapalauna; father of Pul
                                        Miauna; grandfather of Yolaina

Ilhataina................................Lightning Man

Jihkulu ....Large Owl Woman; chief of Kaitsiki's
                                        village

Jupka ....Butterfly of the Wild Silkworm Woman;
                                        Hitchinna's mother; Yolaina's grandmother

Kaitsiki.................................Squirrel Woman

Kalchauna...............................Lizard Man

Ketipku ....Little Striped Skunk Woman

Lawalila.................................Hawk Man; Yolaina's adopted brother

Matdasi ....Spring Salmon Woman

Pahnino ....Ocean Shell Woman; Demauna's wife

Pakalai Jawichi.........................Water Lizard Man; Bohkuina's son;
                                        Topuna's adopted son

Periwiri Yupa ....Black Oak Acorn Woman; Hwipajusi's wife

Pul Miauna ....Colored Bow Man; Igupa Topa's oldest
                                        son; Dari Jowa's brother; Hitchinna's
                                        husband; Yolaina's father

Six Toes ....Chief of Black Rock Village

Sukonia ....Pine Martin Man

Topuna...................................Mountain Lion Man

Tsanunewa ....Wren Woman; Lawalila's wife; Periwiri
                                        Yupa's daughter; Hwipajusi's adopted
                                        daughter

Tsulwalkai ....Red Obsidian Man

Tuina....................................Sun Man

Ututni ....Wood Duck Man

Weanmauna.............................Hidden One; Hwipajusi's youngest adopted daughter
Wihlaina ....Chipmunk Woman; Dari Jowa's wife
Wirula....................................Red Fox Woman
Yolaina ....Bravest Man

CHAPTER 1

A Birth

Pul Miauna, son of Chief Igupa Topa, lay next to his wife Hitchinna. Heavy from carrying his child, she was awkward in all movements, but now she slept peacefully. As the sun shone through the door and silhouetted her beautiful, brown face against the tule mats and bearskin, Pul Miauna's heart grieved even in love. Watching his young bride, he could not get enough of her. Before she had become pregnant, during her blood times in the women's house, he had missed her. He would sit with the other men and boys in the sweathouse and discuss the horrible news of his slaughtered people, the Yahi, and the lost ones, the other Yana to the north whom the whites had conquered. Those Yana lived near or with the whites, accepted strange living habits, and did as the whites commanded. They chose to live without pride. Peace with the whites was impossible with raids and counter raids, but always he had Hitchinna. Pul Miauna cried silently, not out of immediate pain but out of love and great concern for Hitchinna and the unborn baby. Soon his mother-in-law, Jupka, Butterfly of the Wild Silkworm Woman, would

1

arrive and not leave until a moon after his baby was born, and would probably stay longer. Jupka would take responsibility for the delivery of the soon to arrive baby. She had assisted in the deliveries of many babies and knew how to care properly for mothers after their infants were born. Jupka would bring advice, wisdom, joy, and probably a few problems, but Pul Miauna was grateful that she would come to provide a proper delivery. He knew his only proper role was to run into the mountains once daily for five days before and after the birth of his child. He wiped the mist from his eyes and rose slowly in order not to wake Hitchinna.

He stepped into the pit, dressed in his deerskin loincloth, and then walked up his stairs and into the morning, the chirping birds and warm air. He walked briskly around the bay tree and then up the small trail to the village toilet behind the jagged rocks. After relieving himself, he climbed even higher up the canyon to look for signs of danger, and to his great joy, he saw Jupka and Dari Jowa, White-headed Eagle Man, his younger brother, who was responsible for bringing old Jupka to Tcapalauna. Pul Miauna saw others also, and curiosity and fear and excitement rose in him. Jupka's village near Black Rock on Salmon Creek was too exposed to white people and to their lightning sticks that threw the soft, heavy stones. Six toes, the chief of Black Rock Village, and his hunters sought revenge against the white people, the saltu, the spiritless beasts; consequently, the other Yahi with Dari Jowa were probably seeking protection. They probably knew Pul Miauna was assigned to protect the old, the orphans, and his unborn child. With most of Pul Miauna's village, Tcapalauna, hunting deer and drying venison in the high country around Wahkanopa, the snow-covered mountain to the northeast, he and his wife were also too exposed to danger. Pul Miauna was happy that Jupka would free him from some women's work that he had lately taken on. Heating cooking rocks at that moment was far less functional from his survivalist's point of view than hunting and scouting for white men who would soon be tracking Six Toes and who, even in blatant ignorance, could stumble upon a Yahi camp. The others would soon be in Tcapalauna to make their stories clear.

He hurried down the steep canyon and through the chaparral to his earthen home. He bent down, stepped inside, took some tinder from a large basket, and stepped back outside to the fire pit. He used a cooking stick to uncover the blackened coals from the ashes. After placing the fine, white filaments from the blossom of thistle on the smoking embers, he blew gently. A small flame grew from the smoke, and he patiently added dried grass until the flame grew enough for twigs and small branches. Once the fire was snapping loudly, he placed the round, fist-sized cooking rocks around the flame and added even larger pieces of driftwood. The others would need a meal, and he was proud to have killed a large buck the day before. Fresh venison was hanging in the storage mound. Further, he knew he must not vary his or Hitchinna's diet very much from the traditional foods for a pregnant woman and her husband. His mother-in-law would never let him sleep another night if she feared harm would come to the unborn due to an oversight of an uncaring husband, a husband who scorned the knowledge and wisdom drawn from stories of the Mapchemaina, the First People, from whom all that existed was understood.

Pul Miauna stood, picked up a large water basket, and walked through his village, Tcapalauna, where he was born and where his people, to his knowledge, had always been. The remaining people in Tcapalauna were not to be seen. Perhaps the old women were digging brodiaea bulbs or grinding acorns or finding wood grubs or bathing with the young orphans in Deer Creek. Perhaps they were helping him gather the proper greens for the soup. Mostly, however, he was relieved because of his brother's return. The burden of protecting Hitchinna during her delivery and time of rest and of protecting the old and the sick and young children while the others gathered food strained Pul Miauna. He could not move his wife in the event of a direct attack, and being brave, alert, and cunning was the most he could do, even with his brother's help. Pul Miauna knew the others would obey commands quickly if they had to flee, at least those who could move.

Perhaps he would have to stand and fight and die as many others had, and as he knew, many others would, as in the stories of the Mapchemaina, when the Yolaina, or the Bravest People, sometimes died for justice or noble causes.

He stepped carefully off the trail and onto the round river rocks. After filling the basket and drinking from Deer Creek, he climbed the hundred paces uphill through the toyon and willows and oaks and cedars and foothill pines to his village. He arrived as the others came near the first dwellings, and he saw his wife stepping from their home. She was naked and round with full breasts and extra weight. Her mannerisms and her quiet, supportive attention filled him with love, and when he noticed Hitchinna's slightly bent posture and agonized face, he felt relieved that Dari Jowa had brought Jupka.

"Your time has come?" he gently asked Hitchinna.

"I think so," she replied as the strain left her face.

Even in the best of situations, having a child was very dangerous, and he tried not to remember the swollen eyes and burned hair of other mothers when they placed their still births on funeral pyres.

"Jupka has arrived," he said as the familiar cry of the jay announced the arrival of Dari Jowa and Jupka and the others. He replied with the voice of the kingfisher, and then said, "Lie down, please, and let your mother do the worrying. Our baby will be straight and a fine hunter who will provide us with many salmon and much deer meat when we are too old to do anything but give requests."

Hitchinna smiled and held out her hand for support as the travelers began to arrive.

Jupka was ahead of Dari Jowa as they came directly into view around a yellow pine and earthen home, and she rushed immediately to Hitchinna's side and dropped her deerskin bag. The old woman and her daughter held each other tightly, and Jupka put a hand upon her daughter's round belly.

"The baby kicks like an elk in rutting season," said Jupka to Hitchinna. "Have your contractions started?"

"Yes," replied Hitchinna. "This morning I awoke because of them."

Jupka turned toward Pul Miauna and did not seem to notice the others. "Hitchinna and I must prepare now," she said, "and when you run into the mountains to sing to the Mapchemaina, you must carry your bow and arrows and side spear as well as your fire pouch. You must be brave enough to use wisdom. You must think of life when you sing."

As was usual, Pul Miauna was careful not to look directly into Jupka's eyes. "I am happy you arrived safely." He was keenly aware of the others but stepped inside to get his newest bow of mountain juniper, the quiver made from a mountain lion's tail, and the hand spear with a red obsidian head. He looked proudly on his hunting gear: two bows, two quivers filled with fine, straight arrows and fire sticks, some chipping bones, a sling, three sets of toggles for his salmon spear hidden near Deer Creek, a snare, a deer's head mask, some rope, a fishing net, a basket filled with obsidian and feathers, and his pouch containing tinder, pitch, and shells. As he put the fire pouch around his neck, Hitchinna entered their home to lie on the bearskin bed, and her mother helped her. Pul Miauna looked longingly at his wife's burdened face.

"Yours is the dawn's light, a gift of lupines in the high meadows," he said to her, and kissed her in her pain. "You stay. I go."

"I am so afraid," said Hitchinna.

"You must hurry," Jupka reminded Pul Miauna. "You must save your honeyed tongue for another time." She smiled broadly and showed the four gaps where her teeth were missing.

He glanced once more at his richly provided home and the glazed eyes of his lovely wife, and blessed his fortune. Being the son of a chief and wise man, Igupa Topa, had given him as much as any man before him.

Once outside he took careful notice of the others, who then included two stragglers, a pregnant woman of about six moons and an old woman, probably the pregnant woman's mother or relative; both had short hair. At their feet were coyote-skin blankets, several finely woven baskets, and a deerskin cache. Their wary look confirmed a disheartening story. Another man of about twenty stood proudly by his tied skins, but his milky eyes had rolled upward. Four girls from eight to ten years of age stood quietly near their baskets, and two boys about three stood cautiously by the girls.

"Demauna and Chunoyahi, with whom we hunted last summer, watch our trail for white men," said his brother, Dari Jowa. "Some have died. Other women and girls were taken." He paused and glanced at the rustling leaves of black oak and then into the blue sky. "Six Toes has forbidden anyone to live or to remain temporarily in Black Rock Village and has taken his hunters south to burn homes and to exact revenge for what has been done. Since we are in hiding and waiting, he asks that we protect the helpless." Dari Jowa paused again, looked at the others, and then spoke to Pul Miauna. "When you run to the canyon's rim above our village to sing to the Mapchemaina for the health of your child, make your fire small and your songs quiet. Demauna makes the sound of the kingbird and Chunoyahi the purple finch."

Pul Miauna waited a few moments before speaking. "Venison hangs in the storage mound. Eat well. You, old woman, and you, pregnant woman, will stay with me and take care of my house until your men arrive or until you die or until another man offers to hunt for you. Help Jupka with my wife's labor. You girls must act as women now, and take care of the young boy and the one with forsaken eyes. You must be his eyes. You must gather seeds and roots and pine nuts and acorns. You must prepare food and chew sinew and make baskets. You must dry venison and salmon."

He looked for their eyes, but none returned his glance. All stood and listened and thought. They were good people.

"Prepare caches away from the village and be ready to scatter. I go. You stay."

Pul Miauna walked to the storage mound and removed a rabbit-skin pouch, which he hung on his back by his quiver. The pouch contained acorn bread and smoked salmon. He took a water basket, also, for the bluff was hot and a long way from running water. He walked to Deer Creek and set his gear by the stream. Although the breeze was faint, he could just hear rustling leaves amidst the sound of white water. A jay flew into a buckeye, and soon its fledgling called from a foothill pine. A slate-gray water ouzel flew from its verdant, mossy nest near the spray of a small, upstream waterfall and landed on a boulder in midstream. The bird dipped up and down every few moments and cried bzeet, bzeet, bzeet in rapid series, tauntingly, making him pause before bathing and drinking. The bird's bobbing made him think of lizards on the hot rocks of canyon walls and of how all of existence was interrelated with stories, mind symbols, stories for everything, stories of Water Ouzel Man and of Lizard Man and of how even though arrows were shot at them to the point of raining like a great storm, none could hit them. Too bad, thought Pul Miauna, that the Yahi cannot always dodge the stones of lightning sticks as easily.

Pul Miauna climbed in the water and sidestroked his way to the middle of the stream's deep, cool pool. There he relaxed as a dead man would and floated slowly downstream, and next he dived to the bottom and swam as a salmon would toward the shore. Pul Miauna placed his gear upon his body, filled the water basket, drank deeply, and then poured the remainder into the stream. He walked downstream in the shallow water and cautiously left no tracks or watermarks upon the rocks. Once around two turns in the river, he filled his water basket, stepped onto a grassy bank, and carefully observed all he could see for any sign of a white man, but all he saw through the trees was the golden grass of the canyon shimmering in the heat waves. He picked out his favorite perch on the canyon's rim and began his run.

He was strong and a tireless walker. The canyons and steep mountains and cliffs had relentlessly opposed his every step for his entire life, but the run to the canyon's rim through the mounting heat would be merciless. He noticed the deer trails he would use on the side of the canyon, and then began his run. He stepped on large, secure boulders whenever possible, especially when he was forced to leave deer trails and to run a zigzag across the fall line. The trees, rock formations, and brush provided him with some protective covering, but often he ran in the open. His pace was deliberately slow, but still his legs and lungs burned. His tongue dried quickly, and even though he shifted his basket regularly, his arms and shoulders soon felt heavy. He never stopped, however, for he did not want to bring bad luck upon his unborn child.

Gradually, the canyon descended below him, and drenched with sweat, he continued up the draw leading to the high ground and little Dry Creek. Once the ground leveled off, he made his way through the manzanita, foothill pines, and buck brush to the point overlooking the trees hiding Tcapalauna. He kneeled in the shade of a rock formation, set the basket down, and breathed heavily. As he wiped the sweat from his face, he stared in all directions for any sign of danger. In the great distance across the valley of white men where the Wintun Indians used to live lay the coastal mountains, where none of his band except Igupa Topa had ever been. The loud demon belched smoke in its journey south near Daha, the great river of the valley; other movement, however, was normal and of nature: hawks and buzzards in the morning's updrafts, quail darting from a nearby thicket, large black ants upon a rotting foothill pine.

Pul Miauna drank deeply and sat down. All was well, and the rest was welcome. He had to build a fire and to sing for his unborn child. Pul Miauna gathered some dry wheat grass from the thicket and returned to the rock formation where he removed his pouch, spear, and quiver. He took the fire stick and board from his quiver, and placed the thistledown in a small notch leading into the drilling hole of his cedar fireboard. Next, he set a small amount of wheat grass about the hole and picked up his long fire stick of hard, straight, dry buckeye. With his left foot he held the fireboard and placed his fire stick through the grass and into the board's hole. He balanced himself comfortably with his right knee, placed his hands at the top of the shaft, and twirled the stick back and forth in his palms as he pressed downward. The rhythmical, hard pressure soon brought his hands to the bottom of the stick, where with deft movements, he released the stick entirely and returned his hands to the top of the shaft to repeat the twirling process many times. The fire stick changed little in its vertical position; Pul Miauna did not use haste in obtaining fire. Rather, his perseverance, concentration, and delicate control of movement coaxed the cedar board to grind away and to fill the hole's notch with the smoldering powder that ignited the thistledown.

Soon a small fire was snapping, and Pul Miauna sat in the shade where he relaxed and thought about nature. His tools came directly from his immediate surroundings; however, his was not the new way. He knew others, especially Six Toes and his hunters, who used the stolen lightning sticks of white people. Pul Miauna had shot a lightning stick and had tried on white people's clothes and had eaten sheep and horses and cows and donkeys. He had helped others burn barns and homes. He had traveled north to scout when the Southern Yana had been attacked. The vision of sitting in the brush and helplessly watching blue coats and other whites shoot and capture the exposed Southern Yana would not leave his mind. The barbarous whites, the spiritless saltu, never stopped coming into the foothills, never stopped hunting the Yana, and never stopped skinning the hair from the heads of dead warriors, raping women, and shooting children. The whites were worse than Skull People, Putokya, who destroyed many First People. The blue coats had marched the Southern Yana across the valley. A few had escaped and had returned to the hills, and their stories were of rape, sickness, murder, and starvation, as if the Yana were of no value. The sick had been left to die by the sides of the roads, and none had been allowed to move freely or to hunt. Their food was foreign and not meant for people. Pul Miauna was happy that his father, Igupa Topa, had ordered him to stop hunting whites, for using stealth had proved successful in keeping his tribe alive. When he wished to seek revenge against the whites as he had done for several years, he remembered that most of Tcapalauna was still alive.

Pul Miauna remembered his wife, Hitchinna, lying painfully in labor. He hoped that his running into the mountains to sing would help Hitchinna, but the mystery of birth was left to women who had to bear children. He knew Jupka and Hitchinna would move to a hidden and comfortable spot near Deer Creek. When the baby was born, he or she would be dipped in the cold water. The water would bring life to a healthy baby, a gasping newborn, striving to live. In his heart Pul Miauna hoped for a son, but a daughter would please him also. Pul Miauna added more wood to the fire, took another drink of water, gazed about cautiously, and then sat quietly to sing.

Pul Miauna's song deviated only slightly from a single tone, was well paced, and had a descending melodic movement. His father, Igupa Topa, taught the song to him in the sweathouse when he was a young boy, long before the saltu descended with their wagons and mules and lightning sticks from the east across the Yahi's country. He repeated the song twenty times, as his singing custom required.

"Mapchemaina, Mapchemaina, make my child strong."

The simple song's repetition gave him a concentrated peace of mind.

When finished singing, he wondered about survival in the Yahi's world. Wisdom, love, cunning, bravery, stealth, knowledge, intelligence, strength, and skill were required for survival, and he wanted his unborn child to be named accordingly. His mother-in-law thought that he should consider bravery and wisdom the most when naming his unborn child, but Pul Miauna had to laugh to himself because many people were given nicknames. Before Pul Miauna was married, he was often called Ututni, Wood Duck Man. He was handsome and had his choice of several brides, but Hitchinna stole his heart. Pul Miauna thought again of naming his child after one of the Mapchemaina who had descended into this world as a fallen creature. The grizzly was brave and powerful and dangerous, but the grizzly was too easily angered and could be trapped and killed. Surely a man should be wiser than a grizzly bear. Perhaps the newly born child should be named after the mountain lion that liked to hide but could be dangerous none the less. A Yahi, however, needed to be more intelligent than any animal if he or she were to survive. No characteristics of any name seemed to fit the qualities needed in the new and dangerous world.

Yolaina, thought Pul Miauna after letting his mind rest a few moments, must be the name. The Yolaina were people and were brave, and the Yolaina made possible the existence of the Yahi. Although many of them died, none died vainly. The Yahi had lived on their land for time eternal because of the Yolaina, the bravest of the Mapchemaina, and surely if the Yahi were to continue to survive, those who did would have to be as remarkable as the Yolaina had been.

Pul Miauna was relieved. His last few days of running every morning into the mountains to sing for his unborn child had been fruitful, and no matter whether the child was a boy or a girl, he would name the child Yolaina.

He put out his fire with rocks and dirt and scattered the ashes with a dead manzanita twig. He drank from his basket and repacked his fire stick and board in his quiver. He would walk to Little Dry Creek, refill his water basket, hunt rabbits, and scout the nearby land for saltu. Perhaps Demauna and Chunoyahi could be found. He would listen for the kingbird and the purple finch. He then would walk carefully back to Tcapalauna, feast heartily, take a sweatbath, and wait for news of his infant, his own Yolaina, and in the mornings for the next five days after Yolaina's birth, Pul Miauna would run again to the canyon's rim and sing for the newly born child. He would sing for peace so that his child might gather food or hunt in his or her rightful land.

*   *   *

After the contraction left Hitchinna's abdomen, she breathed heavily and waited for the new pain to come. All day and deep into the night, the contractions had worsened, and still the baby had not come. Hitchinna felt the child on the verge of ripping her vagina. Her water had broken, and the child had mostly escaped the inner womb. The smell of blood and of the womb intermingled with the campfire's smoke. Hitchinna did not know if she could bear another contraction, and was a bit delirious. All day she had heard the kind and patient words of Jupka, her mother, and knew Jupka had suffered the same pain when she had given breath to Hitchinna, but the rinsing of her face and the drinking of smashed manzanita berries and water and the hearing of advice about relaxing and breathing meant so little in her pain.

Hitchinna looked helplessly across the low burning fire at the face of the strangers, the pregnant woman and her mother. Sometimes they fetched wood or water or prepared food for Jupka and themselves, but mostly they sat quietly and watched Hitchinna's labor. The young woman must have wondered in awe about such pain, since she would have to suffer the pain in three moons. Hitchinna did not know their names, but as the day wore on into night, a bit of their story was told. Apparently, Black Rock Village had been attacked a week before, for an unknown reason, by settlers on the edge of the valley to the south, the ones who had tried to track and to kill the Yahi before. Six Toes, the fierce and skillful hunter and chief of Black Rock Village, was sworn to revenge. He would kill in retaliation for the murdered of his village, especially the young. The details must have been tragic, but Hitchinna's pain and absolute fatigue left her too dazed to be concerned with more than her own survival during delivery.

When the new contraction came over Hitchinna's stomach, Jupka spoke excitedly. "Push, push, you must push. I see the baby's wrinkled crown of wet, black hair again. You must push very hard."

Hitchinna held her breath, pushed very hard, and squeezed a piece of driftwood and the hand of the old woman holding her head and shoulders. The old woman squeezed back and wiped Hitchinna's brow with dampened deerskin. Gasping for air in the middle of her contraction, Hitchinna screamed, "No. No."

"Push. You must push. Your baby will come now. You must push," said Jupka in a loud voice.

"I…ah…ah…cannot," grunted Hitchinna breathing heavily.

"You must push. The baby will come," said Jupka excitedly.

Hitchinna once more held her breath, closed her eyes, and pushed with all the strength she had against her opening pelvis. She felt the air turn stale in her lungs.

"Push. Push. You must push hard," yelled Jupka.

Hitchinna felt the baby's head surge through her torn vagina, and she gasped for air and cried out in pain.

"Push. You must push," said Jupka. "The baby's body is still in you. Push. Push."

With closed eyes and held breath, Hitchinna once again pushed, and as the contraction left her, she felt the baby slide free of her.

"You have a boy," said Jupka, for the child was visibly in her hands.

Hitchinna relaxed a bit against the arms and legs of the old woman, and panted deeply. "Is he healthy?"

Jupka laughed warmly, laid the infant upon the deerskin, and quickly finished clearing the infant's mouth. "He looks healthy to me." She doused him with cold clear water from a basket. The child cried and stretched and turned from the color of gray river rock into a pinkish brown. Jupka tied a deerskin thong around the umbilical cord and held him up for Hitchinna to see.

"When you have another contraction, push out the child's womb," said Jupka. "We need to see it all. Any left in place would cause a fever."

"The contraction is coming," said Hitchinna.

Over the baby's new cries Hitchinna pushed, and as Jupka pulled slightly on the cord, the afterbirth slid free from her torn vagina. Jupka picked it up, put her hand through the tear where the newly born had been rejected and inspected it carefully in the light of the flames. The excreted remains of the baby's first home was complete.

"Relax now, my dear Hitchinna," said Jupka while placing a flat piece of driftwood under the umbilical cord, and cutting it with the chipped edge of a hand-sized obsidian stone. Jupka then placed the excess cord and afterbirth in a small basket for burial and stood and held the child in the firelight for all to see. The old woman holding Hitchinna's head in her lap looked on in great joy. A smile creased her wizened face, and her eyes glistened with tears and glanced from the baby to her own daughter. Her daughter seemed tranquil and interested, but she showed signs of elation and fear.

"You have much to experience," said the old woman.

"You mean I have too much to experience," replied the daughter.

The old woman looked back at Hitchinna. "The gift of life is precious."

"To the river, now, my little one," said Jupka to the baby. "I must dunk you thoroughly." The baby had excreted a thin, green liquid on her forearm, and firelight danced on its slick, moist body. Jupka turned and walked by the pile of driftwood, over the pebbled beach, and into Deer Creek. Once in the water to her waist, she repeatedly submerged the baby boy.

The child howled and stretched against the dunkings, but when Jupka finished, she held the child to her breast and carefully stepped over the slick river rocks. Once back at the fire, she handed the crying child to Hitchinna.

"He will lose weight before your milk arrives," said Jupka.

"He is healthy?" asked Hitchinna. The child was slick and helpless. His umbilical cord lay on Hitchinna's breast.

"Very," said the old woman admiring the baby. She touched the child's glutinous skin. "He howls as do wolves in mating season."

The pregnant daughter added wood to the fire.

"His eyes are closed," said Hitchinna.

"He will learn to see," said Jupka. "He will learn all there is to know in the Yahi world, a day at a time, slowly. He will learn more than hunting and stories of the Mapchemaina, however, for he must learn to see with his heart in vengeful times."

*   *   *

Pul Miauna and Dari Jowa sat across from Demauna and Chunoyahi in the men's house of Tcapalauna. A small fire cast a flickering yellow light on the tule mats, skins, posts, and cedar-bark walls. A man of many seasons, Ilhataina lay crippled on a rabbit-skin blanket. He had been wounded twelve years earlier when the first white men raided his Salmon Creek Village. Demauna and Chunoyahi had muzzle-loading rifles with them, as did most of the hunters of abandoned Black Rock Village. The two men had entered camp that evening with news of the killing of two settler girls and of the kidnapping of a boy who would be used to lure the trackers away from the Yahi women and children and then would be stoned to death. Further, a man hauling a load of wood on a wagon had been shot to death with an arrow from each man. Cabins had been burned and looted. A mass meeting of the white men had already been underway when the young women were shot and robbed of their clothing, and as surely as the moon rises and sets and grows from blackness to pure brilliance, the settlers of the valley would form many tracking parties to hunt the Yahi. Demauna had received this information from two hunters who had left further vengeance to others in their party. The hunters had talked to a docile Yahi ranch hand to the south and had left Six Toes north of Deer Creek. They wished to find their families on upper Deer Creek and feared being hunted. They wanted to keep their families continually moving far away from the trackers and lightning sticks.

"Our people grow smaller every year," said old Ilhataina to no one in particular, but he then glanced at Pul Miauna. "How will you keep the white men from killing your new son? They could be coming now and will be coming at day's break."

Pul Miauna did not reply. He was not sure what course to take. He did not dare move Hitchinna, who was weak and far from healed. His baby could barely suckle. His mother-in-law, Jupka, was too old to travel quickly, and Ilhataina could only be moved a short way. The new blind man, Gowila, could not be moved easily either. Perhaps they could hide while the others—the young girls and boys, the elders, and Chunoyahi and Demauna—could walk upstream as quickly as possible. Maybe they could warn Igupa Topa and the other men, women, and children near Wahkanopa.

"We must split up," he finally replied. "Those who can move readily will go upstream with Demauna and Chunoyahi. You, Ilhataina, will hide with Dari Jowa and me. We will take the blind man, Gowila. When you need help to move, he will be your legs, and you will be his eyes. The pregnant woman and her mother can either hide with us or walk upstream. Jupka, Hitchinna, and my baby will hide downstream in the chaparral with us. When Hitchinna heals enough to travel, perhaps when the moon is full, we will travel upstream to the high country. By then the white men will grow hungry and tired. They will be in the valley."

"The white men will never stop pursuing us, even at unexpected times." Chunoyahi sighed and gazed at the small fire. "Still, your plan is the only one to take."

Pul Miauna watched his brother, Dari Jowa, look intensely at Chunoyahi and then admiringly at Demauna's lightning stick, but Dari

Jowa was following Igupa Topa's request not to own a lightning stick and to use one's wits to avoid detection and to provide for the tribe.

"Your plan is good," said Dari Jowa. He picked an arrow from his quiver and examined it closely: the witch hazel, buzzard feathers, sinew, obsidian, and blue and red stripes.

"Tell me, Chunoyahi, does your lightning stick make up for the arrow?" The arrow rested ominously in Dari Jowa's hand, and his eyes moved from Demauna's lightning stick to Chunoyahi. As Chunoyahi stirred the coals and added wood to the fire, the shadow of the arrow danced on the bark and posts of the men's house.

"Yours is a question without an answer," replied Chunoyahi, a displaced Hat Creek Indian and an accepted member in any Yahi village. "The white men fear the lightning stick more than the bow, but your question is this: how will the Yahi survive? Perhaps the lightning stick is better than the bow. Perhaps Igupa Topa's hiding is better than Six Toes' revenge. Perhaps we should battle until all the saltu are dead or until all the Yahi are dead. Perhaps some should fight, and some should hide. Perhaps we all should hide. I no longer understand or am able to make a decision. I fight, and I hide. I carry the lightning stick, and I carry a bow.

"The men who have lost wives and children and relatives want lightning sticks. They burn the hair from their heads and cover the stubble with pitch. They feel that the white men will go away if we burn their homes and slaughter those who encroach upon our land. Those in mourning are not hunters of reason, however.

"Pul Miauna's plan is good. Those who can travel must do so, and those who cannot must hide in the brush of a steep canyon."

Chunoyahi and Demauna stared at Pul Miauna sitting patiently, and as Dari Jowa slid his arrow in the otter-skin quiver, he and Ilhataina took notice of Pul Miauna.

"Then make ready to leave," slowly replied Pul Miauna. He stood, picked up his bow and quiver, and waited a few moments before leaving.

He wanted to express how he felt at the moment, but the proper words escaped him. What could one say about having to hide in the brush like a wounded deer? They could not live in their homes, the places of their births. They could not walk across unmolested land and gather food as their ancestors had. They could not fish many traditional holes and lie on the large river boulders in full view of the surrounding canyon. They could only trade with neighbors to the east, the Shoshone and Paiute, for obsidian and lightning sticks, because the Wintuns and Atsugewis and Maidus served white men or were dead.

Pul Miauna left the men's house to walk to his one-room, earthen home. With four women and a new son to attend, he was no longer alone, no longer Wood Duck Man, the lusty hunter, whose sisters took care of his cooking as many women came to claim his heart but left lonely with baskets of dried venison and salmon for their efforts. He stepped into his home, carefully set his bow and quiver near his other belongings, and took off his loincloth. He lay next to Hitchinna and his new baby. Although he tried not to think about his wife's mother, Jupka, and the other two women sleeping in his home, he felt their presence in the blackness. The older woman's breathing was too noisy. He did not readily fall asleep. His mind wandered in fear and in joy. He was a father who had to hide instead of hunt and to cower instead of fight.

In the darkness his baby seemed not to be alive, but he gently reached out, touched the rabbit-skin bundle, and lifted his son's tiny, warm hand.

"For you, my son, and your beautiful mother, I will hide in the brush, and I will make sure we eat and live," he whispered. He laid his son's hand back on the rabbit skin, closed his eyes, and sensed how exhausted he was from running, gathering wood, hunting, making jerky, working on arrows, carrying water, and taking care of all those who could not take of themselves, and gradually his mind wandered over random thoughts and blackened.

Pul Miauna awoke to his son's crying and Hitchinna's movements. She began suckling him. Pul Miauna still could see little in the darkness, but he slowly reached over and touched Hitchinna's face.

Hitchinna responded gently and kissed his hand. "You are the best of men, and I am very proud to be the mother of your son."

"Will you be so proud when we move into the brush at sunrise?" asked Pul Miauna in the most quiet of whispers.

"Not even the moon, the tricky old man of the sky with his poisonous tobacco of dried skin and crushed bones, could cause my love to change. You have given me a son, and my heart shines like an abalone shell under the high sun."

"In that case, I promise to complain no more. After the whites have gone, however, we will travel to the high country and spend the rest of the summer with Igupa Topa and the rest of Tcapalauna. We will have much venison, and then we will gather many acorns. We will live in our warm earthen home through the cold winter. You will make baskets and blankets, and I will make rope and arrows. We will watch our son grow in peace."

*   *   *

With the last of their belongings firmly tied in skins to the end of the long cliff rope, Pul Miauna threw the bundle into the rushing white water. The bundle quickly disappeared down the white water and around the huge, smoothly worn boulder. Dari Jowa, Pul Miauna's brother, pulled the bundle to shore on the opposite side of the boulder; there, Ilhataina, Gowila, Jupka, the old woman, her pregnant daughter, and Hitchinna waited for Pul Miauna and his son, who lay crying and bundled up on a boulder in the water's riffling shoreline. Soon the rope flew over the boulder again, and Pul Miauna tied the rope around his upper chest, picked up his son, and flipped the rope from the boulder into the water. One more he looked upstream where Demauna and

Chunoyahi stood in the shallow water. Their lightning sticks rested in their arms, and they waved to Pul Miauna. Pul Miauna waved back, held his son high above his head, grabbed the rope firmly, breathed deeply, and stepped into the roaring water. The current fiercely surrounded his entire body, and his foot scraped against an unseen boulder. Pul Miauna was not sure if little Yolaina had been submerged, but he worried little. As soon as he washed between the cliffs, he felt the rope tug on his chest, and his head emerged into the air. His son's skins were wet; the crisp air filled Pul Miauna's lungs; and the white people could go live with the Putokya, the Skull People, for all he cared. He and those he loved and cared for were hidden safely in the dense chaparral of the steep canyon, where cliffs stopped travelers from above, where brush turned humans into four-legged animals, and where white water roared between steep boulders like black clouds. At the water's edge, Dari Jowa took the soaked, rabbit-skin bundle from Pul Miauna, who climbed onto the grassy shore and removed the rope. He saw that Yolaina's small, puffy, cloud-gray eyes were wide open. With his black, short hair wet against his scalp, little Yolaina cried in open revolt.

"You may yell about being a man now," said Pul Miauna quietly unheard. "Later, though, you must act as a man."

Pul Miauna watched Ilhataina lead the blind man on his hands and knees through the brush, and watched Hitchinna remove Yolaina from Dari Jowa's arms. She sat in the grass and untied the wet, rabbit-skin blanket. The little one's arms moved awkwardly and touched her breast. Hitchinna suckled the child from her swollen breast, and smiled up at the others: the old woman, her pregnant daughter, Jupka, Dari Jowa, and Pul Miauna. Dari Jowa touched the old woman's shoulder and motioned for her to take her daughter and their skins and baskets and to follow the young blind man and the old cripple through the brush. Ilhataina knew of a place not too many paces downstream and on the southern hillside where he, as a young man, and other hunters had killed a grizzly bear in its winter's drowsiness, and he wanted to show the others. The old woman and her daughter took their belongings and began crawling after them. Dari Jowa finished wrapping the rope into a neatly tied coil, and then added the rope to his bundles of arrows, bows, skins, and sundry hunting items and tools. He followed the pregnant woman into the brush. Jupka got on her hands and knees, shoved her cache she had brought from Black Rock Village into the brush, said something no one could hear over the white water, smiled broadly, and slowly followed Dari Jowa into the brush.

Pul Miauna could not help but laugh. Jupka's old breasts swayed back and forth like an opossum hanging from a blue oak in the moonlight. Pul Miauna laughed for other reasons, also. Who could find them in the denseness of nature, in a world with so many hiding spots? Soon they would be eating, sleeping, and living with security as the world about them swirled with the hatred of the white settlers. As Dari Jowa and he had watched the movements of the white murderers in the past, they would watch their movements again. He put his arm around his wife. Her long black hair was wet against his biceps, and she held Yolaina's little hand with a finger. He suckled ravenously and kicked Hitchinna's stomach. Pul Miauna would have to wait before meeting his father, Igupa Topa, in the high country, but Pul Miauna was impatient to show him his new grandson, Yolaina. Hitchinna put her arm around Pul Miauna's waist, and the young family sat hopefully in hiding among the rocks, grass, toyon, buck brush, and manzanita, out of sight, happily.

CHAPTER 2

Autumn in the High Country

Yolaina lay naked on a rabbit-skin blanket and played with a deer-hoof rattle. The aspen leaves above him crackled in the light breeze coming off Wahkanopa, and sunlight danced delicately through the branches and over his backside. As he gurgled and drooled and rolled over, his mother noticed his deep brown eyes and his raven black, straight hair. He was no longer a tiny, glistening newborn. He was a human with a mind of his own, especially at night when his hunger drove him to cry for Hitchinna's breasts. He was learning to enjoy sips of broth from venison soups and the cooled acorn gruel from the large bubbling baskets. In fact, Yolaina seemed to enjoy pine needles, pitch, grass, dirt, rocks, and anything else he could manage to get in his mouth.

Hitchinna finished slicing the venison stripped from the back of large buck hanging with other dead deer not far away. She cut the meat against its grain and set the last of the strips in her flat, low-rimmed basket. She stood, walked to the nearby fire where she had prepared a rack of straightened and peeled buckeye. Hitchinna carefully placed each piece of meat on a straightened stick until each stick was laden. The sunlight, heat from the fire, and smoke would cure the venison, and the jerky would be stored to help her village, Tcapalauna, against the long nights of winter. Hitchinna remembered her last winter well. She and Pul Miauna were without child and were together to make love when they wished. Then her moon blood stopped, and her belly began to rise. She remembered how the cold wind blew and how clouds at times filled Deer Creek Canyon. She remembered how the colored bow arched across the canyon above Tcapalauna when the sun broke through the storm clouds. New life turned the golden canyon brazenly green, even as the barren twig of the wild rose bent in the foggy wind.

Yolaina rolled off his rabbit-skin blanket and onto the grass. He howled for attention. Hitchinna left her work to pick him up; he was always hungry. As Hitchinna picked up her baby boy, she noticed the camp of her people: children playing or helping their mothers, and women tending fire, preparing food, gathering wood, and cutting meat. The men had gone to lie in wait for more deer. Chikpina, the old woman from Black Rock Village, left her cutting when she saw that Hitchinna was suckling Yolaina. Her daughter, Chuna, was lying in the shade of cottonwood tree at the meadow's edge. Chuhna could hardly move. Her belly was larger than Round Mountain, and her child kicked as if it had as many feet as a whole circle of dancers celebrating a full harvest of acorns, pine nuts, and dried salmon. Chikpina slowly made her way to Hitchinna, and they sat with their feet hanging over the bank of the small stream. Her hair had grown a bit longer. To their backs was the large meadow, and to their fronts were beaver-gnawed trees, the forest, and, of course, Wahkanopa and a few puffy clouds. Chikpina appeared to be nervous, but Hitchinna did not press her for information.

"As you know, Chuhna's baby is due, and her husband was killed in a raid. He was a brave man and could carry much weight over many canyons. He always gave me the liver from whatever he killed, whether it was an elk, a deer, an antelope, or a turkey. He was quick to smile and full of hot-blooded passion."

Chikpina paused and glanced at Hitchinna as if a response were in order, but Hitchinna let Chikpina speak on her own. She did smile at Chikpina, however, when Yolaina tried to eat a ladybug that landed on his hand.

"Her husband is dead," said Chikpina, "along with many Yahi from Black Rock Village. The canyon above Salmon Creek is filled with our cremated dead. Your village has more people now than the others, and I believe your men are brave and also wise. I see Pul Miauna hunts deer instead of men. I hear Igupa Topa speaks of living through the long winter ahead instead of burning a settler's home. Not enough men are left to hunt and to kill settlers at the same time. These are hard times."

Chikpina paused again, for still her meaning was not clear. She was too uneasy.

"You are a lucky woman. Your son is straight and healthy; your husband is handsome, strong, and loving. Pul Miauna has without question proved himself to be a great man. He shares with us just as Chuhna's husband did. He asks for nothing in return and treats Chuhna with much warmth. I wish for Pul Miauna to marry Chuhna. Her baby will soon arrive, and whether the infant is a boy or girl, the baby will need a real provider, a man of love and wisdom. You get along well with Chuhna, and Pul Miauna already hunts for both of us, anyhow.

"You, of course, would always be first wife. I have discussed Pul Miauna's possible marriage with Jupka, and she laughed and said Wood Duck Man would have little difficulty handling two wives."

Hitchinna laughed. "Pul Miauna is certainly a man. I think only my shyness captured his heart. As to your question, I would be happy to keep both of you in our home. With two grandmothers around, Wood Duck Man would find plenty to keep him busy. Now, though, you must ask him, but I know he likes you both. You are also a great friend to

Jupka. We will have a dance tonight before Chuhna's baby arrives so that Chuhna's baby will have a provider."

Chikpina smiled broadly and stood quickly. Her twinkling eyes were like glistening rapids when the spring's sun breaks over the canyon's rim and flashes between the pines, cedars, and oaks shading Salmon Creek. "We will be like swarming lady bugs on the bare branch of the rose in the warm sun. Chuhna will be quite happy."

Hitchinna watched Chikpina hobble quickly to her daughter, Chuhna, Spider Woman, the great weaver of rope and baskets. In the stories of the Mapchemaina, the First People, Chuhna wove a great web so that the morning star, Halai Auna, could climb into the sky to her father, Wakara, Moon Man. Wakara was shot into the sky on a great, flexible tendon; Wakara was trying to ward off Pun Miapu, son of Colored Bow Man, from marrying Halai Auna. Pun Miapu had the great strength of Igupa Topa in his heart, however, so Wakara was caught off guard and was shot into the sky. Only Chuhna saved Halai Auna from never visiting her father again.

Hitchinna hoped that Chuhna would have a baby girl, for Hitchinna wanted to name the baby Halai Auna, Morning Star Woman. Besides, Hitchinna was tired of dodging Yolaina's urine and would prefer a little girl. She switched Yolaina to her right breast, and noticed the sun would be down soon. Pul Miauna and the others would soon be back in camp.

Hitchinna noticed the other women watching her and Chikpina. They knew that Chikpina had been planning a marriage. Chikpina was old and quick to point out she could not walk around the canyons without a real home too many more seasons. She was a bit of a fly, however, and after she became used to the people of Tcapalauna, she was quite vivacious. Anyhow, the people of Tcapalauna loved her stories, and the gossip she had to tell about the remaining people of Black Rock Village was always welcome.

Soon, Hitchinna thought, we will leave the high country and gather with the remainder of the Yahi to collect acorns on upper Salmon

Creek. There they would collect pine cones from the tall pines, heat out
their pitch, and beat out their nuts. They would dry acorns and salmon,
and they would feast and dance and sing. They would rejoice in the
coming storms that would drive the white men and their lightning
sticks from the great canyons. Hitchinna swished a fly and noticed that
many men, including Pul Miauna, were crossing the meadow's edge.

Both Igupa Topa and Pul Miauna were carrying a deer with its legs
tied around a long pole, but seeing Pul Miauna tromp around a
meadow with the remaining men of Black Rock Village was unusual. Six
Toes was in the lead and next to him was Dari Jowa, little Yolaina's
handsome uncle. Hitchinna recognized only Hapawila, Demauna,
Chunoyahi, and Tenna from Black Rock Village. Two others she did not
know, but those two and Tenna had short hair, a result of burning their
hair in mourning after the raid on Black Rock Village. Their hair was
about as long as Chikpina's and Chuhna's. All the men from Black Rock
Village had lightning sticks stolen from dead white men or traded from
the Paiutes of the desert to the east with the stolen gold coins from
burned cabins.

Hitchinna knew their lives would be in upheaval, for always Six Toes
was in the forefront of trouble. Six Toes was the loudest Yahi that
Hitchinna had ever known, and she had known him since childhood
when Jupka was still young and when Black Rock Village lay peacefully
in the tall pines by the deep, lazy pools surrounding the giant, ragged,
huge Black Rock, and when their only enemy was the Wintuns, the valley saltus whose lives were soft and whose fears were great.

Hitchinna watched Six Toes carefully to see if his demeanor had
changed, but he was forceful and took large steps. Hitchinna remembered Six Toes as a boy, always fighting those who teased him about his
foot. His powerful anger led to his rise as accepted chief. Hitchinna felt
sorry for him, for his huge foot, and for his quick temperament. She
knew that trouble was at hand.

A chill was in the air, and Yolaina began to cry. Hitchinna stood, picked up the rabbit-skin blanket, and wrapped her baby boy. Along with the others in camp, Hitchinna made her way to the men and especially to Pul Miauna since she had not seen him in two days. Little Yolaina still cried and was ready for another nap, but first Hitchinna had to hold Pul Miauna and to hear of Six Toes' fighting.

When Hitchinna and Pul Miauna met, he and his father, Igupa Topa, set the doe near the other hanging carcasses. Pul Miauna removed the quiver from his back and gave both howling Yolaina and Hitchinna a large hug. He held little Yolaina in his hands, then threw him in the air and caught him at the last moment. The rabbit-skin blanket flew to the ground, but Yolaina decided to stop crying for the moment. Pul Miauna then held them both again and whispered in Hitchinna's ear.

"Every night when we men sat around a campfire and told stories, most of them lies, I thought of you, and always my heart glowed like stars of different colors."

"I love you, and I hope you are as active as your tongue," replied Hitchinna as she looked around. Demauna and Chunoyahi were with their wives. Six Toes was surveying the camp and demanding a meal. Chikpina and Chuhna were still together under the cottonwood tree, but they were looking at Pul Miauna and Hitchinna. Hitchinna did not know if Chuhna's request of marriage would be accepted, but she felt some apprehension at that moment. Perhaps sharing Pul Miauna in matrimony would not be good, but men were becoming scarce. Hitchinna picked up the rabbit-skin blanket and gave it to Pul Miauna for Yolaina.

"My son," Pul Miauna said, "I see you have been faithful and have protected our camp well. I am pleased." He wrapped Yolaina but left room to tickle his round belly.

"Yolaina has only protected his stomach," laughed Hitchinna, and then she heard Six Toes telling the women of his village to make ready to move camp the next day. Apparently, the blue coats were coming again. Hitchinna looked with concern at Pul Miauna.

"Is this true?" asked Pul Miauna. "Did you protect your stomach?" He laughed and tickled the little one's belly. "Did you eat any rocks or frogs or bugs?"

"The blue coats are coming?" asked Hitchinna with concern.

"Do not worry my lovely woman. The blue coats are not hunters. They are stupid. They are more obvious than the soaring condors and blinder than river rocks. They come up all the canyons at once, but none of us is in the canyons. They leave sentries behind as they go in search of us. We will dry our meat and hide for a while, and the blue coats will never see us."

"Poor Chuhna," replied Hitchinna. "Such news is unsettling to a pregnant woman so heavy with child. I know."

"Do not worry about Chuhna. Ichpul, Frog Man, wants her," replied Pul Miauna with a smile.

"Ichpul," said Hitchinna with disdain. "How did he get such a name?" She looked at the hunters whom she did not know, and then she knew. He was about twenty-five years old, but his mouth protruded and his eyes were bulging. His short hair did not help his appearance, either. He was too little.

"Chuhna will never marry such a man," replied Hitchinna with a glint in her eyes.

*   *   *

Pul Miauna set down his bow and arrows, and looked about him at the forest in its entire splendor. He loved the autumn smells deep within the pines and firs. The bubbling, white mud sputtered in the air, and when the wind shifted, he smelled sulfur from the steaming holes in the earth. The tiny, steaming, off-blue lake lay in full view of Wahkanopa, but Pul Miauna was questioning his reasoning abilities at that moment and was not paying much attention to the forest.

"How could I have Chuhna? No man should have two mothers-in-law, two wives, and two babies to feed all at once, not even Wood Duck Man, Ututni, the lusty hunter," mumbled Pul Miauna. I will need a round house the size Wahkanopa, Pul Miauna continued thinking, and no village homes are now safe to use. Winter is coming, and the blue coats still swarm in the canyons like yellow jackets. Then, however, Pul Miauna thought about the shyness in Chuhna's eyes the night of the dance, and how Jupka was so excited about the birth of Chuhna's new baby girl, Halai Auna, and about her friend, Chikpina, having the same son-in-law. "How can one man please so many women?" muttered Pul Miauna. The time would come the following winter when Chuhna would want to make love, though, and maybe the rewards would be great. "At least I am young enough to enjoy two women," he said out loud with a large smile. He removed his fire drill and board from his best quiver, made from a mountain lion's tail, and for the fifth and last time after the birth of Halai Auna, Pul Miauna prepared to build a fire and to sing to the health of Yolaina's new little sister.

Soon Pul Miauna and Dari Jowa would take their little band downstream to the east where Igupa Topa had taken the rest of their village to wait out the blue coats. At least the blue coats were too stupid to bring dogs, and they lacked tracking ability and stealth. Pul Miauna remembered how the blue coats, the mighty white warriors, rode their horses up the road from the valley to the ridge between Deer and Salmon Creeks. Pul Miauna, Dari Jowa, and Igupa Topa were among the hunters that lay in wait for them. Igupa Topa shot the first arrow through their chief's hat and into a large pine. Dari Jowa shot the second arrow into a mule, and then the fight was over. The blue coats scattered in all directions toward the valley. While running, they shot their lightning sticks into various objects like trees and rocks, and two even hurt themselves scampering down the side of Salmon Creek Canyon. One blue coat knocked himself out and broke his own arm. Demauna and Chunoyahi stripped him of everything that he owned and left him naked to walk back to the valley. The blue coats were very funny saltus, spiritless beings. A valley half-breed told Six Toes that the settlers also laughed at the blue coats. The settlers and the Yahi at least had that much in common, besides open disdain for each other, but Pul Miauna wondered why anyone would organize such worthless hunters. At best the blue coats were only good for rounding up enslaved Wintuns or docile Yanas working on ranches to the north. Pul Miauna wondered if any among the blue coats had pride in his heart, but he had to stop daydreaming and had to sing for Halai Auna.

When Pul Miauna made his fire, he placed his cedar fireboard, fire drill, and tinder pouch back in his quiver. He wiped the sweat from his brow and walked through the soft white clay to rinse his face in the sulfuric water. He felt like dancing for that last sing, so he did. Taking short shuffling hops on each foot, Pul Miauna danced around the small fire twenty times, once for each repetition of the song to the Mapchemaina, the First People, from whom all the Yahi and all that existed came.

"Now little Halai Auna will be safe and straight. She will live a full life. I, however, will sway back and forth in the wind blowing from the mouths of five women," Pul Miauna mumbled. "Chuhna is a fine woman, but poor Ichpul, Frog Man, never even had a chance to arrange a wedding. Maybe I can build two round houses, one for me, for Yolaina, for Halai Auna, and for the one woman wanting something at the time, and one for the other three women thinking of chores for me to do. How will I ever chip enough arrowheads to bind to enough arrows to shoot from enough bows to kill enough game to feed so many mouths?"

Pul Miauna stood, listened to two stellar jays cawing back and forth, and walked into the forest to gather more wood for his fire. Once the fire was again burning well, Pul Miauna took a bundle of five pealed buckeye shafts from his quiver. He untied the leather thong and extended each shaft from his right eye. He had carefully selected each shaft for its straightness and width, but each shaft had its own quality. When carefully observed, each shaft was crooked, as if it had a will of its own, but Pul Miauna heated each shaft at each curve. He bent each one carefully against its curves, for although buckeye was light, strong, and hard, it was also brittle and would readily snap. Pul Miauna's new arrows would not be ready for use until the end of the following spring, when each shaft would be totally straight and when each arrowhead would be held in place with a mixture of pitch and charcoal chewed sinew from a deer's shoulder. Each shaft would also have three carefully placed and cut feathers from the wing of a large bird, also secured with sinew and glue. Each shaft would be used many times to kill many deer, that is if Pul Miauna were lucky enough not to break or lose it.

As he continued gathering wood for his fire and straightening his shafts, he thought again about his new son and how worthwhile life was. True, he had to hide, and he did not know where he would live next winter, but he was never quite so content. His little son was handsome and troublesome and happy. Yolaina even laughed out loud when Pul Miauna sneaked up behind him, jumped up, crossed his eyes, and blew out in such a way so as to smack his lips together. Jupka said Yolaina would sit up in another moon, and would crawl in three moons. Too bad he did not come out of the ground as the baby did in the story of the Mapchemaina, the First People. Where the old lady spat a baby grew, and within seven days he was a fully-grown hunter, capable of protecting the old woman for the rest of her life. She did not need to fear her enemies any more, for the child could not be killed. The many hunters who tried to kill the baby died themselves. Pul Miauna wondered if peace would ever return to the Yahi again. Six Toes believed that if enough whites were killed in revenge for their murders, peace would be achieved. Igupa Topa thought peace was impossible, but survival was not.

"These matters are beyond true reasoning," mumbled Pul Miauna, "but if I am found, I will sink arrows through the hearts of those who hunt me."

Pul Miauna placed his five unwieldy shafts together, and then tied the deer-hide thong around them. The straightening process would be gone through many times before the shafts would be worthwhile. Maintaining his hunting arsenal was an endless process. After packing his quiver neatly, he began walking back through the forest to the camp. He also had to climb the slope of Wahkanopa that same day to pull a limb from a windswept high mountain juniper, the first step in a year-long process of making his next bow. He hoped to be back in time for the festivities celebrating the birth of little Halai Auna.

"Being Wood Duck Man is not so bad," said Pul Miauna as he stepped around some manzanita and over a fallen cedar. "At least I have others to protect and two women to share my passion."

*   *   *

The campfire was small but adequate. Its blue, orange, and yellow flames sent small sparks into the wind, and the pine cones that Six Toes had thrown into the fire when he had made a place to sit down snapped loudly and shot embers far from the fire pit. Fires, however, were peaceful to Pul Miauna even while he listened to Six Toes. The nights had become progressively colder, but at least the snow had not come yet. Pul Miauna was wearing full winter clothing, including his new deer-hide moccasins, a gift form Chuhna. He put more dry limb wood in the fire as Demauna and Chunoyahi came from the women and children. Pul Miauna did not want to hear what Six Toes had to say; he preferred to listen to his father, Igupa Topa, whom he loved and respected and followed. Pul Miauna would listen, smile, and be thankful Igupa Topa was speaking. Speaking with Six Toes was like trying to shoot an arrow into a hawk gyrating high in the wind down Salmon Creek Canyon. The hawk would just scream and glide away, and the arrow would be lost deep in the forest on the other side of Salmon Creek. Pul Miauna looked at all the men one at a time: Chunoyahi, Six Toes, Demauna, Hapawila, Ahalamila, Tenna, Ichpul, two others whom he did not know well, and, of course, Igupa Topa, Dari Jowa, Gowila, and Ilhataina. Five other men from Tcapalauna had gone scouting and were to begin building winter homes on the south side of Salmon Creek in the woods near a small feeder stream across from the large, destroyed round house in the meadow from where one could see the sun set in west of Black Rock. Pul Miauna looked at the deep brown eyes of his father, Igupa Topa, whose hair was white and long, whose face was deeply wrinkled, and whose patience and leadership were obvious. He wore his best shells, and his buckskins were warm in the wind. Six Toes was stern, as usual, with a lightning stick across his lap, and he had a white man's earring above his leather thong in his right ear. Beneath his buckskin was a white man's shirt. He waited for Igupa Topa to speak, for he was at Igupa Topa's fire and had eaten Igupa Topa's venison and acorn mush and pine nuts. Six Toes waited impatiently, however; his eyes did not speak peacefully.

"We talk again, my young warrior; I am glad. You are welcome at my fire. My venison is yours; my salmon is yours. If you should break your last bow in our struggle with the men, then I would give you one of mine. You have always done well to fool our enemies, and many of your hunters have died in our struggle to keep the Yahi alive. We appreciate your skill in watching the enemy to protect our women and children. Now, speak your mind with the straightness of a well-made arrow," said Igupa Topa.

Pul Miauna almost smiled at the ease in which Igupa Topa spoke with Six Toes.

"As you know," said Six Toes, "the blue coats have left the mountains and canyons, and winter approaches, perhaps the hardest winter the Yahi will ever face. Many are dead from this summer, and villages have disappeared. You have gathered food, and you protect many people. Most people think you are wise. You look wise. Certainly, our winter will be easier because of your leadership than because of mine. I have not gathered food. I have burned cabins and killed settlers. The war will begin with a fury again when next summer arrives. Perhaps we can drive the settlers away forever if we burn the homes they rebuild this winter. We cannot sit as they hunt us and steal our land. We must continue to fight. Only in this manner can we secure our land and be free to hunt in peace. For our survival I ask that you command some of your hunters to join me taking back our land when the spring moon is full. Otherwise, the white man will stalk you with the viciousness of Putokya, Skull People."

The fire flickered off the yellow leaves of a cottonwood tree, and wind turned the orange coals white.

"You give me much to think about," said Igupa Topa pleasantly, "and after the five hunters from Tcapalauna have built our new winter camp and the large storms have arrived, I will gather all my hunters together, and we will speak of these matters at great length. Perhaps then I can answer you better."

"Old man," replied Six Toes, "speaking with you is always like jumping in Salmon Creek and commanding the water to lie still."

"I have been a chief too many years," replied Igupa Topa. He smiled. "I will send over bearskins. You keep this fire. Perhaps tonight you can decide upon a winter's camp and decide, also, among those women and children left from Black Rock Village whom you wish us to take in the morning. I fear we will be snowed on, and I wish to break camp early. We must travel slowly; our responsibilities are great."

"Old man, how come I like you so much?" asked Six Toes with admiration in his voice.

Six Toes reached into the neck of his deer-hide garment and pulled on a leather thong. Out came a white man's hunting knife and a fancy leather pouch, tightly stitched. Six Toes removed the knife from the thong and extended it to Igupa Topa. "This is a gift, old man, for feeding so many."

Igupa Topa stood quietly for an extra moment and raised doubt as to whether he would accept the gift. Not to do so would be a great insult, even if the knife were too great of a gift, and still Six Toes extended the knife and stared into Igupa Topa's eyes. When Igupa Topa extended his hand and accepted the large knife, Pul Miauna smiled. Peace was among the Yahi, no matter how temperamental Six Toes was.

"We go now," said Igupa Topa, and he turned and walked back to the women's fire and to the makeshift, cedar lean-tos. Pul Miauna and the others followed him.

Pul Miauna had to laugh at the blind man, who wanted to know exactly what the gift was. He wanted to touch it, to marvel at its strength. How someone could get so excited was beyond Pul Miauna, but the knife was a great gift. Pul Miauna would wait until the proper time to examine the knife, however, perhaps when the new men's house was built and when all the men would make up stories to see who could get away with the most lying. Ilhataina was the worst joker of all, and before one even knew a story had gone astray, one would hear that the stars were made from fallen leaves and that Ichpul, Frog Woman, stole fire. Once back at the main fire, Gowila helped Ilhataina to sit in the pine needles, and Igupa Topa gave them the knife to touch.

"You must be careful," said Igupa Topa. "This saltu's knife is very sharp and hard."

Pul Miauna noticed Hitchinna's impatient expression as she sat on a log near the fire. His other women were happy, and Jupka and Chikpina were weaving baskets. Hitchinna removed Yolaina from inside her skin where she had been feeding him and keeping him warm. She wrapped him with a rabbit-skin blanket and handed him, crying, to Pul Miauna.

"Take your son, and teach him when to pee," Hitchinna said, still disgruntled. She removed her top in front of the fire and turned it inside out. She then walked into the moonlight toward the headwaters of the

Feather River, and in the freezing wind she rinsed herself and her deer-skin top. With his back to the fire, Pul Miauna carefully admired her beautiful full breasts and her long, braided black hair.

"Little Halai Auna would not pee on Chuhna like that, Yolaina," said Pul Miauna. "Now your poor mother will have to be sweet-talked a full moon before she will smile again, that is if she does not freeze to death before she gets back to the fire. You know her name means Wildcat Woman for a reason. She is quiet and beautiful, but she must not be made angry," said Pul Miauna. "Besides, she would not urinate on you when the cold north wind blows through the high country and when the stars twinkle like roaring white water in the sunshine. Oh well, at least I have Chuhna to keep me warm tonight." Pul Miauna tickled his son's belly, turned toward the fire, sat down, and placed Yolaina on his knee.

Pul Miauna watched Igupa Topa admiring Chikpina and Jupka's basketry. He then walked to where Pul Miauna sat, and joined his son and grandson at the fire. He took Yolaina gently into his withered, old hands, and Yolaina stopped crying.

"Have you learned to climb the steep canyon to where the sun sets early and a spring continually seeps from the ground?" Igupa Topa asked Yolaina. "One can find a true limb of mountain juniper there."

"No," answered Hitchinna for her gurgling, drooling son. "You tell your grandfather that you are only a mommy's boy and want only large warm breasts to suckle." Wrapping herself in a deerskin, she sat next to Pul Miauna in the pine needles. She rested her head on his shoulder, and he put his arm around her.

"Well, even a little hunter needs to appreciate the finer things in life," answered Igupa Topa with a smile on his face.

CHAPTER 3

Death at Three Knolls

Pul Miauna arrived back in camp in the late afternoon. He had a turkey with him, but no one seemed to care because Yolaina and Halai Auna, the rowdiest three-year-olds he had ever seen, supposedly knocked over a basket of a neighbor's acorn mush. The woman, Jamuka, Acorn Worm Woman, was not swayed with part of Chuhna and Hitchinna's acorn mush. Pul Miauna could see no solution, especially when Jamuka would not accept his turkey for the damage the two three year olds had done.

"Your children are out of control," she scolded Pul Miauna and waved her stirring stick. "They need to learn greater respect for the work of others. Perhaps they should go without food a day, and then the little ones would not knock over a hard day's work."

The sun was too hot for Pul Miauna to argue with Jamuka, but at least with over a hundred people gathered together, food was plentiful, not that Jamuka needed any extra food. She was as round as a full moon.

Even Hitchinna had much to say about the spilled mush, and Pul Miauna listened carefully to every word. Fortunately, Chuhna was weaving baskets and rope in the makeshift women's house, for she was having her blood time and was not around to tell Pul Miauna what she thought about the two wild three-year-olds. Pul Miauna had heard plenty already, and even though he had much on his mind, he took Hitchinna's advice and decided to talk with Yolaina and Halai Auna.

"Come," he said to them," let's swim and then have a talk." He held out his pointing finger on each hand. Yolaina took the left, and Halai Auna took the right. They walked through the trampled brown grass, down the embankment, onto the gray river rocks, and into the water near a small sandy beach. The river there was too swift for swimming, and large boulders lay under the white water. A small spot behind a large boulder near the beach was suitable for cooling off in the extreme heat, however. "Up you go," said Pul Miauna. He held both children in arms and waded out to his waist. "Hold on now; we are dunking all the way under."

"No," screeched Halai Auna, but she was quickly doused.

Pul Miauna walked them back to the shore and set them down. As he splashed water on a couple of boulders so that they could sit on the heated rocks, Yolaina began the conversation.

"She tried to take my spear, and then she kicked me."

"Who did, Jamuka?" asked Pul Miauna.

"No. I did not," yelled Halai Auna. "That was my spear."

"I made it," said Yolaina.

"You gave me the spear," countered Halai Auna.

"Where is the spear now?" asked Pul Miauna.

A pause followed, and Yolaina said, "Mother broke it and threw it in Salmon Creek."

"You must have been pretty troublesome for Hitchinna to break your spear and to throw it in Salmon Creek. Who turned over Jamuka's acorn mush?"

"It was an accident," said Halai Auna, who knew she and Yolaina were never punished for accidents.

"How did it happen, though?" continued Pul Miauna.

"She grabbed my spear and would not let go. Then she kicked me, and we fell over a rock. The spear tipped over the mush," said Yolaina.

"It was an accident," said Halai Auna.

"Well, this accident would not have happened if you two had not been fighting," said Pul Miauna. "I fear you have learned improper behavior. Perhaps you should listen to the story of the two sisters, Haka Lasi, Loon Woman, and Tsore Jowa, Eagle Woman."

"It was still an accident," said Halai Auna as she played in the sand with a stick.

"Perhaps," said Pul Miauna, "but listen carefully anyhow."

"Haka Lasi and Tsore Jowa lived with many brothers in their father's house, some distance from Jigulmatu. After a great time Haka Lasi, the younger sister, fell in love with her brother, Wildcat Man, Hitchinna. She saw him in a dream and said, 'I dream of Hitchinna; I dream that he is my husband.' That night all the men came back from hunting and at daybreak they all went for a swim. Tsore Jowa made food for them.

"Haka Lasi, however, took a large staff with her to the top of the sweathouse and said, 'Where is my husband? Send him to me. We must go on a journey. Send me my husband.'

"All Haka Lasi's brothers knew she was not married. They said 'You have no husband here. All the men in this sweathouse are your brothers.' But Haka Lasi continued: 'Send me my husband.'

"The eldest son…"

"Look," interrupted Yolaina, "a butterfly." Indeed, one was sunning itself on his toe and then flew away.

"The eldest son said," continued Pul Miauna, "that he would go up to Haka Lasi and see what she had to say.

"'You are not my husband,' said Haka Lasi. 'Do not come near me.' Haka Lasi drove him back into the sweathouse and said again, 'Send me my husband.'

"Her father, Juka, Silk Worm Man, sent all his many sons, one at a time to the top of the sweathouse until only one son, Hitchinna, was left in the corner, sleeping and wrapped in wildcat skins. Said Juka, 'Hitchinna, Haka Lasi must want you, for you are the only one left.'

"Haka Lasi replied, 'Yes. Send me Hitchinna. We must go on a journey.'

"Hitchinna said not a word. He washed himself, dressed nicely, and went to Haka Lasi, Loon Woman. 'The sun is high. We must go quickly.' They traveled a great distance, and all the while they sang to Hitchinna. At night Haka Lasi built them a bed, and they lay down. Hitchinna could not sleep, however, for he was frightened. He got a rotten log, put it on Haka Lasi's arm, and covered it. He then ran with all his might back to the sweathouse and arrived about sunrise.

"Chuhna, Juka's sister, heard this news and was terribly worried that Haka Lasi would kill everyone in the sweathouse, but Chuhna was a great weaver of baskets and could twist fine ropes. One of her baskets was as big as a house, and one of her ropes was attached to the sky. She said to Hitchinna, 'You must all climb into my basket and let me pull you to the sky. Haka Lasi will not follow us there. If she finds us in the sweathouse, she will kill us all.'

"Metsi, Coyote Man, was the first. 'I will be in the bottom of the basket.' All the others followed Metsi into the basket. Then Chuhna rose on her rope and pulled the basket after her into the sky. All were gone from the sweathouse. It was empty.

"When Haka Lasi awoke and saw the rotten log instead of Hitchinna, she said, 'I will catch you wherever you are.' Haka Lasi ran back to the sweathouse, but she could find no one and no tracks. She was furious and burned the sweathouse to the ground. It was a heap of burning embers. Then she saw the great basket almost at the sky, very near the sun.

"Metsi, Coyote Man, became curious. 'I wonder how high we are,' he said, and he poked a small hole in the bottom of the basket. That instant, the basket burst apart and everyone, except Haka Lasi's sister, Tsore Jowa, fell from the sky straight into the burning embers. Tsore Jowa was on the top, near the outside rim of the basket when it broke, and she was able to catch hold of the sun and to save herself.

"Haka Lasi saw all the men were burning in white hot embers. Haka Lasi was glad. She made a net and waited near the fire. Soon a body burst open, and a heart flew into her net. Then another body burst apart, and its heart also flew into her net. Soon all the hearts except two, her father's and her oldest brother's, were in the net. Juka's heart flew high out of the fire, almost to the sky, and landed on an island in the Klamath River, and the eldest son's heart flew high to Wahkanopa's sister peak to the north, Wahkalu. Both became men again, but were buried to their necks and could not eat.

"Haka Lasi strung the hearts around her neck and went to a lake east of Jigulmatu, but it was not deep enough. She then went to Crater Lake northwest of Klamath Lake. She wanted to live in the bottom of Crater Lake.

"The two Fishing Bird brothers, Tsanunewa brothers, heard…"

"I am hungry," said Halai Auna, who could sit still no longer, even though she had enjoyed the story to that point.

"Wouldn't you like to hear how the Tsanunewa brothers helped Tsore Jowa kill Haka Lasi and bring her brothers and father back to life?"

"No, I want some acorn mush," said Halai Auna.

"Well, it is probably cool now," said Pul Miauna thoughtfully. He loved them dearly and often wondered about their training and safety. "But first you must tell me what you will do if the white men begin shooting at us. Do you remember our plan?"

"We run to this beach and hide behind this big boulder," said Yolaina.

"And what do you wait for?" asked Pul Miauna.

"We wait for you to throw a rope across Salmon Creek, and we ride across the creek holding your hair," said Yolaina.

"And then," continued Pul Miauna, "what do you do next?"

"We run from tree to tree until we cannot be seen," said Yolaina.

"And then we walk up the feeder stream and to our winter's home to wait for you and mother and Hitchinna," added Halai Auna.

"That is correct. I am so proud of you. Give me a hug."

He hugged them both warmly.

"I have decided on your punishment," added Pul Miauna as Yolaina squirmed free to urinate in the stream.

"No," said Halai Auna.

"Yes," added Pul Miauna. "Do you see Hitchinna, your beautiful mother, up at the fire roasting the delicious turkey? See, she says you must be punished. She says you must be careful, and your mother is very temperamental. We must not upset her any more, at least not today." Pul Miauna tickled Halai Auna's bare belly.

"Stop," replied Halai Auna, pushing Pul Miauna's hand away. "I don't want to."

"Here is your punishment: You must give your portion of blackberries to Jamuka."

"No," cried Yolaina with instant tears running down his cheeks.

"And you must say you are sorry," added Pul Miauna.

"Halai Auna did it," sobbed Yolaina.

"It was an accident," whined Halai Auna. "I don't want to give blackberries to Jamuka. She's ugly. She yelled at us."

"If Jamuka does not want the berries, you must set them on the ground at her feet. If she kicks them into the dirt, you must pretend they were never yours, that you do not miss them. You come with me now, and stay close by. We will visit with Hitchinna. I will tell her what must be done," said Pul Miauna, but he knew making the children give up their blackberries was easier said than done.

*   *   *

Igupa Topa arrived back in camp in time for dinner. He and his family feasted on watercress, turkey, and acorn mush. When Igupa Topa heard of Halai Auna and Yolaina's punishment, he walked them over to Jamuka, who sat with her two children and husband. Jamuka calmly accepted the blackberries from the children, but Igupa Topa's smile helped. Yolaina and Halai Auna both acted well, for they wanted blackberries the following evening. One night without blackberries was enough.

Pul Miauna watched all this with great amusement, and the merriment of children running around a camp of so many people pleased him immensely. After dinner he took Hitchinna to watch the sunset at the old, burned men's house in the sloping meadow a short walk from where they were camped next to the river. Chikpina and Jupka cleaned up and watched over Yolaina and Halai Auna. Pul Miauna knew the members of Tcapalauna would have to move the following morning, for having so many people congregated together was very dangerous. Not many men were in camp, either. Dari Jowa, Demauna, and Chunoyahi were still drying meat around Wahkanopa, and other men had been gone several nights to exact revenge on a particular settler's woman. The white man lived far to the south near Concow.

As Hitchinna and he watched the setting sun over Black Rock, Pul Miauna was very pleased even if life was a struggle about which his ancestors could not have dreamed. Who could have imagined when he was a boy that such a great struggle would have killed so many of the Yahi so quickly? As a man, Pul Miauna had known no other life than that of struggling against the vengeance of the saltu.

"This is a good spot," commented Pul Miauna. "Above us many oak trees are about to rain enough acorns to feed us well many winters. Blackberries are in abundance at the small feeder streams and springs. The sides of the canyon have tall pines where many deer lie in the shade next to the large ferns and small brooks. A few years ago many hundreds of people would meet here to celebrate such abundance. I wish I could dig out the dirt and burned timbers of this once sturdy sweathouse, and that we could live here in peace. I wish we could just grow old and always sit like this on the open hillside and in the light of setting sun."

"Your words always dance lightly around a great fire, my husband. Dreaming too much is not always good."

"I know, Hitchinna. I know."

"Igupa Topa swears he has seen the sun fall into the great water. Do you believe him?" asked Hitchinna.

"Yes. He is old and well traveled. He traded with many villages in all directions well before the settlers arrived. He knows much."

"How come, I wonder, the sun does not go out?"

"You know the story, *The First Battle in the World*, in which Bohkuina made a road under the great water and under the earth back to the east. The road is smooth without rocks, and in the east is where Tuina, Sun Man, rests before he and the tiny dog in his hair follow the road across the sky again. You know that is why bright shells lie upon the shore of the great water. Tuina bubbles and boils the water with his great light, and turns the shells every color of the colored bow. When Tuina crosses his road in the sky, colors dance from his shells. I tell you truly, Igupa Topa has seen Tuina sink into the great water, and Igupa Topa has collected the bright shells from its sandy shore. Even you admire what few abalone buttons Igupa Topa has left. You must be careful not to admire them too much. Those buttons remind him of a time when he was young and strong and a great hunter." Pul Miauna held Hitchinna even more tightly.

"Those buttons are very beautiful. Yolaina and Halai Auna fight to see them. Igupa Topa is a good grandfather. He tells them too many wild stories, however, and when they cause trouble, he just laughs and smiles and hugs them. He says he wants to hunt no more. He says he only wants to eat Tcapalauna's food and to play with his grandchildren, even if he has to hide in the brush."

"He is a chief with two fully grown hunters. It is his right. He brings much harmony to the Yahi, and he is the wisest of the chiefs," said Pul Miauna with concern for his father's health.

"He almost needs a cane. In the mornings he walks like a broken stick to the stream for his bath. Then he goes back to the other men so that he and Ilhataina can laugh and tell dirty stories to Gowila. They make bows and arrows and tell more dirty stories. Then they want fresh roasted meat and much acorn mush for their morning meal. Then he plays with the children and swims in the stream. He talks with many people throughout the day. He listens to many problems."

"He does like dirty stories," commented Pul Miauna, who also liked to listen to the old men's dirty stories. In fact, Pul Miauna liked to talk about sex in great detail with the old men in a sweathouse, and always Igupa Topa and Ilhataina liked to hear sexual jokes.

Pul Miauna paused before he spoke next, for the moment was so perfect. "Tomorrow we will climb north out of the canyon and into the brush of Antelope Creek."

"May we stay another day? We have much work to do. Chikpina and Jupka are so happy, and they do not enjoy these climbs. Chuhna still has her blood time."

"I am sorry. Igupa Topa has already decided, and besides, as you can well see," added Pul Miauna as he nodded for Hitchinna to glance downhill toward the stream, "Six Toes and his vengeful hunters have now arrived."

Hitchinna looked, and Six Toes had arrived, along with Malwila, Topuna, Tsanunewa, Bohkuina, Ketchowala, and Bill Sills, the halfbreed in his white shirt of saltu's cloth. All had lightning sticks. All had come from avenging hundreds of Yahi and Yana deaths. All were on the run from the saltu who tracked the Yahi.

*   *   *

Hitchinna and Pul Miauna sat in front of the small fire on the embankment near the river's border. Yolaina and Halai Auna slept on a bearskin. Hitchinna sat between Pul Miauna's legs, and he had his arms around her. The night finally cooled enough for Pul Miauna to cover the children with a rabbit-skin blanket. They were always hard to put to sleep. First, one would twist and ask a question, and the other one would roll on top of the first. Then they would talk some more, or they would fight and cry, especially if they were too tired. The day had been hectic for them, however, with all the other children about.

"Look," said Hitchinna. "They are so peaceful. Their hair is long and black, and they breathe quietly. One would never know that each of them thought that everything in these canyons belongs to him or her. Each must fight daily for all, especially anything belonging to another child."

Pul Miauna was not thinking about the sleeping children, however; he wanted to melt magically into another world without conflict so that he could be alone with his wife forever. He held her tightly and said nothing.

"Truly we are meant for each other," said Hitchinna. "I would climb a hundred canyons with weight enough for ten women, and would hide in the brush forever to be with you. I would bear you fifty children if I could. You are the finest man alive. I know. I look at them all."

Pul Miauna smiled at her joke. "You need only do half the work you are already doing, and for my love, you need to do nothing at all. I cannot help but love you. You stole my heart when I became a man, and I have been passionately out of control ever since. A man is helpless when such a love takes over his heart."

Hitchinna stood and helped Pul Miauna to his feet. Pul Miauna stoked the fire with small branches, for it was nearly extinguished. Then Pul Miauna and Hitchinna lay next to their two children, Halai Auna and Yolaina. Hitchinna covered Pul Miauna and herself completely with the deerskin and lay with her head on Pul Miauna's shoulder.

"Will our children know peace in these canyons?" asked Hitchinna.

"They do not know fear now. They know only simple discomforts, such as hunger and tired feet."

"But this killing, will it ever end?"

"I do not know, my woman. I truly do not know."

"What did Six Toes bury in his fire pit this evening before he took embers from Igupa Topa's fire?" continued Hitchinna.

"Billy Sills calls them *coins*. Many were taken from the killed white women at Concow. Six Toes buys lightning sticks and soft stones with them from the Paiutes. Billy Sills helps with the transactions."

"Billy Sills was born because a white man raped his mother, and he was raised like a dog. His mother is dead, and he is very angry. Many hundreds of all types of Indians have been killed, peaceful Maidus and Wintuns, mainly, but also those Yana on the ranches to the north. Billy saw drunken men rape and shoot his mother. The white men took the little gold *coins* they had earned. The rancher and his wife did nothing to help Billy's mother. Then Billy stole the rancher's lightning stick and came to Six Toes. Billy says no Indian is safe, no matter who he is or where he is. Billy Sills wishes to fight until he is killed. He says only fighting is honorable. Six Toes likes him very much, but Billy Sills is rash. He knows too many of the white men's ways, and has too little patience," said Pul Miauna. "He teaches Six Toes to speak the white men's tongue."

"What did Igupa Topa say after he heard all that was said at the fire?" asked Hitchinna.

"Igupa Topa said that Six Toes' baby son will be a great leader some day, just as his father is, and that Billy Sills needed a new shirt, for his white shirt can be seen from a great distance and is a threat to the Yahi."

"That is all?" asked Hitchinna. "The talking lasted a long time."

"Others talked. Igupa Topa listened. The stories were not pleasant. Billy Sills bragged of stuffing a woman's liver in her mouth and of cutting the hair from her head. You do not need to hear more of such loud and evil talking. Billy Sills is just a tormented boy, but he believes as many Yahi do, that revenge is necessary and good, that justice can be served only through revenge."

"We will begin a new journey with the morning's light," said Hitchinna, "far away from Six Toes."

A dog began ferociously barking slightly downstream from where Six Toes had made his fire, but it soon ceased. Pul Miauna sat up to search the moonlight for any sign of danger, but nothing could be seen or heard. Perhaps the dog was barking at an errant bear. Pul Miauna became too tired to care, and all he saw was the dancing shadows of branches across the sparkling, moonlit white water. He lay back down, covered his head to avoid the moonlight, and turned on his side. Hitchinna turned on her side also.

"Good night my love," said Pul Miauna. "May you dream of warm spring days and budding azaleas."

"Good night," replied Hitchinna. "I love you."

*   *   *

The loud thunder from the many lightning sticks pierced the gray light of the early morning, and Pul Miauna jerked from his calm sleep as if waking from a dreaded dream. He saw Six Toes run from the men's fire to the fire of his wife and new baby boy. He saw Billy Sills snaking his way from tree to tree down the rounded knoll, and screaming children and women ran toward the stream.

Pul Miauna thought of stringing his bow, but Hitchinna rolled behind the embankment with Halai Auna in her arms.

"Hurry!" she screamed. "Bring Yolaina!"

Pul Miauna grabbed his quiver, and quickly helped Yolaina from where he sat under the deerskin and stared, abandoned to fear at seeing his tribe murdered. Pul Miauna picked up Yolaina in his left arm and ran toward the river after Hitchinna and Halai Auna.

"They are shooting people," yelled Yolaina.

"We will cross the river and escape," said Pul Miauna as they reached the small sandy beach behind a large boulder. He laid down his bow and arrows. Hitchinna was there, close by, and helped to hide the children behind the boulders. Pul Miauna picked up his coiled rope with the rock attached to its end and twirled it above his head. The rope glided across the creek, landed among many boulders, and became lodged.

"Take the children across the river," yelled Pul Miauna to Hitchinna as he turned to look back at the fighting. A white man was running down the knoll to inspect Malwila, lying still by a large black oak. "You must come," she yelled.

"No. Others need help," said Pul Miauna. "You go."

Hitchinna waded into the frigid water and pulled the frightened children along.

"Hold on with all your might, Yolaina. Hold on Halai Auna. When you get to the other side, run and do not stop." As he spoke, several dead children and women scraped under the rope and floated downstream.

Pul Miauna saw the disgust on his wife's face as he helped Yolaina and Halai Auna hold on to her hair, but he too felt thoroughly sickened at the dead bodies. Hitchinna kicked off in the rapid white water and made her way safely to the other shore, and the children held tightly to her hair. Though the distance from the shore to the trees and beyond was short, Pul Miauna watched Halai Auna stand almost paralyzed with great fear as Hitchinna jerked Yolaina and her to the trees.

Pul Miauna watched until Hitchinna, Yolaina, and Halai Auna were temporarily safe. Looking downstream, he saw Ketchowala reloading his lightning stick, but others among Six Toes' hunters were already dead. Ichpul and Tsanunewa lay sprawled out on the hillside. Pul Miauna looked in the other direction for the rest of his direct family, and Igupa Topa rolled from behind a live oak and into the boulders. Not far away both Gowila and Ilhataina were lying on the ground with blood oozing from their bodies. Many women and children were on the ground also. Pul Miauna looked to find Chuhna, to see if he could save her, but she was far away and sitting in the open, naked. She was singing and crying and holding her foot and watching others scream and die. Pul Miauna could do nothing, but as Igupa Topa arrived behind the large boulder, Pul Miauna turned and saw Hitchinna screaming from behind a black oak for him to cross Salmon Creek. Pul Miauna pulled the rope taut, and Igupa Topa and he waded into the river. Pul Miauna grabbed a boy by the hair as he floated by, and surprisingly the child grabbed his hand. When Pul Miauna pulled him into his arms, he noticed the child's foot was shot. Igupa Topa took the child from Pul Miauna, grabbed the rope, and began kicking his way across Salmon Creek's white water. Downstream Pul Miauna could see white men shooting the swimming children and women who were still alive when they were washed into a pool with a steep bank on the opposite shore. When Igupa Topa reached the far shore, he picked up the boy, and with all the strength in his old body, he ran to the trees of the steep hillside. Pul Miauna saw Igupa Topa's hand partially explode, though, as if it were a snapping ember in a hot fire, but still the old man carried the boy to Hitchinna.

Pul Miauna again pulled the rope taut, for he was next if he were to live even another moment. He glanced to his rear as the saltu were descending the hillside and shooting wounded victims again. Pul Miauna entered the white water and kicked with hard stokes as he pulled on the rope. A dead woman crashed between two boulders and onto him; he held on tightly, however, and emerged once more into the air and close to the opposite shore. He kicked water rapidly, and soon his feet found footing where the water was a bit calm. He looked back toward the north shore where he had just left, and a white man stood on the grassy bank near the fire pit that Hitchinna and he had used the night before, and leveled a lightning stick at him. Pul Miauna took one more step, gazed into Hitchinna's horrified face and at Igupa Topa's retreat up the hillside. Igupa Topa held his bloody hand close to his body. Then Pul Miauna felt a searing heat through his chest and fell. He lay in the sand without the power to move and looked back at the man who shot him. Another man in fancy black clothes joined the man on the embankment and leveled his lightning stick at Pul Miauna. Pul Miauna tried to look to where he heard Hitchinna's screams, but a ferocious shock hit his head. He was only briefly aware of a descending blackness.

*   *   *

Hitchinna wiped her tears and tried not to think of the early morning massacre. She kneeled before Halai Auna and Yolaina in the small, earthen home they had used for the last three winters. All were much in shock, and Halai Auna was crying.

"Where is father?" asked Yolaina. "Is he dead? Did the lightning sticks kill him too?"

"Yes," replied Hitchinna with swelling tears in her eyes, "but listen to what I have to say. I have staked Igupa Topa and the boy to the ground because I must heal their wounds. When you hear them scream, do not pay attention and stay in the house. They will scream only a short time. I will be quick."

"No," cried Halai Auna. "Do not leave."

"I have to, my darling. You do not want them to die also, do you?"

"No."

"Then stay here and be strong. You must. Soon we will all cry together. There will be much time for grief." Hitchinna removed the large hunting knife from its skin, stood, and walked up the stairs to the fire near where Igupa Topa and the boy were well staked, flat on their backs, to the ground. She placed the knife's blade in the fire, and looked at Igupa Topa's face, calm as usual, but pained.

"First, burn all the exposed flesh on the boy's foot. Be quick and be forceful, for he has bled too much. Do not listen to his screams."

"No. Let me up. Do not burn me," he screamed.

Igupa Topa let the boy talk and whine, and he continued with the last of the instructions. "Then reheat the knife and cut off my hand, neatly between the joints, as if you were cutting the hooves from a deer before hanging it upside down from a strong oak branch. I have seen you do this many times. I know you can cut well. Do not listen to my screams. Be forceful. My bones in my hand are all shattered, and I will die unless you cut it off. Then reheat the knife and burn all the flesh to stop the bleeding. When we are calm, you can let us up. You must be stronger than you have ever been to do this, Hitchinna. I once removed a smashed foot. The man's screams haunted my nights, but he lived many moons."

Hitchinna looked at the large knife a moment and waited for the coals to finish heating its blade. The boy, not much older than Yolaina, lay begging to be let up. Hitchinna removed the knife from the coals, held the boy's foot firmly as he screamed, and cauterized the wound, first the bottom where the flesh was much torn, and then the top. At first the boy screamed and jerked his foot, and then he was silent and calm and blank. He had passed out.

"Mother," cried Halai Auna from the entrance to the earthen home.

"Go back in," screamed Hitchinna with much fear and anger and anxiety in her voice. She placed the knife's blade back into the fire, and glared at Halai Auna until she retreated.

"Check his wound carefully now that he is still," added Igupa Topa.

She removed the tourniquet from his ankle and looked at the boy.

"He will live, Hitchinna. You did well. Now me. Cut off my hand. Place the piece of driftwood under my wrist, place your knees on both sides of my wrist, and be graceful and quick. Do not stop. Do not listen to my cries. I am old and do not need my hand anyhow. Now hurry before I beg as a little baby for you to stop. Be quick while I still have honor left in my heart. Give me some leather to bite."

Hitchinna placed a piece of leather in the old man's mouth. She then removed the knife, placed the driftwood under the wrist, knelt on the shattered hand and forearm, and with as much speed as possible, cut off the hand neatly between the joints. She placed the cut off hand in the fire along with the knife blade, and tried not to listen to poor Igupa Topa as he wailed and writhed in his agony. She waited what seemed like an eternity and watched the blown-apart hand burn and the knife become very hot. She then burned Igupa Topa's stump, and he passed out, a blessing. She removed the deerskin tourniquet on his forearm, and then she walked slowly back to the children to cry and to wait before cutting the boy and Igupa Topa loose.

Hitchinna did not know a beautiful, warm morning could hold such grief, for she had lost Jupka and Chuhna and Chikpina and her loving husband, Pul Miauna. Hitchinna herself wanted to die then, to plunge the white man's large hunting knife deep within her own breast.

Little Yolaina and Halai Auna were at the door of the house, both in great shock at the horrible screams they had just heard. Hitchinna dropped the large knife and went to them, held them very closely, and sobbed and sobbed and sobbed. She did not even have the willpower to burn her hair or to collect pitch to put on her stubble; such was her grief. She did not know how she could even continue to breathe.

CHAPTER 4

The Men's House

Demauna, Chunoyahi, Dari Jowa, Igupa Topa, Yolaina, and Lawalila, Large Hawk Man, sat together in the men's house. Lawalila had become a part of Tcapalauna when Igupa Topa fortuitously pulled him from Salmon Creek by the hair of his head and helped him hop up the south side of the canyon to the safety of the winter camp. Lawalila's foot was maimed but caused him no pain, and he walked with only the slightest of compensation. Yolaina and Lawalila were eager, new companions of the men's house, no matter how humble when compared to Tcapalauna's large house of the past. Yolaina and Lawalila were proud that Igupa Topa, even over the stern look of Hitchinna, admitted them to the house. They were allowed a spot to keep their tools, weapons, and skins, and they could sleep there away from the women. They could learn more about the ways of men, including all the nuances of the men's tongue and all the knowledge required to make proper hunting gear: bows, arrows, knives, slings, spears, nets, ropes, decoys, snares, and poisons. They could also participate in the conversations, which, with

Igupa Topa's keen wit, were becoming as riddled with symbolism, underlying truths, and sexual puns as was his face with wrinkles. Yolaina and Lawalila could not smoke, however, for Igupa Topa thought they were too young. Yolaina and Lawalila did not care about smoking anyhow. They were more than happy to be sitting on the tule mats and skins and to be taking instructions on how to make weapons and tools.

Dari Jowa was carefully shaping the last uneven spots from his newest bow of mountain juniper with a piece of smooth sandstone. He had been working on the bow for about six moons and would soon back the bow with chewed sinew and salmon-skin glue.

"Now that you are members of the men's house," said Dari Jowa to the wide-eyed six year olds, "you should perhaps begin making bows." Dari Jowa glanced at Igupa Topa, and noticed the great love and pride in the old man's heart. "Perhaps when the sun rises in the morning, we will go together and find sturdy limbs from healthy trees and make ourselves fine new bows. What do you say, Yolaina?"

"Yes. I want a bow," said Yolaina, "and I want arrows. I want to bring Hitchinna a large buck. She will be proud."

"I want to shoot a large buck also," said Lawalila.

"Should we make bows of yellow pine, black oak, or mountain juniper?" asked Dari Jowa with a straight face. It was a trick question, for yellow pine made a worthless bow.

"Black oak," said Lawalila, for he much admired Demauna's bow of black oak.

"Black oak is a good choice," said Dari Jowa, "and it is easy to obtain. Maybe I will use black oak also. How about you, Yolaina?"

"I want mountain juniper like the one you are making," said Yolaina, for he loved his uncle dearly.

"Then tomorrow we will pull one branch of black oak and one branch of mountain juniper from the trees, but I must warm you, Yolaina, we must hike into Deer Creek Canyon to my favorite tree of mountain juniper in order to find a proper limb. I will help you pull the limb from the tree, but you must carry it a long way back. Maybe you would like to use a limb of black oak instead. Black oak makes a fine bow."

"Pul Miauna always used mountain juniper," replied Yolaina.

A short silence filled the earthen room, for speaking of the dead was not good. The children, however, were not scolded; they were allowed to forget their dead naturally and would be taught not to speak of painful events by example. No one fed human energy into the boy's remembrance of his father. The children seldom mentioned the dead, for the spirit world filled their minds with many fearful stories already. Outside great gusts of wind periodically roared over the brush covered earthen dwelling. Chunoyahi added two pieces of wrist-sized limb wood to the fire. Demauna removed some deer-hide thongs from a bundle of five arrows that he wanted to heat and to straighten. Igupa Topa was more than happy to fill the silence, however, for Dari Jowa had just put himself in a position to be teased.

"I thought I heard you say at last night's fire that you would hike downstream to Matdasi's new camp past the flat mountain near the feeder stream and high shallow cave, and there you would ask old Matdasi, Spring Salmon Woman and chief of that camp, for permission to marry Kaitsiki, Squirrel Woman," said Igupa Topa quietly but with a smile on his face.

"You are correct, Igupa Topa, I heard him also," added Demauna as he removed a small piece of cedar from his septum. "Have you lost courage?" asked Demauna of Dari Jowa.

"The winter will be long, and I will have plenty of time to be with a woman. Now, however, our two new men need to make bows. After we gather our limbs, I will go to Matdasi's new camp."

"I believe last week you needed to search lower Deer Creek for a possible new winter camp, and the week before that you needed to search for broken glass to make arrow points," said Chunoyahi. "No. I think Dari Jowa is afraid to ask for Kaitsiki to marry him. Maybe he is afraid that Squirrel Woman will scamper up a tree and away into the forest forever."

"Kaitsiki will not scamper away in fright. She loves me. Her eyes speak with great lust, and her heart sputters like the hot, bubbling mud pits of Wahkanopa, just for me."

"Dari Jowa is not afraid," said Yolaina, who was not keen about matters of love.

"Dari Jowa is a brave man," said Chunoyahi softly to Yolaina. "He, for instance, would face a grizzly bear with his bow and arrows and hand spear. He would face a whole canyon full of blue coats. He would probably even cross the mountains in winter to search in the east for obsidian, but the tiny sparkle in Kaitsiki's eyes sends the fear of thunder through his heart."

"You see," added Demauna, "a woman has the power to turn a hunter into a coward afraid of his own reflection in still water."

"After we have our limbs, I will rise the next morning, bathe, dress in my finest skins of wildcat and beads, and paint my face, and by the light of Matdasi's fire that evening, I will ask for Kaitsiki to be my wife. I am not afraid," said Dari Jowa, who should have known he was simply adding another cooking stone to the already boiling basket.

"Those are truly brave words," added Igupa Topa with a smile. "Yes. Even last night I heard brave words such as those, words about how Kaitsiki would soon be filled with desire. I love such brave words."

"You have built a fine house for Kaitsiki, Squirrel Woman, to store her acorns," said Demauna, "but since she does not know of your love, the house is still empty."

"She knows of my love," replied Dari Jowa. "I sent her a fine crystal filled with many colors. Hwipajusi, Whistling Swan Man, a hunter of Matdasi's village, took it to her for me. We hunted together a little while this fall. He told me that Kaitsiki spoke of marriage and that she mentioned me. She loves me, and she speaks of me with the love of a young woman. She will be mine."

"Very brave words indeed," commented Demauna. "But maybe she has married someone else. Maybe she thought the crystal was from Hwipajusi. Hwipajusi is not afraid of women. He has three wives."

"Hwipajusi is my friend. He gave me the heart from his elk to bake. He knows that Kaitsiki loves me. Kaitsiki knows I will soon arrive in her camp to ask for her love in marriage."

"I would like some babies to fill our camp again with joy," said Igupa Topa while rubbing his left ear with the stump where his hand had been severed. "Is Kaitsiki a good woman to have babies?"

"I must admit," said Chunoyahi while adding another piece of limb wood to the fire, "that Kaitsiki looks as if she could bear many children. In fact, she looks so good that if Dari Jowa loses his nerve one more time, I think I will go down to ask her to marry me. I could use another wife. Wirula is not as lusty as she once was. Maybe Kaitsiki will make her jealous, and I will get the love I need."

"Enough of this. As soon as Yolaina gets his limb of mountain juniper, I will leave the following morning, and I will bring Kaitsiki to her new home. I will fill her with babies."

"May I go?" asked Yolaina.

"No. I will go alone. You can stay with Lawalila and make your bow, and I will silence these forked tongues myself." He put his smooth grinding stone in its pouch, and carefully placed his bow next to other completed bows. "Kaitsiki will be mine. Her heart glows like a full moon in winter for me. She will be mine." Dari Jowa stretched out on the bearskin and gazed at the small blue flames at the edge of the fire.

*   *   *

"Careful," reminded Dari Jowa, for he did not wish his little nephew to harm himself after the long struggle to pull the limb from the tree. The ascent up the crumbling off-white, damp rock was difficult enough when one had the use of both hands. Where weight was placed on the side of the steep boulder, it often gave way, and the climber was left to slide down the mountain. Dari Jowa's knee had a sizable hunk of flesh gouged from it to prove the point. Dari Jowa sat on the upper bank where all the dirt below had given way to the spring that seeped from the mountain and exposed the rock. The mountain juniper were just below them, deep in the shade even though Tuina, Sun Man, and the dog in his hair were only three-fourths of their way across the road at the sky. "Move the branch before you move yourself, and make sure three limbs are placed before you move the fourth. Good. Very good. You look like a mountain goat, and I look like a wounded rabbit." Dari Jowa watched Yolaina with great pride. He had provided for the little one ever since Pul Miauna had been killed below Three Knolls of Salmon Creek. Yolaina continued to struggle up the embankment with the limb of mountain juniper. The bow he would make would be worthless and misshapen, as were all first bows, but Dari Jowa would never tell that to Yolaina. Yolaina slipped but was not scraped, and he was much relieved and breathing deeply when he finally reached Dari Jowa. They still had to be quite cautious because the mountainside above them was steep and covered with pine needles. If they were to slip, they would fall over the bank and onto the rocks below where the spring began. Soon, however, both had dragged their new limbs of mountain juniper through manzanita and to the safety of the pines just above the ridge. They were safe.

"I am very impressed with your branch," said Dari Jowa. "I honestly did not think you could carry such a strong limb up the bank. "Do you think it will make a better bow than Lawalila's branch of black oak?"

"I know so. Demauna makes a fine bow of black oak and, and his bow is strong and shapely. His bow, however, is not as quick as one from mountain juniper, and cannot shoot an arrow as far. Look at my bow." Dari Jowa removed his bow from the otter-skin quiver. "Notice its color and smell and weight. It is the bow of a hunter, and yours will be made of the wood from the same tree as this one. When you look at your limb, envision your bow beautifully arched beneath the bark. Your bow is trying to escape, trying to reflect your patience. You must be the master of smooth stones." Dari Jowa took the bow from Yolaina. He placed the tip of the bow over his right foot and the arch of the bow in back of his left knee. With his left hand he bent the top tip of the bow until he could tie his bowstring of sinew in place. He gave the bow back to Yolaina. "Feel the strength of the bow."

Yolaina struggled against the taut sinew to little avail. "Will my bow be this strong? I cannot bend it." He was disheartened.

"No. Your bow will be the proper size for you, for the size of man you will be next year, and you will be able to pull it fully and kill much game. A bow must be exactly the correct size to match the hunter, and each year your new bow must become large enough to match your strength." Dari Jowa removed his fire drill and fireboard from his quiver.

"We must spend the night away from Tcapalauna. I will make us a fire. You can collect wood and sticky, red manzanita berries. Then you can keep the fire going, and I can hunt for whatever answers the call of a wounded rabbit. Sometimes a hungry bear answers such a call, but we will roast whatever shows its face. It would be fun to take Hitchinna the skin of a wildcat, since that is her name and since she is so fond of the yellow, speckled skin."

"I am hungry. I hope you will not be gone long."

Dari Jowa placed the fire drill through the tinder into the darkened hole of the cedar fireboard. He deftly twirled the drill, but he stopped briefly and looked at Yolaina.

"Yolaina," he said briefly before he began drilling in earnest, "a full hunter never brings home much game."

         *   *   *

The night had been hard on both Dari Jowa and Yolaina. The cold wind had howled through the tops of the trees and had even knocked over a large snag at too close of a distance from their camp. The snag could have killed them both. They did not have enough warm clothing and skins to stay even moderately warm, and neither of them got much sleep.

"Such is the life of a hunter, Yolaina," said Dari Jowa, who had spent many cold nights away from the men's house.

Yolaina was just happy to be heading home. The rabbit from the evening's meal had left his stomach many hours before, and the smashed manzanita berries in water were not enough to make him full. Manzanita berries were mostly seeds, and the drink was not meant to be a meal. He could not wait to get back to his mother's acorn cakes and baked meat. Surely Hitchinna would have something fully cooked for him, maybe a roasted haunch of bear. Demauna had been trying to organize a bear hunt before Yolaina and Dari Jowa had left camp. Demauna had said that he wanted to provide a proper place for Dari Jowa and Kaitsiki to make many babies. When Yolaina and Dari Jowa came near to the settler's road between Deer Creek and Salmon Creek, Dari Jowa became much more cautious than when they were walking freely through the woods and over dead logs and between the brush.

"If we were to be spotted in the open here, perhaps we would die," said Dari Jowa who had almost been seen on the road before. They advanced cautiously and stopped near the road where they could hide in the brush. A large amount of quacking came from above, and they looked upward into the swiftly moving clouds and threatening sky. Many ducks were flying overhead between the patches of darkening gray.

"Where do the ducks go?" asked Yolaina.

"Now they go to the south. I do not know where. Many places, Igupa Topa says. He has more stories about ducks than one can imagine, especially the wood duck, the most handsome duck of all."

"Pul Miauna was called Wood Duck Man. He was handsome."

Dari Jowa paused a moment before he replied, but he decided that if he did not use Pul Miauna's name, he would assure that Pul Miauna's spirit would remain in its world. "That is very true. He was handsome, and he had much skill as a hunter. He knew much about women and was brave in their presence. He could get much love from them. He was very brave when compared to me. I do not know exactly what to say to women. If I tell them the truth, I fear they will run away. Wood Duck Man, though, he used lies and sweet words, and women did not care what he said. They loved him."

"Will you use sweet words when you ask Kaitsiki to marry you?"

"I do not know any. I will simply ask her. I will act as my name, Dari Jowa, implies. I will swoop into her camp like a white-headed eagle and grab her with the talons of my love as if she were a large lake trout about to eat a wasp on the surface of the water. Except," continued Dari Jowa, "I will not eat her. I will…" A mounting fear made him stop. "I hear a wagon." He and Yolaina hid behind some thick brush by a large granite boulder and a sugar pine.

"We should never have talked here. Never talk near this road again. If the driver of the wagon sees us, I will have to sink an arrow into his heart, and then the saltu will hunt us again. I have seen this man before. He carries a lightning stick always. You must be very quiet. Do not move. Lie like a lizard in the shade of gray river rocks."

"Will he shoot me?" whispered Yolaina. His eyes reflected a deep terror.

Dari Jowa stood behind the tree and removed his bow and two arrows from his quiver. While stringing his bow, he whispered, "Say nothing more. Do not move."

The wagon was in full view, and the man was singing a strange song with many strange sounds. If the wagon stopped or if the singing stopped, Dari Jowa would peek from behind the tree and brush, and perhaps sink an arrow into the man's chest. All depended on stealth. Dari Jowa looked down at little Yolaina, next to his branch of juniper, and winked. Yolaina would be a fine man some day. Dari Jowa sat in a crouching position and put an arrow on the string. He became one with his skills at that instant, and his ears guided him as they often guided him when he sat patiently behind a deer blind of rocks to listen for crackling leaves and pine needles. The game in which Yolaina and Dari Jowa were involved was perhaps deadly, but in such a game, much was to be learned. Dari Jowa looked with a great pride upon Yolaina in all his fear, and the wagon kept rolling by with its large log of cedar and with its singing white man with the fat belly. Yolaina never flinched or looked up at the man. He lay still as Dari Jowa had asked. Dari Jowa could now talk at great length in the men's house about how Yolaina got his branch and was trickier than Metsi, Coyote Man. When the wagon was positively gone from view, Dari Jowa and Yolaina crossed the road to a very safe distance before they stopped for Dari Jowa to unstring his bow and to pack his quiver.

"Maybe I should have shot him," reflected Dari Jowa humorously, "but I do not know if my arrow could have pierced all that fat. You did not see him, but believe me, he was about as big a grizzly bear, but more ugly."

"I could smell him," said Yolaina. "Do all white men smell like that?"

"Probably," said Dari Jowa. "I have never seen a white man bathe, and the dead ones I have seen all smelled very badly. I think they dislike rivers."

*   *   *

With the breaking of light across the canyon, Dari Jowa was the first out of the men's house. He plunged beneath the small bathing area made in the rivulet for such a purpose and scrubbed all over. Then he left and entered the new winter's home he had recently finished. When he came out, he was truly a sight of beauty. His hair was tied in the back, and he wore his beaded skins of wildcats, and his face was painted with two stripes on both sides of his cheeks, two stripes of red and blue, from the pigments used to mark his arrows. He had his quiver made from a mountain lion's tail, and had a wrapped bear-skin, a gift for Matdasi, the chief of her village, whom Dari Jowa would have to sway with what little charm he had, that is, if he wished to marry Kaitsiki, Squirrel Woman, of his dreams.

Dari Jowa ate with Hitchinna, Halai Auna, Yolaina, Lawalila, and Igupa Topa before he left, and he took a small amount of dried salmon with him. All in the camp were quite happy for him, and all wanted to sing, to dance, and to laugh with him and Kaitsiki upon their return. Wirula, Red Fox Woman, Chunoyahi's wife, made Dari Jowa drink something, something which would give Dari Jowa strength, but something which also made him gag and which also made Igupa Topa almost fall down laughing. Apparently, Igupa Topa had had to drink such a mixture before, and he did not think highly of it. Igupa Topa always made light of Wirula's potions. Soon, however, Dari Jowa left to marry Kaitsiki.

Hitchinna was tending a small fire during the cool morning, and was cracking the small pine nuts that she and others had gathered not long before. Such work was time consuming, but all food gathering was an eternal process, from gathering seeds or digging roots to washing greens in the stream. Always the mouths were hungry. Sometimes Halai Auna would help, but she was soon bored and was still too young to have very many responsibilities. Yolaina would also help, but since he was a member of the men's house and was Dari Jowa's hunting companion, all he wanted to do was make a bow. He was trying to get the bark off his limb for much of the morning, and Hitchinna watched him carefully. Truly, he was a fine boy, and she knew that some day he would be an excellent hunter. He took great pride in all he owned and did. After a while he became tired and hungry again, however, and went to the men's house to eat some dried salmon. Lawalila had gone to listen to Igupa Topa in the men's house where it was warm, and Igupa Topa had him gathering wood for much of the morning. All of the children were blessings to Hitchinna. They gave her strength and love, and they depended greatly on her and the others for survival.

"Please put some more wood on the fire, Halai Auna," said Hitchinna.

"It's Yolaina's turn," said Halai Auna.

"You can see that Yolaina has been working hard all morning. He is shaping a new bow from the limb which took one night's travel to get."

Halai Auna was not sure such logic was good, for Yolaina had shared many of her chores before. She also missed him at night. They used to tell stories and to pretend and to play games and to sing and to dance. The nights were not the same without Yolaina around. Now she had to visit with Demauna's wife, Pahnino, and Chunoyahi's wife, Wirula. Halai Auna also missed Lawalila, but not so much as Yolaina. Yolaina was her brother, and she felt a loss of the heart.

"Yolaina thinks he is a man," said Halai Auna.

"You better hope he keeps thinking that way," said Hitchinna. "We will need him to be a good hunter some day. One might surmise that hunters are lazy, that they just sit around. You watch them, however, and they are always working on something, an arrowhead or salmon spear or fishing net, always something. Spending cold, hungry nights alone by oneself in the woods sometimes happens. Sometimes a hunter does not kill a deer and must bring a family nothing to eat until his luck changes."

"Yolaina is not working now. He is talking to Igupa Topa and listening to stories by the fire."

"You do not know what he is doing. He might be learning to chip points."

Yolaina walked out of the men's house and to the fire where Hitchinna and Halai Auna were shelling pine nuts. He sat on a log near the cooking stones, and then he stood, walked to Hitchinna and Halai Auna, and touched Hitchinna's shoulder.

"Mother, what is passion?" he asked.

Hitchinna stopped shelling a moment, added a piece of wood to the fire, and could think of nothing except that Yolaina's question had caught her totally by surprise. "Ah...passion is a strong feeling for or about anything," she replied, but she knew Igupa Topa and the other men had been filling Yolaina with stories.

"Are you passionate?" he continued.

"Sure. I am filled with passion. I desire with great feeling, for instance, that both you and Halai Auna will always be safe. I am filled with passion when I finish a beautiful cooking basket."

"Are you filled with passion when you see a man?" continued Yolaina.

Hitchinna could feel her pulse rise, but did not wish to show her feelings to the young ones. She would try to be calm. "I have normal feelings about men," she replied and tried not to think of Pul Miauna, for such thought caused her grief.

"How come you do not marry again?"

Hitchinna sighed, stopped shelling, and stared at Yolaina. He was innocent and young and full of way too many questions for such a brisk morning. "For many reasons, I guess; however, some of them are personal. Do you talk about my being single in the men's house?"

"Igupa Topa says you are a passionate woman. He says passionate women should be married."

"What do you think?" asked Hitchinna.

"I do not know," replied Yolaina.

Hitchinna continued shelling the pine nuts. "Truly, I tell you that I am passionate, and sometimes I wish I were married. However, I must then make some more acorn mush, so I do not have much time to think."

"May I have some acorn cakes for me and Lawalila and Igupa Topa? Igupa Topa sent me for them. He is hungry," replied Yolaina.

"They are in the basket by the cooking sticks," replied Hitchinna who was beginning to think that maybe the stories in the men's house were not good for her young boy. When Yolaina emerged from their home,

Hitchinna spoke to him. "You tell him to be careful, or I will tell him the story of Loon Woman, who had to stick her head under the water before she swallowed each bite of food."

"Tell me," said Halai Auna.

"Run along, now. Tell Igupa Topa what I said," she told Yolaina evenly, with just a glint of hilarity in her eyes.

*   *   *

The men's house was a bit too smoky, so Yolaina lay down on his skins. Night had just fallen, and the wind was not calm as it usually was at that time. The wind would surely bring in a storm, and as it swirled about the top of the men's house, it forced the smoke down the central cedar post. Demauna was combing his long, black hair, and Chunoyahi was chipping arrow points from a green, glass bottle that he had found on the white man's road. Chunoyahi was careful that the chips fell onto his deerskin, for they were very sharp and should not be left lying about the floor. Igupa sat smoking, a habit he had long been fond of, but he said it was not healthy. Lawalila opened the skin covering the entrance to the men's house and entered. The fire turned bright yellow about the coals, and Chunoyahi had to stop chipping a moment to close his eyes and to move his head to avoid the small sparks shooting from the flames like meteors across the night's sky. Lawalila gave a basket to Igupa Topa.

"Hitchinna said these were for you, said they were from Loon Woman. I told her Loon Woman did not live with the Yahi of Tcapalauna, but she smiled and said that Loon Woman had just stopped by for a few moments on her way to Deer Creek so that she could stick her head in the water before swallowing."

Demauna broke into laughter, and Chunoyahi smiled. Yolaina did not know what was funny, but he was happy when others were. He laughed. He liked stories about Loon Woman.

"Let us see what Loon Woman has sent this old, one-handed chief then. Let us see if it is a worthy gift." He opened the large basket, peered in dramatically, and gazed back at everyone. "Yes. This is a fine gift." He stood, set the large basket near the fire in the center of the room, removed a warm acorn cake, and dipped it in the small basket of hydrated blackberries. "This Loon Woman is definitely my kind of woman. There is a cake for everyone." Igupa Topa tasted a cake with great delight, for he loved such surprises.

"Hitchinna probably made these for Dari Jowa and his new bride, Kaitsiki," said Chunoyahi reflectively. He wondered, as did the others, where they could be, for Dari Jowa should have arrived by that late in the evening. Maybe Kaitsiki was having her blood time and should not travel. One should always avoid taunting a grizzly with the smell of blood. Many arrows from several bows were warranted for such a kill; a single hunter should never try to kill such a large and temperamental beast. Maybe Kaitsiki said no, or maybe Dari Jowa had to wait in their camp for a celebration. Dari Jowa was always wise about traveling, however, and never took risks. Perhaps he was avoiding the white men roaming the hills on their horses to gather cows and sheep, such pathetic animals, even though tasty. Any hunter could kill one. Cows and sheep were so stupid they almost jumped on the arrows.

Chunoyahi took a cake and dipped it in the blackberries. "If Dari Jowa is not back by the dawn's light, I will hunt downstream past the flat mountain and near the steep canyon for birds. I hear turkeys are big there."

"I hope Loon Woman stops by again soon," said Demauna. He loved the cakes also.

"Hitchinna made the cakes," said Yolaina. "I know. I saw her working extra hard all day so that we will be able to sing and dance and talk when Dari Jowa and Kaitsiki arrive. I saw her." He climbed off the skin to dip his cake in the blackberries. He had been eyeing the blackberries all day.

"Yes," said Igupa Topa, "I would like to eat a turkey. Hitchinna bakes them well. You go tomorrow early and kill turkeys near the feeder stream of the bluffs. Travel north out of the canyon first, however, for trees are there, and one is always hidden. Besides, Dari Jowa told me he would bring Kaitsiki back by that route."

"I think I might travel west, downstream, to hunt deer tomorrow, near the table mountain. I think maybe that would be wise. I hear deer there are almost the size of elk. I will see," said Demauna.

"Good idea," said Igupa Topa. "We could use fresh venison to help us through the coming storm."

"May I go," asked Lawalila, for Demauna had chosen to teach him to hunt, as Dari Jowa had been teaching Yolaina.

"No," said Demauna. "I must travel alone, travel fast. I must try to kill a deer and hurry home before the storm arrives."

"Is Dari Jowa okay?" asked Yolaina.

"When a hunter is gone," said Igupa Topa, "many sit at night and wonder about him. I must tell you, though, I know of no better person to travel alone, or with Kaitsiki, than your uncle. I have been with him since he was born. I taught him all I know, and then he taught me new things he had learned on his own. When a cold snow puts out his fire, another fire lights in his heart. He never complains. He is a good man."

The speech was too sensitively delivered, though. Igupa Topa was concerned. All stared at him, and he sat back on his skins, ate the rest of cake, and looked at his pipe. No one spoke immediately.

"You are right," said Demauna to Igupa Topa. "Dari Jowa is the best of traveling companions; he always carries more weight than other men. He never complains, not even about women, but that will probably change soon."

The laughter had returned.

"Probably just as soon as Kaitsiki sees that she needs tule mats and more skins," said Chunoyahi. He laughed out loud, for he knew many of the prices a woman demanded.

"Dari Jowa will probably climb through the muck on the shores of a cold lake in winter to gather brown, dead tule fronds just to keep Kaitsiki quiet. When he kills a turkey, she will want venison. When he kills a deer, she will want wood grubs. Passion makes a man do strange things," added Demauna. "I…"

Dari Jowa pulled back the skin from the entrance and put all doubts about his safety to rest, but his paint was gone and his demeanor was bleak. He did not wear his wildcat skins over his shirt. He placed the quiver and the bundled bearskin he had taken with him the morning before as a gift for Matdasi, Spring Salmon Woman, chief of Kaitsiki's tribe, on his skins near his hunting gear. He took a limb from the fire's edge, for always limbs were on the edge in case someone wanted a coal to start a fire or to light a pipe or to shape some wood.

"I need to start a fire for Hwipajusi, Whistling Swan Man. He will stay a while in my house. He is very cold and hungry. I will be right back with the horrible news," said Dari Jowa. He left, and cold wind again blew into coals.

"This will indeed be horrible news," said Igupa Topa. "Yolaina, Lawalila, maybe you should go prepare Hitchinna. Tell her we will soon tell her bad news, but that Dari Jowa is in good health."

"I want to hear," said Yolaina, who sensed he was being treated like a boy instead of a man.

Igupa Topa looked at him and then Lawalila. "Then will you go Lawalila? Bearing bad news is hard to do."

Lawalila thought about Igupa Topa's words. "I will tell her and wait there, but I want to know everything also."

"Good. You will," replied Igupa Topa, "and soon."

"I go," said Lawalila, as if he had just accepted a manly act, and he left.

Dari Jowa again entered the men's house and took a seat very near the small fire. His hands were red and chapped. He saw the remainder of the blackberry juice in the small basket and drank it ravenously. He reached into his deerskin shirt and pulled out his tinder pouch. He opened it, reached in, and removed the crystal he had given Kaitsiki. He stared at it blankly. "In my quiver are feathers of the white-headed eagle, feathers of my name, Dari Jowa. They were with the crystal in Kaitsiki's hut. They were to be her husband's, Dari Jowa's, but Kaitsiki is dead," said Dari Jowa with tears welling in his eyes. He paused, and then looked up at Yolaina. "Yolaina, get me some meat and acorn cakes and blackberry juice, if some is left, and some pine nuts. Get me much food. I have never been so hungry. Tell Hitchinna that Hwipajusi also needs food. Go quickly. Hurry back. Tell Hitchinna all are dead in Kaitsiki's village."

Yolaina quickly scrambled from his supine position and left to get the food.

"When I arrived at their camp from the small feeder stream above, all were dead. The coyotes were so full they were lying near the huts watching buzzards and condors fight over the carcasses. I could not tell boys from girls or women from men. The hair was cut from their heads, as is the white man's fashion. Many gray marks from lightning-stick stones were near the cave's entrance. There seventeen of the small, mostly skeletons lay. Most of the baskets and skins and tools were gone. Truly their spirits will be lost in these canyons for a while. We must be very careful never to leave food or water lying about at night. In the middle hut I found the crystal and feathers, and Hwipajusi confirmed that is where Kaitsiki slept."

"How many were killed?" asked Igupa Topa plaintively.

"I counted thirty-three."

"How did Hwipajusi survive?" asked Demauna.

"He was using the village toilet when the man called Anderson and the other white men with leashed dogs arrived in camp. They followed his and Malwila's deer hunting trail from the day before. Matdasi said that with so many mouths to feed hunting continually was always wise."

Yolaina entered the men's house with a steaming basket of venison soup with much watercress floating on top. Lawalila also entered. He was holding acorn cakes and another small basket of blackberries.

"Does Hwipajusi have food?" asked Dari Jowa.

"Yes," said Yolaina. "He is very ugly."

"I know," said Dari Jowa. He picked up the basket of soup and drank. He removed some watercress with his right hand and some venison with his left. He ate with great appreciation of such a fine meal. "Hitchinna is the best cook in the world," commented Dari Jowa between chewing. He grabbed an acorn cake and dipped it in the blackberries.

"Hwipajusi is totally covered with pitch. All of him. He is singing, 'I have killed many people,' over and over. He sticks dirt and rocks and twigs in the pitch. He ruined your wildcat cape," said Yolaina. "It is stained with pitch and dirt."

Dari Jowa swallowed the cake and paused a moment before speaking to Yolaina. "Last night when you lay sleeping in this men's house and when the cold crept in through the door and smoke hole and into your toes, Hwipajusi was sobbing at my fire. He saw many white men blow large holes in his wives and children. He feels, in retrospect, that he was not cautious enough and that he might as well have been the one to shoot so many women and children. He probably would have died had I not forced him to eat my salmon, covered him with my cape, and made him sing at my fire. Now he will heal and become whole again. I have seen Hwipajusi when he was happy and hunting and full of many stories. Last summer when I arrived in the high country, Hwipajusi and his family were already there. They fed me. Hwipajusi made hunting a pleasure. In a couple days, he will be more philosophical than he is now. He will see that he was not to blame for the madness of the saltu, and that nothing can stop white men from hunting the Yahi. The white men are cursed with an evil spirit. Billy Sills, the half-breed who died with your father and so many others not too far from here, said the white men only have one First Person, an evil spirit who makes the white men steal land and kill Yahi. I do not know of this hatred personally, but I do know I will not let such a spirit kill my good friend, Hwipajusi. What I own is Hwipajusi's. I do not see pitch on my wildcat skin cape; I see laughter in Hwipajusi's heart."

CHAPTER 5

Five Bows

"Maybe you are right, Hwipajusi," said Dari Jowa quietly. "Never have I gathered so much meat so easily." The bright moon cast crisp, gray shadows on the ground, and herding the cows was very funny. Yolaina, Lawalila, Demauna, Chunoyahi, Dari Jowa, and Hwipajusi were spread out along an imaginary line, and they simply walked toward abandoned Bay Tree Village. The five cows stayed just ahead of the four men and two boys and within shooting distance of an arrow at all times. The cows plodded through and around all obstacles and took the easiest route they could away from the men and straight to where they would be shot in the meadow of Bay Tree Village on Salmon Creek, half a morning's walk from Black Rock. "No wonder white men are such bad hunters," continued Dari Jowa. "Cows are more stupid than dirt."

"They are tasty animals, too," said Hwipajusi. "They have big hides, but I prefer deer sinew to that of cow."

"The winter was too long this year. We should have hunted more often," said Demauna. He walked not far away on the other side of Dari Jowa.

"We had plenty of dried meat until the remnants of Black Rock Village joined us," said Hwipajusi. "Too bad they could not have brought all their food with them at once. Their chief, Bohkuina, Silver-Gray Fox Man, is old, though, and the women and children he takes care of are too many. He says he aches too much to hunt in the winter. At least they stored many acorns. Bohkuina has too many fine women and children. I think I will marry one or two and take in the orphaned boy. He needs a hunter to teach him how to walk behind cows." Hwipajusi laughed out loud.

"I wonder if cows know how to start a fire and to jump in a boiling basket, also," said Dari Jowa. "They know how to walk to their deaths so congenially. Can you imagine five antelope walking just ahead, plodding through the brush like grizzly bears, just waiting to be shot in the middle of Bay Tree Village?" He laughed.

"I think I will ask the fattest woman with the most acorns and the most little girls to marry me," said Hwipajusi. That way when the girls get old, I will have plenty of bargaining power with Yolaina and Lawalila, here, and probably you too, Dari Jowa. That way I will no longer have to walk behind cows. I will have all of you bring me one deer and one hide every moon. My women will think I am a great provider. They will sew me fine clothes and make many acorn cakes. I will sit not far from our winter camp and watch the sky turn rosy pink over Black Rock every night. I will not let you marry my daughters or sit in my sweathouse unless you agree to my terms."

"What do you say to that, Yolaina?" asked Dari Jowa.

"Those are hard terms," said Demauna, "but Yolaina and Lawalila will probably think they are fair."

Yolaina stepped carefully over a rock onto the slippery pine needles of the steep canyon. "I do not like women that much. Feeding

Hwipajusi would take too many deer. Hwipajusi would get too fat, like the woman he wishes to marry." Yolaina carried a strung bow, his second, and ten arrows in a quiver.

"What do you say to that, Lawalila?" asked Dari Jowa a bit more loudly, for Lawalila was the farthest away. "Will you give one deer and one hide every moon to Hwipajusi for one of his daughters?"

"Hwipajusi will have to kill the deer himself. I do not need a woman," he replied. "Hitchinna and Halai Auna already cook for me."

"I will remember these words well," replied Hwipajusi, Whistling Swan Man. "You will wake up one morning in about four or five years, and you will say, 'I feel like Wood Duck Man. I must become the greatest hunter in the world so that I can win Salmon Woman's heart.' I will say, 'Lawalila, you must bring me two deer a moon for a year before I will allow you to marry my fat daughter.'"

"Spread out some more," said Demauna. "The cows are getting close to the meadow. Come in from all sides and shoot them before the stupid beasts try to cross Salmon Creek."

All the hunters moved quietly then and did as Demauna had suggested. They sneaked upon the meadow from all sides, and from behind the laurel trees and brush and boulders, they loosed their arrows. The cows quickly fell, mostly dying right in front of the oval of ten summer homes, then used occasionally to aid travelers or hunters, as was the occasion. The hunters then entered the meadow and began the hard part, butchering the ignorant beasts and hauling them far upstream so as to be not tracked or seen or caught. Double packing would be required for so much meat.

Dari Jowa removed his two arrows from the cow he had shot. One of the points had broken on a rib bone, but his arrows were both sound. He glanced at Yolaina and saw the boy carefully pulling his last arrow from his cow. Dari Jowa did not know if Yolaina's bow was strong enough to kill a cow, but apparently even the bow of child could do so. "How are your arrows?" asked Dari Jowa.

"I lost one," replied Yolaina. "It flew into Salmon Creek."

"I hope you can shoot better than that in four years," said Hwipajusi, who had deftly killed his cow with one, clean shot to the heart. His was the strongest bow, for he was the largest man. He was also the oldest and could have been Dari Jowa's father. "Otherwise you will not be able to provide me with three deer every moon for the rest of your life to marry my daughter, even if she will be a little too fat and have pimples."

"Do not listen to Hwipajusi," said Demauna in a loud voice because his cow had tried to run away at the far edge of the meadow. "He is getting old and tired and is thinking of ways to make young men work; however, he does not own all the women. Plenty of women are around. In Jihkulu's camp are most of the girls, and most of them are not fat. They are pretty. I have seen them many times. I took them three deer this winter. I know. I think I need another wife, and I have been looking at all the women carefully. My wife, Pahnino, says our camp is too small. She says I should have another wife."

"See," said Hwipajusi, "you and Lawalila will not have any women left in four years. Demauna and I will marry them all."

"Hitchinna says you joke too much," said Lawalila. "She says you laugh all the time. She says maybe you should marry the Ichpul Sisters, Frog Women, and then maybe you would not tease so much."

As the conversation continued, Dari Jowa watched Yolaina take his sharp piece of cutting obsidian from his neck pouch. Yolaina was wasting no time, and Dari Jowa was happy for expedience. He greatly feared what would await them in the next day's light if they were too slow. Yolaina cut the hooves off first, and then began cutting the inside of the upper legs of the prostrate cow from the cut off hooves to the chest and belly. There he made an incision the length of the cow and began to cut the hide from the carcass. They would use the hides to carry all the meat they could cut from the bones. Much of the innards and bones and head would be tossed into Salmon Creek. Wasting that much good food was a necessity, but still a shame as far as Dari Jowa was concerned. Yolaina and Lawalila were much slower than the men, but the boys were there mostly to learn. That night's hunt was their first, even if it were for cows. Lack of sleep, stumbling over slippery boulders, having one's feet feel like Wahkanopa's snow pack in mid winter, carrying heavy weight, and avoiding the saltu's lightning sticks were making Yolaina into a strong character. Perhaps he would always be known as Yolaina, the bravest of the Mapchemaina, the First People, but Dari Jowa knew how easy getting a nickname could be, especially with a chief like Igupa Topa and a prankster like Hwipajusi to entertain everyone in the men's house.

"I bet Dari Jowa is thinking of going to Jihkulu's camp, Demauna," said Hwipajusi. "I bet you got him all excited, talking about the pretty girls that live there. I know that deep inside his heart lies a strong passion for women. He has been a bachelor too long, but now his heart is prancing like a baby mountain goat in a lush green meadow."

"That is right, Hwipajusi," said Dari Jowa as he began cutting meat from the hindquarter and throwing it on half of the laid out skin, "and as soon as we get back, I think I will go to Jihkulu's camp and marry three women. Then I will build my house next to yours. I will make love to all of them many times a night, and they will keep you wake. They will keep you all awake, and I will not move unless you give me two deer, one antelope, and ten turkeys a moon for the rest of your life."

"Now I have the liver," said Chunoyahi. He set it on his cut up meat. "I think we need a fire, and I think we need roasted liver. Our meat will take all of tomorrow to get back to Tcapalauna." He walked to Salmon Creek to wash his hands and arms. "I do not think hunters should fast to kill cows. Killing cows is about as ritualistic as taking a nap. Also, I do not want Lawalila or Yolaina to shrink on the walk home." He paused. "Hwipajusi's belly, however, is beginning to become as soft as his brain, and he will probably not want roasted liver. Hwipajusi probably thinks tonight is a great hunt, and when we arrive back at Tcapalauna, he will talk of waiting many hours in a blind and barely getting his shot off in time because he was daydreaming about women."

"Good idea," said Dari Jowa, who would not have been the first to suggest they eat. "We should be full for our day's travel. Escaping from this village is the most important task, and that could take more than a day."

*   *   *

Near nightfall Dari Jowa arrived back in the men's camp from the feeder stream. He had been by himself scouting their rear to see if they were being followed, if any dogs had managed to find their scent. Their camp was within half a morning's walk of Tcapalauna, and they could have arrived safely there that day. Dari Jowa, however, insisted they stay gone another day to check their rear before actually going to camp with the meat. They could afford the time and caution; they could not afford to lead white men to their primary winter's quarters, especially with Bohkuina's arrival. No one argued with Dari Jowa's logic. All the men, Demauna, Chunoyahi, and Hwipajusi, wanted to eat well and to sleep on furs in front of a warm fire, but they also did not wish to question Dari Jowa's emphatic attitude. They all felt and knew they were safe, but Dari Jowa wanted to be positive. Igupa Topa had trained Dari Jowa, and Igupa Topa was chief, the oldest Yahi. Less than a hundred Yahi were then alive and many of them because of Igupa Topa's wisdom. Besides, when Hwipajusi looked disappointed at Dari Jowa's decision, Dari Jowa looked as if he were about to string his bow. Hwipajusi did not need to be reminded about what a wrong decision would mean, however. Hwipajusi had only been wholly happy a few months. Only recently had his hair been growing long, for he had spent many horrible months not being able to forget the mass murders he had witnessed as a helpless bystander with all his bows in a summer's hut.

Chunoyahi had killed a deer in Dari Jowa's absence, and a roasted heart and liver from the deer were lanced on a stick over the flame. The meal made all the men very happy. They joked until it was time to sleep, and different individuals kept the fire going all night in shifts according to the position of the moon in relation to a stick poked in the ground. Thus, they avoided the frigid night air that stiffened their bundles of meat and the deer hanging from a tree. In the early morning they began the double packing of meat to the ridge just above Tcapalauna, but three men went back for the deer. One, Hwipajusi, scouted down the feeder stream to investigate their trail one more time. Hwipajusi volunteered to make sure Dari Jowa did not misunderstand his intent of the day before, and Hwipajusi took pride in himself as a hunter. He never wished to be caught again, either. Dari Jowa and Chunoyahi took the deer from the tree, strung its legs over a pole, and walked it back to where the original piles of meat were stored just before being taken down the little feeder stream near Tcapalauna, as Igupa Topa was fond of calling his moving village. The piles of meat were gone by the time they arrived, so Demauna, Yolaina, Lawalila, and perhaps others had already taken them to Tcapalauna. Dari Jowa and Chunoyahi soon walked down the rivulet and into camp with the deer.

In the little village, however, much was wrong, for Yolaina, Lawalila, and Demauna were not there. Hitchinna and Halai Auna were crying in their home, and only about half of the people from Bohkuina's village were sitting about with dazed looks. Dari Jowa stood in the doorway of Hitchinna's home and went to her side. He said nothing but put his arms around her and Halai Auna.

"What is happening?" asked Dari Jowa finally.

"Igupa Topa is dead. The man from Acorn Hollow shot him. He was with the man who lives near Bay Tree Village and two others. They had dogs and were hidden in trees as Igupa Topa led Bohkuina and the children and women down Salmon Creek. The women had the remainder of their nuts and acorns and dried berries. A white man motioned for the women to squat, and his lightning stick cracked the sky four times. I heard the shots from our fire. The fourth shot killed Igupa Topa. He lies on rocks at the stream's edge. The men captured Bohkuina's wife, daughter, and grandchild. All the others are scattered or are here. The white men have gone downstream. Bohkuina has followed them. He wants to surrender to the white men. All of his people are to surrender at Igupa Topa's body upon Bohkuina's return with the white men."

"Where are Yolaina, Lawalila, and Demauna?"

"When Yolaina heard, he left quickly to see Igupa Topa. He was crying. Demauna took Lawalila to make sure that Yolaina is safe."

"Why are the white men not chasing us through the woods with their dogs?" asked Dari Jowa.

"I do not know. They just left downstream. They could have killed many more. I do not understand," replied Hitchinna.

"I am so tired and sad," said Dari Jowa, barely able to speak with his naturally quiet voice cracking. "I will go cry now and collect pitch. We cannot even claim Igupa Topa's body and burn him properly until Bohkuina is finished with whatever he is doing."

Outside the dirt mound, Dari Jowa went to Chunoyahi and spoke. "Watch over Igupa Topa's body in Salmon Creek. Do not let animals eat him before Bohkuina brings back the white men. We must bury Igupa Topa properly. Hunt. Take care of the women and children. Bring back Yolaina and Lawalila. I go. I must get pitch," said Dari Jowa between almost choking stops in his breathing. Then he grabbed his bow and quiver near the deer and went into the woods to find old stumps or damaged trees where the pitch had collected in large clumps.

*   *   *

Yolaina stood at the forest's edge near a tall cedar and a newly budding buckeye tree. New shoots of what soon would be bright flowers were at his feet, and a water ouzel and its mate chattered loudly as they flew from boulder to boulder in the stream below. Above, the sky was blue, and windswept, billowy clouds could be seen above Salmon Creek Canyon's north rim and above the caves where many Yana were buried.

Small gray, puffy birds landed in the buckeye tree and then scattered quietly away. Little could be heard above the rushing water and wind in the trees. Barren oaks still had no sign of spring in their twisted boughs, and hordes of ladybugs flew in the air and gathered around the rose bush thorns. Twigs and limbs and pine needles and oak leaves were scattered on the ground. A kingfisher swooped swiftly over the water and out of sight, and hawks glided high above in the strong upward current. Yolaina noticed little then, however, except Igupa Topa's dead body lying face down in the stream's rocky shoreline. A red spot was on his deerskin shirt. The stump he had for a hand lay in the tiny waves lapping the dark-gray, moist sand. His long, gray hair washed lazily back and forth in the undulating water covering most of his head.

*   *   *

Bohkuina, the elder of the remnants of Black Rock Village, Silver-Gray Fox Man, brought his young son Pakalai Jawichi, Water Lizard Man, one of his two hunters, Topuna, Mountain Lion Man, and Chikpitpa, Young Weasel Man, probably a nickname, to speak in the men's house of Tcapalauna. Dari Jowa sat lethargically on the sleeping ledge where his skins kept him warm. His hair was burned short, and pitch was still thick on his head. Yolaina and Lawalila sat at his feet and under the wildcat-skin cape, long ago abandoned to pitch when Hwipajusi had almost died of exposure. Both Yolaina and Lawalila had short hair and pitch-covered heads. Demauna straightened his arrows on his spot next to Dari Jowa. Hwipajusi tended the fire, and Chunoyahi sat in his spot across from Dari Jowa and near the entrance. Much was to be decided, supposedly, for the men felt many emotions and had many beliefs. Bohkuina wanted the meeting to be formal. Everyone who wanted to speak would be able to do so. Bohkuina wished everyone to reach a consensus. Bohkuina, Pakalai Jawichi,

Chikpitpa, and Topuna sat where space was available. Bohkuina waited a respectful amount of time and then spoke.

"The men of Tcapalauna have always been wise, friendly, and helpful. None of our people has been cold or hungry in your village. At first I was angry when my people did not meet me at the killing sight when I brought the white men back. Surely, I felt the white men would accept our surrender, for they did not kill me. When no one appeared after I called over Igupa Topa's body, I jumped into the woods and ran away. I can see plenty of reasons to fear the white men, but others have surrendered to them and have escaped to return to the mountains. Surrender is possible. If we are to survive at all, we must find a way to surrender. I say that each of five men should present a bow to the one who did not shoot Igupa Topa, and that we take some women who wish to go with us. The children I wish to leave with you. When we know we are safe and well, we wish to come for them. We hope the saltu will be just, but we should be sure. Why, at this time, however, would the white men want to kill us? We are less than seventy-five people, mostly women and kids, and we have not retaliated for their killings. We should give the man who lives over the ridge from Bay Tree Village five bows as a peace offering. We should try to end the killing and to learn the white man's ways. Topuna, Chikpitpa, and I will go tomorrow. We have decided. We wish two of you would come." Bohkuina had nothing further to offer and waited for someone to speak. A long silence filled the room.

Hwipajusi spoke first, for he had decided after Igupa Topa's death that trying to surrender might save the Yahi, if possible, and he had already informally discussed surrendering with Bohkuina after the white men had left for the second time and had shown no enthusiasm for tracking the Yahi to Tcapalauna. Also, Hwipajusi felt that the white man who had a cabin at the headwaters of Butte Creek and the hollow where they would surrender was basically a harmless individual. Hwipajusi had observed him on several occasions. "I will go with you, Bohkuina. Perhaps you are right."

Demauna put one arrow away, pulled another from his quiver, and checked it for straightness. "I will consider very carefully what you say. Bohkuina, for you are the chief of Black Rock Village. You very well could be correct. Maybe we can get the white men to stop hunting the Yahi. I will let you know by the time you leave tomorrow."

"I prefer sinking arrows into the saltu, myself," said Chunoyahi. "I used to enjoy watching the filthy, stinking men's expressions when they first saw the quivering arrows sticking from their chests and realized they had but moments to live."

"You go. I stay," replied Dari Jowa. "When you have reunited with your wife and child and grandchild, and when you have a white man's home with clear obsidian and wood walls, and when you are happy and eat well, come find me. Say, 'Dari Jowa, look; I am happy and well; bring my children. The white men are good to us. We have a warm, dry home and plenty of white man's food. Come sleep by my fire and eat well with my family. We have plenty of room for your skins. We have plenty of room for all of Tcapalauna. We will only have to hunt for pleasure in the summer, for cows are everywhere about us.' Then come to me, and I will see for myself."

Bohkuina did not respond; his deep brown eyes were silhouetted in wrinkles and gray hair and leather thongs in his ears and nose. He was a patient man when he chose to be. He looked at Yolaina and Lawalila, boys of eight, but boys who had seen enough tragedy to be old men. He wished to give them a chance to speak, even though he would not take them.

Yolaina spit in the fire. "I will be a hunter with Dari Jowa, White-headed Eagle Man, my uncle. I will bring venison to my mother, Hitchinna, and my sister, Halai Auna. I will watch the snow turn the light gray river rocks black and white and cover the cedar boughs. I will watch the roses turn pink and the sun set over Black Rock. I do not wish to be at the mercy of murderers." Tears filled his eyes.

"And you, Lawalila?" asked Bohkuina.

"I stay. You go. Enough has been said," replied Lawalila. "I already have a cursed foot."

"Then we will smoke," said Bohkuina, for from his deerskin shirt he had already taken his pipe and dried tobacco. He twirled the leaves with one hand, stuffed the bowl of his elk-antler pipe, and handed the pipe and a branch from the fire to Dari Jowa.

Dari Jowa accepted the pipe and branch. He lit the bowl, puffed a couple of times, and handed the pipe to Topuna, a good hunter and quiet man with too many wives. Dari Jowa liked smoking once in a while, especially with the three distinguished hunters of Black Rock Village, even if Bohkuina was in direct variance with his thoughts.

"Old man," said Dari Jowa as the pipe continued around the room, "I hope I can serve Tcapalauna as well as you serve Black Rock Village. I hope to lie peacefully at your fire, but if all does not go well and you can escape, you come to Tcapalauna. I, Dari Jowa, will keep you fat with venison in your old age, and will keep you toasty red in the men's house when the wet snow lies in white streaks along the narrow ledges of the tall cliffs."

"Good smoke," said Hwipajusi, who always held the pipe too long.

Dari Jowa looked in back of himself at his three bows. He also had two bows and bundles of arrows hidden in caches in Deer Creek Canyon. He removed his newest of mountain juniper, a truly strong piece of aesthetic beauty, from his otter-skin quiver, and then looked with great compassion at Pakalai Jawichi, who stood almost quaking like a yellow aspen tree in a strong north wind.

"How old are you, Pakalai Jawichi?" asked Dari Jowa as he stood to string the bow.

"Five years and three moons," replied the boy.

"You have the name of Water Lizard Man. He is slippery and hard to catch in the deep, cold water. He has a handsome, reddish color, also," continued Dari Jowa. All the others watched carefully. Dari Jowa removed an arrow from his mountain lion's tail quiver, the one with his

most beautiful and most even arrows, and he handed the arrow to
Pakalai Jawichi. This arrow is made with the feathers of my name,
White-headed Eagle Man, Dari Jowa. The feathers once belonged to a
beautiful woman I loved very much. You keep the arrow. It is yours. Set
it over there next to Yolaina's belongings." Dari Jowa nodded his head
toward the spot behind Topuna. Pakalai Jawichi did as was requested
and joined his father.

Dari Jowa then looked carefully at Bohkuina and said, "Here is my
newest bow. Take it."

The old man hesitated. He did not understand such a gift.

"You take my bow. You can be proud to give this bow to the white
man. He will know you tell the truth if you give such a fine bow. Take it."

Bohkuina finally accepted the bow, but he was still unsure of Dari
Jowa's meaning. Dari Jowa looked back again at Pakalai Jawichi and
waited moment.

"Pakalai Jawichi, when your father gives my bow to the white man,
know in your heart that if the white man kills your father, I will hunt
him. I will get very close to him, and when he sees me, he will only have
an instant to see your arrow sink between his eyes and through the back
of his skull."

*   *   *

After Bohkuina, Topuna, Chikpitpa, Demauna, Hwipajusi, and
Demauna's wife, Pahnino or Ocean Shell Woman, and six women that
Hitchinna barely knew left to give five bows to the white man,
Tcapalauna was not the same. All those left in camp, mostly children of
varying ages, had much on their minds, and wished that peace might be
achieved. Half of the added children, ten in all, were orphans and their
ages ranged from three to fifteen years old. The only other camp of the
Yahi that Hitchinna knew about was to the west, downstream, on the
other side of the mountain near a large overhang and feeder stream.

Demauna said they were doing well, but had few hunters. Hitchinna thought she had been busy before when she shared cooking for fewer people with Pahnino, but Wirula, Chunoyahi's wife, was the only fully grown adult woman left to help with the cooking. Hitchinna did not mind, however, because the camp was gayer than it had recently been, and she and Wirula gave the children many tasks, from gathering wood to practicing all the skills needed for survival. The older girls were a great help, especially Halai Auna, Morning Star Woman, Hitchinna's adopted daughter through Pul Miauna and Chuhna. Hitchinna did not know what would happen if both she and Wirula had their blood times together, but somehow everyone would survive. With so much work to be done, though, she became forgetful of Igupa Topa, buried respectfully after the funeral pyre near the destroyed men's house where she spent her last evening with Pul Miauna and where Igupa Topa had spent many carefree nights as a young man when times were peaceful. All in the camp discussed what would happen to the brave people who had gone to negotiate a peace with the white man. Dari Jowa had gone hunting with Chunoyahi, for food had to be kept in great supply. He felt somewhat healed from Igupa Topa's death, also. Yolaina and Lawalila remained in camp to play with the other children and to impress Pakalai Jawichi with their newly learned, manly skills, such as hunting squirrels. The day was cold, however, because the wind stopped blowing from the west and started from the north, a sign of possible snow or rain in the early spring. Mostly, the children played near the fire, which they attended, and they were happy when Hitchinna called them in the family house to eat. Each received a handful of pine nuts, all the acorn mush they could eat, and a hunk of freshly roasted cow meat. Outside the crisp sun sparkled lightly on the melting frost and scattered patches of snow.

Wirula had promised to tell the children a story after breakfast, and so around the small fire they sat, respectfully, of course, without fighting since few knew her and since they had been warned to be very respectful. Their parents had carefully reared them in the best Yahi customs. The three-year-old was a bit unruly, for he thought that he owned all in the world and could not understand why others used his belongings.

"This is my favorite story," began Wirula, "called *Sukonia's Wives and the Ichpul Sisters.* She sat upon a sheepskin at the back of the dark, family house, so all could see her clearly by looking away from the door's light.

"Wrinkled, gray-haired Jahtaneno, Shell Creature Man, had a great amount of daughters, and two of his daughters were not married.

"At that time Sukonia, Pine Martin Man, had a large sweathouse and many people to serve him, for he was a great chief of the Yahi in our beautiful canyons.

"One day wrinkled Jahtaneno called his two unmarried daughters to him and said: 'I want you to walk to Sukonia's house. I hear he is very rich with baskets of all kinds of food and with many bright shells. Walk to him. I hear he has no wife, and he may marry you. You get up very early, bathe in Salmon Creek, comb you hair, and go see Chief Sukonia, Pine Martin Man,'

"The two sisters did not reply to old Jahtaneno, Shell Creature Man. They were respectful, said nothing, and obeyed their father. They rose early the next morning, bathed well in Salmon Creek, combed their hair, and painted their faces red, for young people painted their faces red. Their mother gave them each a fine basket filled with dehydrated blackberries, acorn cakes, and dried salmon; she hung beads around their necks.

"'If any man meets you on the path,' said stiff, old Jahtaneno at parting, 'do not look at him. A richly dressed man wearing many beads will come toward you and will speak. Do not talk to him, for he will be Metsi, Coyote Man, the trickiest man alive.'

"Jahtaneno's daughters left and began to sing:
    '*Au ni a, au ni a, mo a we, he lo,*
    au ni a, au ni a, mo a we, he lo.'

They went northeast and remembered other words old Jahtaneno, their father, had told them. He said, 'This side of Sukonia's house and just a short walk from it, is a fine house, a great mound of dirt. Two old ugly maids, the Ichpul Sisters, Frog Women, live there. Go by their house quickly. Do not stop. Do not talk to them. Do not go in, because if you do, the Ichpul Sisters, Frog Women, will kill you there. The daughters walked quickly and kept singing:

'*Au ni a, au ni a, mo a we, he lo,*
  au ni a, au ni a, mo a we, he lo.'

"Metsi, Coyote Man, heard Jahtaneno's daughters singing and said to himself, 'I like that song. Those young women sing well, and I like what they sing. I think they are going to Sukonia's house, for Pine Martin Man is a great chief and is a rich bachelor.'

"'Now appear before me otter skins, many beads, and beautiful shells.'

"Metsi always wished for many beautiful things, everything he wanted.

"Jahtaneno's daughters walked on and on until they came to where Metsi was standing by the side of the road. The youngest sister was in the lead, but she only looked at Metsi once. The oldest daughter, however, looked at Metsi twice, and then three times. She said, 'I think that is Sukonia.'

"The youngest daughter replied, 'Your father would not say so; he would say that is Metsi, Coyote Man.'

"The oldest daughter did not listen, and stared many times at the stranger. 'No. I am sure that is Sukonia, Pine Martin Man and chief,' she said.

"'Come with me,' said the youngest daughter as she continued on her way. 'Have you lost your eyes? That is Metsi, Coyote Man.'

"The youngest daughter had walked some distance away from the oldest daughter who had stopped entirely and stared at Metsi.

"'Which way are you going?' asked Metsi.

"'Our father, Jahtaneno, sends us to see Sukonia, great chief of these lands,' said the oldest daughter.

"'Oh,' said Metsi and thought a moment, 'I am chief. You are to come with me. I will start home very soon.'

"The oldest daughter was very happy, and she said 'My sister is ahead on the path, and she is waiting for me. I will tell her, and then come here.'

"The oldest daughter ran very quickly to the youngest. 'I will go with that man. He is chief; he is Sukonia. He told me so, and I believe him.'

"The youngest sister replied, 'You must be totally out of your mind. That is Metsi. He is no chief. He is not Sukonia.'

"The eldest sister finally continued with the youngest sister, but she wanted to go back to Metsi and to go with him. She liked his fine otter skins and beads and ocean shells. His words were like music from a flute in her ears. She believed all of his words, and even though she went with her younger sister, she walked against her will.

"'Father said two black bearskins hang over the front door to Sukonia's sweathouse, and we should stop there. That is where we are going.'

"Toward evening, however, they came to the place where the Ichpuls lived, the Frog Women.

"'Let us stop here,' said the oldest sister. 'I am hungry, and my feet ache and my arms are tired.'

"'Our father, Jahtaneno, told us to pass this house; he told us not to stop here, not to look at or to go near it,' said the youngest daughter.

"The oldest daughter followed unwillingly and sulked as she went along. At last they both came to Sukonia's, for they saw two black bearskins hanging out over the sweathouse. Chikpitpa, Young Weasel Man, Sukonia's younger brother, was on the roof and saw them coming, and Tsore Jowa, Golden Eagle Woman, his sister, was at work making a house. Chikpitpa yelled, 'Two girls are coming. Two girls are coming with baskets.'

"The old man, Sukonia's father, brought bearskins for the young women to sit on, and waited. The young women came in and took the places shown to them. Chikpitpa waited on the ledge, but soon jumped off and ran to one woman and then the next. Young Weasel Man liked them very much. He sat in their laps. He wanted sisters.

"Old man Sukonia stepped outside and yelled to Tsore Jowa, his daughter. 'Come my daughter. Bring food for our guests, the young women who have come to us.'

"Tsore Jowa brought them deer's marrow and other fine food, but the sisters had put their baskets outside the door. On their journey they had said, 'Let the food in you be nice,' and on the way in the door, they said, 'Be large and full.'

"The two small baskets outside the door grew and grew and became very full of every kind of good food. That evening about sunset, Sukonia came home with his men, and Chikpitpa sprang to the roof of the house, and called loudly to his brother. 'Two beautiful young women have come to visit us, and they are sitting in your place.'

"The men came into the sweathouse, and Sukonia sat with the sisters. He liked them very much, the way they sat quietly, the beautiful beadwork on their skirts, the way they looked. 'Have you brought food to our guests?' asked Sukonia, Pine Martin Man.

"'I brought some,' said Tsore Jowa.

"'Oh, bring more,' replied Sukonia. 'We will feast. Bring all kinds of food.'

"The two sisters' baskets were brought into the house, and the young women invited everyone present to try some. All the men ate the food, and praised it highly. Sukonia married them that evening.

"The next morning after everyone had eaten, Sukonia took many to hunt all types of game. That day Sukonia's sisters showed his wives every place in the house and outside it, showed them where the venison, acorns, and roots were kept, and showed them where a spring was kept carefully covered in the corner of the house.

"After several days Sukonia said to his wives, 'I want to know what your father said to you when you were leaving. When does he want you to go back? When does he want you to visit?'

"'He did not tell us to come back at all. He only told us to come here, but we wish to visit with him, to tell him how we live here.'

"'Well, go see him tomorrow. What does he eat? What does he like?'

"'He eats salmon, and he likes beads, furs, and shells.'

"'I will send him some venison, and I will send him beads and furs.'

"'May I go with my sisters-in-law?' asked Chikpitpa, Young Weasel Man, as he danced back and forth.

"'No. I want you here, my little brother,' said Sukonia, Pine Martin Man.

"The next morning the sisters rose very early and bathed and dressed in fine deerskin skirts and beads. Sukonia gave them fat venison and every kind of bright beads and rich presents for their father. The sisters began their journey and got as far as the Ichpul house where the Frog Sisters lived. The two, old, ugly maids were on the path and spoke to Sukonia's wives. For being so ugly, they were kind and pleasant.

"'Put down your baskets,' they said. 'Sit and talk with us.'

"The Jahtaneno Sisters were very afraid and did not want to stop. They feared the Ichpul women; consequently, they did not wish to make them angry. They did what the Ichpul Sisters wanted.

"'Oh, how your hair looks. Let me look at your head,' said one Frog Woman to the oldest of Sukonia's wives.

"'Oh, how your hair looks. Let me look at your head,' said the other Frog Woman to the youngest of Sukonia's wives.

"Together the Ichpul Sisters said, 'Put your head on my lap.'

"Jahtaneno's daughters were afraid but did as requested. The Ichpul Sisters took obsidian knives hidden in the pine needles, and killed Sukonia's wives. They flayed their bodies and put their skins on themselves.

"About sunset the next day, the two Frog Women went to Sukonia's house and sat where Sukonia's wives had sat. They waited for Sukonia, who soon arrived with his men. Chikpitpa hurried into the house to see if his sisters-in-law had returned. He saw the two women. They looked exactly like Jahtaneno's daughters; for they were wearing their skins.

When Chikpitpa, Young Weasel Man, came close to them, however, he cried out at once.

"'Phu! They smell like frogs. The Ichpul Sisters are here! These are old-maid Frog Women!' He cried and then ran to see his brother.

"'Brother!' he cried, 'The Ichpul Sisters are in our house. They have killed my sisters-in-law. The ugly old maids have killed my beautiful sisters-in-law!' Poor Chikpitpa cried bitterly and would not stop.

"Sukonia went to his house where the Ichpul Women wearing the skins of his wives were preparing a tasty venison broth. When it was almost ready, he looked at them carefully. They looked exactly like his wives, but he wanted to test them. Sukonia thought, 'I will ask them to bring me water, and if they go to the hidden spring in my house, then they will be my wives instead of being false.'

"'Bring me water,' Sukonia said to one of them who grabbed a basket, turned toward the entrance, and spoke to Chikpitpa.

"'Come with me for water, my little brother-in-law.'

"'Wait,' said Sukonia. 'You need not go now.'

"She came and sat back by the fire. Sukonia knew those were strange women.

"'Whip me,' said Chikpitpa to his brother, 'I will cry and roll around and kick. I will kick those nasty Frog Women and kill them.'

"When the venison broth was boiling hard, Sukonia struck Chikpitpa with a switch and scolded him. 'Why are you crying? I can do nothing with you crying so.'

"Young Weasel Man rolled on the floor, cried more than ever, rolled around some more, kicked as hard as he could, rolled toward the fire, kicked one woman into the boiling soup, and kicked the other into the burning fire. In this way he killed the false sisters. Chikpitpa was glad. He laughed.

"Sukonia threw the two women outdoors, and he mourned all that night for his wives. The next morning he rose early and said, 'Stay home today, all of you.'

"'Where are you going?' asked Chikpitpa.

"'Stay here my little brother,' replied Sukonia. 'I am going somewhere.'

"Sukonia followed the trail of his wives to the Ichpul Women's house and found their dead bodies. He took out his bowstring of deer sinew, whipped them, called to them, and raised them to life.

"'How were you killed?' asked Sukonia. 'Did you go into the Ichpul house?'

"'We did not go in the house. Those two Frog Women were on the path. We were afraid. They asked us to sit down to talk. We were afraid not to do as they asked, and when we sat down, they killed us.'

"Sukonia took his wives home. When they were in sight of the house, Chikpitpa became very excited.

"'Oh! Tsore Jowa! Your sisters-in-law have arrived!' He ran to meet them.

"The next morning said Sukonia, 'Go now to your father. Take him presents and venison. Be here at sunset.'

"The Jahtaneno Sisters left and took two filled baskets. They were at old Jahtaneno's home at noon. They said, "Our husband told us to be home at sunset. We cannot stay long with you. They took back many presents and met no trouble along the way. The Ichpul Sisters were dead, and Metsi did not meet them a second time. They arrived home at sunset."

Wirula looked very pleased at having kept their attention for the entire story. "That is all; now go get limb wood, a lot of wood, and we will make acorn cakes for the hunters when they return."

*   *   *

Five days passed with no word from Bohkuina, his four men, and the seven women. Chunoyahi, Dari Jowa, Hitchinna, Wirula, and all of the twelve children were very worried. The adults all sat in Hitchinna's family house after the evening meal to discuss what to do while the children tended a fire and scurried about playing games of all sorts. Hitchinna still did not know two of their names, for she had been very busy. The oldest girl among them was still unknown to them, for she was quiet and worked hard on a fine basket of beautiful weave and red, black, and white colors. She had also begun her first blood time and was in the women's house by herself. Dari Jowa decided he alone should travel to scout the hollows and homes of the saltu to learn if the peace seekers were still alive. He was chief, and he saw no reason for anyone else to see dead bodies, if, indeed, they had been killed. Chunoyahi would hunt, and Wirula and Hitchinna would, of course, take care of all the children, a large task. Also, a ceremony and feast would have to be prepared for the unknown young woman, for when a girl became a woman, all Yahi celebrated with much enthusiasm. They would dance and sing and feast and not work or hunt. The young woman deserved the best celebration that could be provided, and all would wear their best skins and paint their faces and put on beads of all kinds. She would be given fine gifts. Pitch was somewhat gone from Dari Jowa, Hitchinna, Lawalila, Halai Auna, and Yolaina's heads, and Igupa Topa was seldom mentioned. His belongings, including lightning stick parts, his large saltu's knife, and some gold coins, were with him in the ground. The discussion had just ended, and Dari Jowa and Chunoyahi were headed to rinse out their mouths and to rub their teeth with their fingers and to have a smoke when the children began making a commotion and a black dog belonging to Pakalai Jawichi began to bark.

Dari Jowa and Chunoyahi immediately ran out the door and toward the men's house where their bows and arrows and hand spears were, but instead of any danger, they saw Hwipajusi carrying a large white man's seed bag. The others were still coming from the feeder stream. Hwipajusi looked as healthy and happy as pink and white manzanita flowers dangling among reddish stems and round green leaves.

"I thought maybe we should take the long way home," said Hwipajusi, "which just happened to be by a couple of white men's storage houses with all these fine seeds in them, clothes too!" He laughed, for he wore saltu clothing under his deerskins.

Topuna and Chikpitpa each carried a large bag of seeds. Laughter engulfed everyone, especially the lonely parents and children. Dari Jowa felt extremely relieved and elated. He did not want them to give up to the white man. The canyons had become too lonely. Hwipajusi was needed in the men's house to make light of all that existed.

"What happened?" asked Chunoyahi of Bohkuina, who looked very old and tired from traveling so many cold nights. Bohkuina stepped to the fire and set down his bow and arrows. He had left a cache nearby the settler's home.

"We gave them five bows as planned, and all went well. We were fed strange but good food. Late in the day we were taken to Acorn Hollow, to the man's house who killed Igupa Topa. We waited with other men, however, for the killer was not home. At night a man threw a rope over a limb to hang us. Many of them laughed and drank the drink which makes them loud and mean. We ran away, and they did not follow us. We have spent three days traveling since then to make sure, and we now live as best we can. After we return from Wahkanopa next fall, however, I think we will move down past the flat mountain with the others. Less snow falls there, and cows are plentiful," said Bohkuina.

"The oldest girl is now a woman," said Hitchinna. "We are planning a dance soon. Now the dance will be full of joy."

"My wife, daughter, and granddaughter are still there," said Bohkuina evenly. "I saw them in his house. She would not have come back, anyhow; she is old and tired and had often said she would like to give up. I wonder why they allow them to live there and would hang us? I think I will go smoke now," said Bohkuina.

"I have never seen this kind of seeds before. Look Hitchinna," said Hwipajusi. "They are brown and big and speckled. Fix these for the dance. I would like to eat these seeds. You can have the fine woven fibers they come in also. You are a great cook, and you deserve such fine fibers."

*   *   *

"Dari Jowa," said Hwipajusi as he shook Dari Jowa in the darkness. The fire had long died out, and the day's new light had barely broken the darkness of the sky through the smoke hole of the men's sweathouse. "Wake up. I am having a vision. I dream I see the unknown, young woman for whom we just danced sitting on a sheepskin outside our sweathouse. I dream she has placed her red, black, and white basket in front of her, and that she wears otter skins and many beads. I dream that her face is painted red and that she wishes to sit on your spot."

"Not now, Hwipajusi, you should not wake everyone so early. You should at least let the sky turn gray first," replied Dari Jowa. His head was heavy on his deerskin pillow.

"The vision will not go away," said Hwipajusi. "I speak with a tongue of straight arrows. I swear."

"I can never sleep after Hwipajusi starts talking anyway," said Chunoyahi as he stood to go relieve himself and to bathe in the frosty morning's, snow-fed feeder stream. "Besides, I wish to hunt deer and to see if the salmon are running below Black Rock yet." Chunoyahi opened the bearskin entrance and stopped. "I have the same vision," continued Chunoyahi with rising hilarity in his voice.

"So do I," said Yolaina, who was sitting up with a clear view out the door.

Dari Jowa pulled the pillow from his short hair. He would be glad when all the pitch was gone. He leaned over to have a clear view of the twilight. Sure enough, the unknown young woman was sitting there just as Hwipajusi had explained. Chunoyahi let the bearskin fall back into place.

"I will start the fire back up," said Hwipajusi to Dari Jowa, "and you can invite her in to see what she wants." Hwipajusi had a big grin on his face which could not be missed even in the darkness, and happiness danced in his voice.

"I told Dari Jowa she was looking at him when he danced," said Chunoyahi. "He would not believe me."

"Now we will see how brave our chief is," said Hwipajusi as he placed tinder on the coals.

CHAPTER 6

A New Wife

"Wihlaina, Chipmunk Woman, might even be a better cook than Hitchinna," said Demauna as Yolaina, Lawalila, Chunoyahi, and Dari Jowa hauled the freshly speared salmon from Deer Creek to Tcapalauna. "Does she ever speak?"

"I told you all I know a thousand times," replied Dari Jowa as he shifted a pole from one shoulder to the next. The salmon were becoming very burdensome. Dari Jowa missed the days when he did not hide and when salmon were dried near where they were killed. The damp air, overcast skies, and sweat from so much work would cause them many problems if they did not reach home by dark, and he wondered why he always placed so much work on everyone's shoulders. "She is the last survivor of Bay Tree Village. That is all I know. She talks to me very little."

"She talks to me," said Yolaina, who was carrying two large fish with Lawalila. "She said I was the most handsome nephew in all of these canyons, and she makes me fine clothes."

"That is because you are a boy and her nephew. If you were a man, she would act like an antelope in a grizzly's den."

"Wihlaina is a good woman with the best of manners," said Chunoyahi. "She brings great honor to Dari Jowa and to Tcapalauna. I say that after the salmon run we hold a dance and honor her for marrying Dari Jowa, who spends too many nights hunting and too many nights smoking in the sweathouse and listening to Hwipajusi. A year is a long time to be married to such a man."

"I am man enough," said Yolaina.

"Well," said Demauna, who was carrying eight fish with Dari Jowa and whose toes were tingling with cold in his wet deerskin moccasins, "when you become an actual man, say in four years, she will still make you fine clothes and think you are handsome, but she will not let you into her house so freely. She will not let you talk to her unless you are outside or with others present. That is her nature."

"A woman always knows when to avoid a man," said Hwipajusi. "Take me, for example. The most Wihlaina, our sweet little Chipmunk Woman, has said to me is, `Thank you,' and that was for the black bearskin, the one from the bear that almost killed me when my first arrow did not reach its heart. `Thank you.'"

"And that is more than you deserve," said Chunoyahi. "She hears the innuendoes of your loud stories too often, and Hitchinna tells her you make light of women too much. You better watch out, or those in Jihkulu's camp will hear too much about you. They will not let you visit any woman there."

"They already know too much about Hwipajusi. When he takes them gifts, all the unmarried, young women bounce through the brush like deer."

"I like it that way," replied Hwipajusi. "That way, see, I get to be alone with the old, fat ones, the ones who do not mind talking and who always cook me nice meals and who have young daughters. See, Yolaina, if you marry a young woman, you have to train her. She knows too little about how to please a man. She does not have suitable skills, and she expects too many gifts and too much hunting from a man. If you marry, say, a widow, well then you have a good woman."

"The rain is starting again," said Lawalila. "I felt two drops."

"If we stop again for rain, we will have to spend the night and maybe lose our fire. That would be very unpleasant," said Chunoyahi.

"I always like walking in the rain," said Hwipajusi, "especially when I get home and see that Hitchinna has a basket full of hot soup with boiled roots and greens and venison. Maybe she will have some white man's seeds in the soup. She will have acorn cakes. All the food will be steaming."

"Keep talking, Hwipajusi. That hot air is keeping my backside warm," said Chunoyahi.

"Maybe we should stop," said Demauna, "and sit in a half circle around Hwipajusi. He could talk, and we could sit as if we were naked on a hot summer's day. The rain could turn to snow, and Tuina, Sun Man, could forget to begin his westward journey across the sky. We would be warm."

"Remind me to tell you my version of *The Finding of Fire* tonight after we have a smoke," replied Hwipajusi just as the rain began to pour. Any pretense they had of staying dry had vanished.

"Take heart, Yolaina," said Dari Jowa. "We will be home soon; besides, our choices are but two, to walk or to die."

"This walking is good training, too," added Hwipajusi, "because you will have to bring me many salmon every spring and fall, or I will not let you marry one of my daughters."

As the rain pounded down, the men continued their chatter and walked through the tall pines to where the land began to decline into Salmon Creek Canyon. There the oaks, foothill pines, and manzanita were prevalent. Yolaina thought that being a man was not the most comfortable of tasks, but beyond participating in the men's discussion, he kept his mind occupied on his surroundings. The rocks always seemed to burst into life during the spring. Patches of blue-gray lichen etched a living on them, and moss of many types then turned to shades of burnt umber and deep green. Beneath rock overhangs, the moss resembled tiny fronds of ferns, and on top of rocks, the moss was thick, soft, and of several varieties. The closer one got to such patches of life, the more the detail presented its beauty. Minute flowers appeared, and perfect patterns of leaf-like shapes were in the patches. The moss also grew on the damp side of oak limbs and trunks. Yolaina noticed how raindrops collected on the tiny six-sided leaves of small plants growing among the green shoots of grass, and also small drops glistened from the ends of pine needles, giving the branches a rich radiance. The grass was filled with shoots of flowers soon to be, and some minute purple flowers had already appeared. The black oak limbs and buckeye branches and redbud all had their magical beginnings poised at the tips of their branches, hints of a forest about to bound into life. The rain quickly soaked Yolaina's deerskin clothing and shoulder length hair; his fingers and toes tingled as they often did. His shoulders ached, and he wondered if he would ever like salmon again. He could feel the cold overtake his body, and concentrating on not making the wrong step on the slick ground and rocks was not easy. Everyone was walking at a fast pace. The gusts of wind were highly unappreciated, but Yolaina said not a word to complain. He looked about and noticed the shades of gray in the sky, and hoped for shades of blue. He saw how the tall pines grew on the northwest slopes of the canyon, and how brush and oaks grew on the southern exposures. During the rain when the men were not returning with cow meat or seeds or other items kept in the white men's storage houses, they were not as cautious, for which Yolaina was extremely happy. Yolaina also thought about the warm, smoky men's house, and about the food he knew his mother would have waiting.

*   *   *

"Mother," asked Halai Auna, "will you get married again?" She was playing with a small, stuffed doll of deerskin, beads, feathers, and paint that Wihlaina had made for her. Wihlaina was weaving a large acorn gathering basket, which would suspend from her head onto her back, and Hitchinna was placing the leached acorn meal she had just brought from the feeder stream into a water-filled basket that she was about to boil. The fire in her family house was burning well, and she had plenty of dry wood. The rocks were very hot, and she had two, large cooking sticks ready to gather the rocks from the coals. Her large water basket was ready to soak her cooking sticks should they catch fire. Hitchinna was totally off guard for such a question; however, she removed the rest of the acorn meal from the leaves and looked carefully at her Halai Auna, who obviously was not a baby any longer.

"There is no one I wish to marry. I am too busy with three children as it is," she said, but the question was honest. Hitchinna had carefully evaded a real answer, which, of course, was painful. Few men were around for her to choose from.

"Maybe you should marry Chunoyahi or Demauna," continued Halai Auna.

Again the thought was painful, for neither of them had ever approached her. They were married. Both of them had been on the best of terms with Pul Miauna, and both considered her to be a bit taboo, someone to hold in high regard, almost like a relative—although the thought of marrying Chunoyahi had occurred to Hitchinna before. He was handsome and a good hunter, and with his white man's ax, he provided many new bow staves from incense cedar for the men of Tcapalauna. He often provided her and the children with food. She had never discussed the possibility with Wirula; she and Hitchinna were very close. In fact, Wirula and Pahnino were boiling venison soup in Wirula's home. Everyone was to eat together when the men arrived from fishing. They would be very cold and hungry. They would probably get caught in a heavy rain, no joke when the sun was setting.

"Maybe you should talk to Wirula or Pahnino about sharing Chunoyahi or Demauna. I like them very much. They are very nice to me," said Halai Auna.

"Why are you such a matchmaker today?" asked Hitchinna, beginning to become embarrassed, especially in front of Wihlaina, who was generally quiet about such matters.

"I just thought that maybe you wanted to get married. I want to get married when I am as old as Wihlaina is. I want to have babies."

"You do?" asked Hitchinna with much love in voice.

"Yes. I want three babies."

Hitchinna picked up a cooking stick and was about to remove a rock from the coals when she heard loud footsteps, like large boulders smashing together at the river's bottom. Pounding scratches came from the door to the main storage mound or smokehouse, and the growl confirmed her most immediate fear, that a grizzly bear had entered camp. She ran quickly to the door and gasped, for they were in very grave danger. Grizzly bears foolish enough to steal food from a camp were out of control and probably ready to kill. Hitchinna immediately grabbed a large handful of tinder from her basket by where Wihlaina still sat a bit in shock. Hitchinna also grabbed a handful of pine needles and small twigs, all neatly stacked in order so that she could readily start a fire. Directly outside her door in two stacks she placed the tinder and pine needles. She grabbed sticks partially burning in the fire and placed them in the tinder and needles; they burst into flames while Hitchinna gathered a handful of pitch, more pine needles, and small twigs. She hurried back to the door and built the fires as quickly as possible into one fire.

"Wirula," Hitchinna screamed, "quickly build a fire in front of your door." Wirula had been staring in a daze at the beast larger than five men, but she instantly followed Hitchinna's advice.

The grizzly took notice of the flames and, of course, would avoid them. He did not wish to tear through a great thickness of dirt and timbers. He wanted their food, especially the fresh salmon hanging through the narrow door of the storage house, or what was left of the storage house. The beast had actually ripped a large cedar post from its well-lodged position in the earth and mound. Soon the fires had connected in front of Hitchinna's door, and she sang quietly to herself so that no heavy rain would fall immediately. She wanted the grizzly to be as full as a round moon before any change in events occurred, and the grizzly was very happy to oblige her. He was feasting mightily on most of their stored provisions and fresh fish, and was destroying every basket in the house to make sure he did not pass up a tasty tidbit. The rack of fresh salmon caught the day before was on the ground, and the grizzly sat in the middle of it, sniffing the air and gorging himself. Hitchinna kept the fire burning, and so did Wirula.

"At least we are safe," said Wihlaina, Chipmunk Woman, "but now the men will have to hunt him. Hunting grizzly bears is not good. Grizzlies are known to snap the arrows sticking from their bodies and to chase hunters through the brush."

"I see him," said Halai Auna as she stared out the door. How can he eat so much and look so unsatisfied?"

"He is chief for a while," said Hitchinna. "All of our work has been to serve him."

"Look at the way he tears at the salmon," said Halai Auna.

"He looks slow and stupid," said Wihlaina, "but he can run much faster through the brush than a man can in the open, and see his wet nose, the way it wiggles in the air. He can smell a man from a journey of two nights away. Only the wind needs to be in his favor."

*   *   *

"I like bear meat," said Hwipajusi to the other men in the sweathouse, "and besides, when you bring a woman a grizzly bearskin, she does not stop cooking for an entire year."

"We will let you have the hide then," said Dari Jowa, "and you can go to Jihkulu's camp where Bohkuina, Topuna, and Chikpitpa are. You can marry the fattest woman they have, with the most daughters too, and bring her to Tcapalauna. We need more women to cook all the food you eat, and to gather more roots and acorns and nuts and berries. We do not want you to lose weight and become a weak hunter."

"Thank you, Dari Jowa. That is very thoughtful of you, but we must kill the beast first. The best way is in the middle of winter when the grizzly is fast asleep. Men should build a great ring of fire around his den, and when he awakens, they should shoot him many times while he is still confused. I have killed three grizzlies in this way," replied Hwipajusi.

"Good idea," said Chunoyahi while shaking his head. "We will feed him every day for three seasons, wait until he hibernates for the winter, and then shoot him."

"You get more intelligent every day, Hwipajusi," said Demauna.

"Well. That is the easy way," replied Hwipajusi with a great laugh, "but I think I will take a hundred arrows, just in case the first ninety-nine do not work."

"Ohhh," sighed Chunoyahi, "the beast walks with the wind, also."

"The wind will change soon. The storm will break, and the winds will be gentle and from the west," said Dari Jowa.

"We could have a big salmon feast and not clean up afterwards. We could leave half-baked salmon in bay leaves lying around our fire, and bowls of blackberries and cooked roots. We could follow his trail and leave small bites of food upon the ground. We could stay home by the fire and dance and sing until he comes. Then we could climb trees and shoot him from four directions. That is until we used up our four hundred arrows and until he shook us from our trees," said Hwipajusi.

"We assume too much," said Demauna. "This grizzly might be a female. She could have cubs and be very dangerous. At even the slightest sense of danger, she could attack."

"Why did a grizzly have to invade camp during the middle of the salmon run?" asked Dari Jowa. "Killing him could take several days. We will lose much of our food supply."

"Maybe we could invite the bear into the men's house for a smoke," said Hwipajusi.

"No smoking," said Dari Jowa. "Not until we kill the grizzly. We must be very clean. We must smell very little."

"May I come?" asked Yolaina.

"No," said Dari Jowa. "I cannot allow you to track a grizzly bear. You and Lawalila must remain in camp, and you must do as Hitchinna does if the bear returns. You must not shoot at it, either. You must watch it eat and tear up camp."

Yolaina did not reply. The quick response and stern voice were enough. A good man, if possible, should always follow his chief's orders. Dari Jowa still looked at him and Lawalila.

"You and Lawalila can help your mother to fix the storage mound and to dry salmon. Much work needs to be done in camp. Do not be disappointed. We must work together to survive as a people." Dari Jowa paused. "I questioned in my heart many times the wisdom of my father when he said to hunt instead of to seek revenge, to scout instead of to hunt, to sleep out all night in a cold wind instead of to walk home, to sit with women and children instead of to hunt, to shoot deer instead of to shoot sheep, to shake pine cones from trees instead of to visit pretty women, to dry meat instead of to chip points. He was chief, and I was his son."

"Maybe you could boil some salmon skins to make glue so that we could back our new bows with chewed sinew. We need our new bows, and they are dry now," said Hwipajusi. He stood up from his skins and added a small amount of wood to the fire.

"I stay. You go," replied Yolaina as he lay down under his rabbit-skin blanket.

"I tell you truthfully, Yolaina," said Chunoyahi. "You do not want to go on this hunt. You will face a bear some day. The bear will be angry and want to kill you, and you will realize in that instant that the moment came soon enough to face a bear."

"Let the bear charge you," added Hwipajusi. "Let it get close so that you do not miss your shot. You will only get one shot, and your arrow must sink into its heart if possible. Do not try to run at that point either. Use your hand spear. Cut the center of its throat with all your might, and wrench your spear back and forth. Who knows? You might live."

*   *   *

"Do not worry so much, Yolaina," said Hitchinna. "The men are doing well. They all know exactly how to hunt and to kill the great bear."

Yolaina did not respond; he continued to pile dirt over the mound where the timber and bark had been replaced. He had not said any words which would have indicated that he had thought about the men; his mother simply knew his thoughts from his behavior because he was too quiet. The day was extremely pleasant, however, especially if one considered the recent snow followed by the heavy rain. Large clouds hung lightly in the brilliantly azure sky. Those near the sun were gray and white and filled with rainbows at their edges, and although the others were large and dark at their bottoms, they were dissipating as the sun followed its road across the sky. The clouds appeared from the north and fell apart just as the dew disappeared from the grass. Their village was deep within the pines and oaks, and only received a little direct sunlight when the sun was high. Yolaina's toes and fingers were cold, and he looked forward to the meal his mother was preparing. He would sit on top of the storage mound and let the sun warm his body. Long lines of ducks and geese filled the air on their trip north. A woodpecker thumped loudly on a snag far from Tcapalauna. A small bird peeped in the distance, and Hitchinna peeped exactly like the bird. She often spoke to the birds, and they would sometimes fly into camp. Above them a spotted hawk soared. Only tiny patches of snow could be seen on the higher ridges toward Wahkanopa, but one had to hike far from camp to see the snow.

"I really should not speak of your father, but I dreamed last night that his spirit left the canyon in peace. He knows he is not welcome. He knows he is dead. He is at peace, though, because he has watched you grow. You are like him, and he loves you so much that he left forever into the proper world of the Mapchemaina. He often had to do what you do right now. When we married, Igupa Topa ordered him to stay in camp often. Igupa Topa would not let him kill white men any more. Sometimes I could see a bit of doubt in his face, but he would sit quietly and chip points or shape his bow. When he spoke, his words were not against his father, but were of beauty and love. He was the most romantic Yahi ever born. I was very lucky to have been his wife, for some women presented him with baskets. However, he sent them home lonely. He certainly earned his nickname, Ututni, Wood Duck Man, even if he did not take advantage of them, and I often saw women smile at him. He was full of compliments for them all, and even married women gave him food. He would bring the food home so that I would not have to cook and we could be alone. I do not think I have ever been so happy as I am this morning, my son. Look above you below the dark cloud."

A brilliant colored bow arched the complete canyon in the light mist pouring from the cloud: violet, blue, green, yellow, orange, and red.

"Pul Miauna, Colored Bow Man, speaks of his great happiness and peace this morning. I had a vision last night that he would. From now to eternity, your father will periodically shine upon us and all the Yahi with the symbol of his name. I think he shines for you. He sees you piling dirt instead of hunting the bear, and his heart glows with laughter. He knows truly you live up to his vision of your name, Bravest Man, Yolaina, who is strong enough to stay home and not to complain. Your father thought that way. He was in no way simplistic, and he saw deeply into matters which concerned us. After you were born, he became even more philosophical than he was when we were first married.

"Your father waited for a day just like this to ask me to be his wife. He waited for a storm to break and painted all colors in the arch of the colored bow across his face. He brought fine pelts of otter and pine martin and wore a mountain lion's skin cape. He had colored shells about his neck and in his ears and nose, and when he stood in front of my father's home in Black Rock Village next to the deep pools and gave my father the skins and spoke words of love and marriage, the colored bow arched the sky. I was very frightened. My heart flopped about like a salmon on a stream's bank."

"Is that really the manner in which he asked you to marry him?" asked Yolaina, who was very impressed with his mother's words.

"Yes."

Yolaina looked again at the brilliant bow above their heads. "Do you really think Pul Miauna sends us the colored bow as a message that he is happy."

"I do. All things are connected. I had a vision of spiritual peace, and life for us is so. Your father shines upon us."

"Do you…," Yolaina said but stopped short as the others came into camp with armloads of wood. They were concerned about having a large amount of dry wood. Every time they recalled the grizzly bear, they thought about how low their wood supply was after the snow and rain. The sunshine gave them all invigorated hope that the wood they were gathering would soon be dry and brittle. The present load was their fourth, and after their fifth load, they would eat and then break the wood into the proper sizes for stacking next to the homes. The sun would do the rest. Until the last windy storm had broken limbs from the snags not too far from camp, wood was becoming scarce, for they had lived secluded in their winter's camp for many seasons by then. Gathering wood directly around camp was becoming a problem, but gathering wood was an eternal process. Wirula, Pahnino, Lawalila, Wihlaina, and Halai Auna were breathing heavily as they entered the circle of dirt mounds.

"A large tree fell not far away," said Pahnino. "Many limbs are broken off."

"When you return, we will have the baked salmon and acorn cakes," said Hitchinna. "We are lucky for the sun."

"Any sign of the grizzly?" asked Halai Auna.

"No. He is probably hiding from the men," replied Hitchinna.

"Just as long as he does not hide in the storage mound, I do not care," said Pahnino as they all left again.

When they were gone back up the canyon's steep incline, Hitchinna continued her conversation with Yolaina.

"I enjoy that you have stayed with us in the evenings for the last three nights, but I know you miss the men's house. Halai Auna misses your company, too. She says so."

"We spend most of our time together already," said Yolaina. "She could not miss me too much."

"Having you around in the evening when we tell stories is what she misses the most," said Hitchinna.

"I like listening to Hwipajusi's stories," said Yolaina. "He makes me laugh all the time."

"I bet he does," said Hitchinna, but she quickly took a gasp of air and held her breath. Twigs snapped just outside their circle. When Hitchinna looked up, however, she did not see a grizzly. She saw a woman over forty, slightly overweight, and with three young girls. She carried a large black and white storage basket of fine weave and wore a wildcat-skin cape. The girls were laden with all kinds of baskets and cooking sticks and women's mats and skins and clothes. She stared at Hitchinna a moment.

"I can only presume this is where Hwipajusi lives," she said. "Is this true?"

"Yes," said Hitchinna, slightly amazed.

"Good," she said. "Which is his house?"

"Ah…," said Hitchinna as she glanced at Yolaina's very broad grin, "he does not actually have a home. He seems to share everyone's cooking about equally, and he lives in the men's house. He has a spot there."

"He does not have a home?"

"No," replied Hitchinna.

"Can you show me his spot?"

"Ah…Yolaina, show this woman Hwipajusi's spot."

"Okay," replied Yolaina, still smiling broadly. "Come with me." He sprang off the mound and ran to the men's house near the very tall cedar. He turned up the black bearskin and escorted the woman and three girls into the sweathouse. "Hwipajusi's spot is here," said Yolaina and pointed to where Hwipajusi had three bows and all of his hunting gear very neatly arranged in back of his skins.

"He has fine otter skins," said the woman as she set her basket on Hwipajusi's bearskin. She touched the otter skins. "Set your belongings there," said the woman as she pointed to the mats below Hwipajusi's bed in the inner circle but away from the fire pit. The girls obeyed her and were careful not to stare at Yolaina. "Now," she said, "we will build a house." She led the way out the door. Yolaina followed them back to Hitchinna.

"Now we will build a home," said the woman. "You are Hitchinna, the greatest cook. I can tell," she continued.

"I am Hitchinna. Ah…I cook all the time for many mouths, but I seriously doubt if I am the greatest Yahi cook. I do wish, however, that you and your children will have breakfast with us. I have baked the largest salmon in bay leaves. It is stuffed with roots and white man's seeds. I have acorn cakes prepared. We will be honored with your presence. You must be hungry from your journey. With so many small girls and such a large load, you must have journeyed for one night. Jihkulu's camp is far."

"We will eat with you, and in return, you must feast in my new home many times. You are sister-in-law of the chief, White-headed Eagle Man, Dari Jowa, a great hunter and wise man. You live among the tall pines, often in the snow. I used to live in Towani with a view of Wahkanopa. Many tall pines are there. I wish often to return to the old days. I can no longer stand living in the brush and eating so much dehydrated cow meat. All winter, though, Hwipajusi brought me fresh venison or turkeys or rabbits, always something good. He loves me. I can tell. I laugh all the time when I am with Hwipajusi, and consequently, I said to myself, 'Go to Hwipajusi and live among the pines. Cook for him. Surely he needs a wife to cook for him since he eats so much.'"

"He always provides much more than he eats," replied Hitchinna.

"He loves little girls, too," said the woman, "so I brought two orphans along with my daughter. Too many children live near the flat mountain overlooking Salmon Creek. Not enough hunters are there, and Jihkulu sends Topuna, Chikpitpa, and Bohkuina after cows because they are so plentiful at the lower elevation. Too many saltu like cows, and trouble awaits the hunters. Hwipajusi says the white men hunt cows all the time because they are such bad hunters and because cows are so stupid, like white men. What do your men hunt today?"

"They hunt a grizzly bear," replied Hitchinna.

"See," said the woman as she turned to the girls. "Go get digging sticks, sharp, smooth ones, and we will build Hwipajusi, Whistling Swan Man and grizzly bear hunter, a fine, big home."

*   *   *

The storm had at least remained broken for several days, and the sky was bright blue for the men's walk home. They had finally tracked the grizzly in a great, aimless circle and to Deer Creek where its den was. The north wind had sent too many delicious smells its way, and after its winter's sleep, the bear had been too hungry not to head directly to

Tcapalauna and to Hitchinna's cooking. The men had paid careful attention to the wind as they had traveled and had been able to shoot the beast when it had awakened in the morning. The beast had chased Demauna up a tree, but too many arrows had been shot from too many directions. They had skinned the beast and had cut most of the meat from its bones to carry in its hide, but Demauna and Chunoyahi carried the beast's skinned hindquarters with a pole.

"I do not know if I should give this hide to woman," said Hwipajusi. "Word will get around that I am a great grizzly bear hunter, and then too many women will want to marry me. I should give the woman I wish to marry a cowhide, and then other women will not become too jealous. They all have cowhides."

"I insist you give the grizzly bearskin to a woman in Jihkulu's camp. I am not so sure the women there like you. They feed you too much, and you tell all of them the same love stories. None of them will marry you unless you give one of them real proof you can hunt," said Dari Jowa.

"They do not care if I can hunt. They have plenty of cows to eat," replied Hwipajusi. "They love me anyhow. You see, all the widows get excited and happy when I show up, even their chief, Jihkulu, Large Owl Woman. I would marry her, but she is too old and bossy. She likes cows too much."

"I agree with Dari Jowa. I hear you say too much about fat women and young girls. I see you come back from Jihkulu's camp with a great smile on your face all the time, and you seem to gain weight. They feed you, yet you do not get married. No woman there trusts you any more, and you must now prove you are worthwhile. You must stop taking advantage of those poor women. You are beginning to give the men of Tcapalauna a bad name," said Chunoyahi.

"All of you are starting to sound as if you have acorn mush for brains," replied Hwipajusi. "Those women know all about the men of Tcapalauna, and they all think we are the most handsome, best hunters of all the Yahi who have ever lived. This is true, and I am not the only reason they think so highly of us, either. Demauna has taken them too many deer. The young girls all love him. He walks into their camp with a large buck, drops it at Jihkulu's door, asks how everyone is doing, glances discreetly at all the old girls and young women, and then struts out of camp without even eating. All I have to do is show up with a couple of rabbits, tell some old, fat widow what a great cook she is, and answer a few questions about mighty Demauna, and they all think we are the best hunters that have ever lived."

"I am just being helpful," said Demauna. "Not enough hunters are there for so many mouths."

"You are just showing off for the young women," replied Hwipajusi. "They know you are a wonderful hunter now, and they all want to marry you. You have said before that Pahnino will let you marry one of them. They know how Pahnino thinks; I told them. The more I tell them, the more they feed me."

"I would hate to hear all you have told those poor women," said Chunoyahi. "You have probably said to the oldest or to the ugliest woman of each house that she is the one you truly love but that each of them should not tell the others because you must be friendly with all of them. Then you eat all their seeds and blackberries and tell them you had to hunt a full moon to kill the fat rabbit you brought them."

"They all ask questions about you, too, Chunoyahi. I have to tell them you only kill half as many deer as you actually do, and even when I lie in such a manner, their eyes glisten like sunshine on white water and their hearts patter faster than a hummingbird's wings. I do not dare tell them the truth about you, or all thirty-two of them would come Tcapalauna to marry you, Chunoyahi, Hat Creek Man, most handsome hunter who ever lived."

Dari Jowa shifted the pole to his left shoulder and looked at Hwipajusi ahead of him and at the bear's paws and once deadly claws on top of the meat. "I am chief. To whom will you give this great bearskin? You must honor a woman of Jihkulu's camp even if she will not marry you because you have used her too many times."

"You are making a mistake, Dari Jowa. Those women will get too excited, and they know you are chief. They will think you ordered me to give the hide to a fat, old, ugly woman because you have many grizzly hides, and then they will come to live in your house with Wihlaina. When you wish to make love on cold nights, the women will be in your house, and you will have no where to be alone. They will stare, and you will come to the men's house and be too grumpy. Maybe I should take the one I wish to marry a squirrel's skin, and then you would be safe."

"I have spoken. I wish a fat, old, ugly woman with many daughters to come live in Tcapalauna. You see such a woman often. She deserves to be treated with honor."

"I have warned you, however," said Hwipajusi. "We should use this hide to cover the entrance to our sweathouse. I know women. Just as soon as one sees this bearskin, I will not be able to rest for many moons. I will have to build a house. I will have to gather reeds. I will have to hunt every day. I must admit, though, that in a few years my daughters will become women, and then I will have to do nothing more. Dari Jowa will become tired of Wihlaina by then. He will come to me and say, 'You are the oldest. I will let you be chief if I can marry one of your young, beautiful daughters.' I will say, 'That is a good idea, but you must bring me two deer, eight turkeys, one cow, and six grizzly bears every moon for the rest of your life.'"

"A grizzly bearskin will probably not be enough to impress the woman in Jihkulu's village. Hwipajusi has probably told her too many lies. We will wait your return with great anticipation," said Chunoyahi as they were entering camp, but he had to stop because Hwipajusi, who was in the lead, had stopped. "Why have you stopped?" asked Chunoyahi. "Let us enter camp to set down our loads."

Hwipajusi did not reply, however, and still did not move. Dari Jowa pushed the pole forward to force Hwipajusi into the center of

Tcapalauna where they set down the meat and hide. The women and children all stopped working on the new house for the new woman and her children. All of the women and children smiled broadly, and then all the men except Hwipajusi smiled broadly. Dari Jowa looked around at Chunoyahi and then at Hitchinna and then directly at the woman.

"After Hwipajusi faced the charging grizzly and sank his arrow deeply into the beast's heart, killing the bear was easy," said Dari Jowa, who then walked to the feeder stream to drink and to laugh. The sight of Hwipajusi's dropped jaw would entertain all of the men for many seasons.

*   *   *

Yolaina, Lawalila, Demauna, Chunoyahi, Dari Jowa, and Hwipajusi all sat in the men's sweathouse, and all were extremely jovial, except Hwipajusi, who was not sure that all had gone as well as he had envisioned the day should have gone. The women and girls had gone to watch the sunset and to make many plans for the wedding that would occur as soon as Hwipajusi's new house was built.

"Wihlaina said she had made extra mats and that you can have them for the floor of your new home, Hwipajusi," said Dari Jowa, "and Hitchinna is sewing you a fine blanket from all the otter skins we have. Everyone likes the new woman. She has quite a personality, just like you, and she is not ugly or too fat either."

"She can cook, too. No wonder you gained weight from visiting Jihkulu's camp. Did you see the way she stuffed leopard lily in that bear's hindquarter and sprinkled it with black salt. She baked it until if fell apart like acorn mush in our mouths," said Demauna.

"You should look in your basket, Hwipajusi, to see what she has brought you as a gift. I have never seen such a fine, storage basket," said Chunoyahi. "The next time you see her, she will want to know that you appreciate her gift."

"She said that you brought her meat all winter and that she knows you love her," said Yolaina.

"I heard her tell Wihlaina that you make her heart warmer than the hot summer's sun on baking rocks and warmer than burning, orange embers on a cold starry night," said Lawalila.

"She said that?" asked Hwipajusi incredulously.

"Yes," replied Lawalila. "She said you made her feel like a young girl."

"And I heard her say that you are the best hunter and kindest man she has ever met," added Yolaina.

"She said that?" asked Hwipajusi again.

"Yes," replied Yolaina.

"Everyone likes you, Hwipajusi, and now you must face the real responsibilities of being a family man," said Dari Jowa. "After all, she does have a daughter and two orphans with her."

"Let us see what is in the basket, Hwipajusi. We have waited long enough," said Chunoyahi.

"What if her gifts are not suitable for a man of my stature?" asked Hwipajusi.

"I will judge her gifts," said Dari Jowa, "but I must tell you this. Her basket alone is an adequate gift for any man. Now open the basket so that we may see inside."

Hwipajusi set the basket near the fire and in front of Yolaina, who sat at the foot of his uncle. "Open the basket, Yolaina, so that we may all see together."

Yolaina opened the basket, and they looked anxiously in. A long, finely woven rope was coiled around another basket. Yolaina removed the basket and set it on the floor, and then removed the rope, which he gave to Dari Jowa.

Dari Jowa felt the rope and examined it quite closely in the orange light of the flames. "This is the most long, finely woven rope of milkweed I have ever seen." He threw the coiled rope to Chunoyahi. "I am very impressed. Let me see inside the other basket."

Yolaina opened the other basket, and everyone stared closely inside once more. The basket contained five, well-sewn, deerskin pouches. Yolaina handed them one at a time to Dari Jowa. Dari Jowa opened the first pouch and removed dried deer sinew for making bowstrings. "This is very thoughtful." He handed the pouch and sinew to Demauna, who sat next to Dari Jowa. The second pouch contained little metal sticks of the material used to make lightning sticks and used to hold white men's homes together. One of them was in a carefully shaped handle of black oak and was to be used to chip obsidian and glass for arrowheads and spearpoints. Also in the bag was a dyed piece of deerskin to be used for covering one's palm when chipping obsidian. "This is another useful gift," said Dari Jowa, who handed it to Demauna, who was still examining the pouch of sinew. The third pouch was filled with bright abalone buttons, beads, and crystals containing the colored bow. "These are very beautiful. Such bright gifts a woman cherishes with her heart." The fourth pouch had a pipe of elk horn and was shaped to fit comfortably into one's hand. "This is the finest shaped pipe I have ever seen." Dari Jowa gave the pouch and pipe to Demauna, who was examining the saltu chipping stick and black oak handle. The fifth pouch was light and filled with dried tobacco.

Hwipajusi jumped off his spot and headed to the entrance before Dari Jowa could speak.

"Where are you going?" asked Demauna.

"To ask the widow to marry me before she changes her mind," Hwipajusi said as he scampered out the entrance and into the twilight.

*   *   *

"All I got was dried venison," said Dari Jowa as he examined the rope again. "Maybe I should marry the new woman. That way Wihlaina will learn her crafts more quickly."

"I have never seen Hwipajusi get so excited," said Demauna. "The widow seems to be a perfect match for him."

"I wonder…" began Yolaina, but Hitchinna's voice came from outside the sweathouse.

"Come quickly before darkness sets. Hwipajusi sent the women and children back from the bluff. He wishes for you to go there. Many fires burn to the west above the canyon. He wants you to see."

"Is it a forest fire?" asked Dari Jowa as they all left to the east, up the canyon, and toward the bluffs where they often kept lookout or watched the sun set.

"I do not think so," said Hitchinna. "Neither does Hwipajusi. They do not make sense."

The men hurried under the darkening sky, and as the evening star first shown over Black Rock, they arrived where Hwipajusi stood. Clearly in the distance across the canyon, many fires burned, and when one walked a short way, some fires disappeared and other fires appeared, meaning that the flames were controlled and somewhat hidden among trees and brush.

"The fires are relatively near Jihkulu's camp," said Hwipajusi evenly. "These fires are probably not good."

"What are you saying?" asked Dari Jowa.

"I will go see what those fires mean tomorrow morning, early," said Hwipajusi.

"No," said Dari Jowa. "I will send Chunoyahi. I want you to visit with your new woman. I want you to get good timbers with me for your new house. Chunoyahi will bring us news about the fires."

"Many Yahi are dead tonight," said Hwipajusi. "I have never been so happy to be given such news."

"We do not know what the fires mean," said Chunoyahi. "Maybe funeral pyres are not the explanation. I will find out tomorrow. You better stay here. You have seen enough grief."

"What other explanation could there be? Count them. If you keep changing positions, you can see many fires. I have counted over twenty."

Dari Jowa walked away from the men, looked all the while at the fires, and then returned. "Over twenty fires are burning, and they are large and controlled. Maybe funeral pyres do not explain them, however. Maybe some saltu is burning piles of brush. White men do strange things."

"White men act strangely all right," said Hwipajusi. "I will stay in camp tomorrow. Chunoyahi, you can count our dead." He walked toward the men's house. Lawalila, Demauna, Chunoyahi, Dari Jowa, and Yolaina watched Hwipajusi walk back into the brush and trees, and looked at each other and then the fires, still glowing very brightly.

"Tell me, Yolaina, Bravest Man, as you look out at what are probably funeral pyres, what do you think?" asked Dari Jowa as the colors of the sunset faded.

The question caught Yolaina off guard, for he felt very confused. "You are chief."

"A chief needs to know what his people think and feel, especially the one he trains to hunt."

"I think many thoughts, and do not know all that we should do," replied Yolaina.

"You must tell me three things you believe we should do."

"We should always keep our camp where cows and horses do not come," said Yolaina after some hesitation, for his answers seemed to become philosophically grounded. "We should always avoid white men. We should live honorably."

"Those are good answers," said Dari Jowa. "I will think about them. Demauna, I wish for you to scout down Deer Creek, back to Salmon Creek, and up Salmon Creek back to here. Hunt birds or rabbits once you are near home. Go for two nights. Watch for white men, and then tell us all you have learned. Let us have a smoke with

Hwipajusi, and see if we can think of pleasant thoughts about the woman and three children."

*   *   *

"I have seen too many skulls today," said Chunoyahi to Hwipajusi, Dari Jowa, Lawalila, and Yolaina. They sat outside around an open fire pit, for the stars were beautiful and the air was only cool.

"How many?" asked Dari Jowa as he glanced at Chunoyahi's house where he could see Topuna, his wife, and Chikpitpa move about. They had just arrived and had burned hair and pitch-covered heads. They sang continually.

"They had already fully buried five, and I helped with the carrying of rocks, and the digging of holes next to the fires, and the final burial of twenty-five more. Bohkuina died carrying bodies away from the over-hang. He was not shot like the others.

"Topuna and his wife were away to be alone, and Chikpitpa and Bohkuina and Pakalai Jawichi were hunting cows when four white men and dogs rode into Jihkulu's camp on horses. They shot everyone there, all the women and children. They cut the scalps from their heads, they stole their belongings, and they left. Topuna watched them cut the hair from his daughter.

"The dead are at least buried properly this time," said Chunoyahi. "They will not be lost in these canyons. The coyotes will not dig them up. I sang twenty times over each carefully covered and hidden grave. They rest forever."

Hwipajusi threw some wood on the fire from where he sat on a rot-ten, smooth section of a tree trunk. "The only Yahi alive are now mem-bers of this camp, Tcapalauna: Dari Jowa, Wihlaina, Chunoyahi, Wirula, Demauna, Pahnino, Periwiri Yupa, her daughter Tsanunewa, the two orphans Ketipku and Weanmauna, Hitchinna, Halai Auna, Lawalila, Topuna, his wife Kadila, Pakalai Jawichi, and I. I count only seventeen Yahi alive. In these canyons we used to have eleven camps in the open. Between the camps we had over four hundred people. We got along well with most of neighbors, except the Wintuns, but the valley Indians were a joke. The saltu came, and now we have seventeen. We fought for a long time, many years, and we have tried to surrender. We have not killed a white man or woman for several years, also. I guess we have but two choices: to fight until they kill us, or to hide and hope they do not accidentally find us."

"We will hide and hope that they do not accidentally find us now," said Dari Jowa.

"That is one very good choice," said Hwipajusi. "I feel extremely sad for Topuna, his wife, Chikpitpa, and Pakalai Jawichi. They suffer and will continue to suffer for a long time."

"Topuna and Chikpitpa might want to kill the saltu or their women and children," said Chunoyahi.

"That is true, and they would be just in doing so. I am chief, however, and I say no one will kill a white man, a white woman, or a white child. I count many white men, especially in the valley, and I have often seen how many men hunt the Yahi when we kill a few of them. We are now very few in number, and if the Yahi are truly to live and to reproduce and to grow, we must hide. We must not taunt the white men."

Hitchinna carried a basket from her home to Chunoyahi, who greedily awaited the bear meat and acorn cakes made partly with white man's seeds. She quickly left, however, for she did not want to be included in the conversation. Hitchinna already knew that Jihkulu's camp was destroyed, and the new guests required a lot of attending.

"A man these days does not eat grizzly bear meat too often," said Chunoyahi.

"I am happy your woman came to Tcapalauna when she did," said Dari Jowa to Hwipajusi. "We have her life and the three children's, also, to be thankful for."

"I look forward to hunting in the high country this summer," said Chunoyahi. "Maybe Lawalila and Yolaina will kill a deer this summer. Let us smoke, Hwipajusi. Go get your new pipe."

A moth flew into the flames, and the wind blew sparks toward Chunoyahi. Dry leaves chattered as they blew across the pine needles and under brush around the circle of homes.

When Hwipajusi returned, Dari Jowa spoke. "I want you to get your wife a couple of skins while the snow is still on the ground, Hwipajusi. Tomorrow morning would be a good time. Scout the high country. Make sure no saltu are there, and bring back your soon-to-be wife some joy. We will have your house finished by then."

CHAPTER 7

Revenge

Yolaina and Dari Jowa made their way up the feeder stream on the other side of the flat mountain. Sometimes even the feeder stream became so choked with brush they had to leave the streambed, but the men skirted around the brush and sometimes into the open for a few paces. Dari Jowa and Yolaina were trying to find Pahnino, Topuna, Kadila or Soaproot Plant Woman, and Pakalai Jawichi. All of Tcapalauna had been gathering acorns on Black Oak Mountain, and they had been shuttling the acorns down the side of Salmon Creek Canyon to Bay Tree Village. From Bay Tree Village they had hiked on the south side of the canyon for a day until they had reached the feeder stream between the massive rock landmarks, Kashmauna and Ocholoko. From there they had hiked up the feeder stream to the tall pines where Tcapalauna was well hidden in the steep canyon. Topuna, Kadila, Pahnino, and Pakalai Jawichi should have been at Bay Tree Village when Yolaina and Dari Jowa showed up there at midday to haul the last acorns to Tcapalauna, but they had not shown up since Dari Jowa and Yolaina had left the camp the previous day. Both Dari Jowa and Yolaina expected possibly to find them dead. Collecting the best acorns in abundance every year had become progressively difficult from a safety point of view for many years. Where the best black oaks grew, cows grazed, and saltu hunted them. They rode their horses and had guns on their sides and tied to their saddles. During the autumn, the saltu chased the cows from the north side of Salmon Creek Canyon to their homes, where settlers burned marks on the cows, killed some of them, and separated some for walking to the valley.

When Yolaina and Dari Jowa finally entered the relatively flat, open grove of black oaks near the top of the rounded mountain, they searched back and forth quietly, except that every once in a while Dari Jowa made the call of the stellar jay. Perhaps the lost people would respond. The search turned up evil news quickly, however, for horse tracks were found. Not too far away from them, blood was on the ground. The blood led into the brush. After a long crawl downhill into the brush, Dari Jowa once again made the call of the stellar jay, and this time Pakalai Jawichi responded. He was in an open clearing waiting to be found, and with him Topuna lay on the ground, dead. The wound in Topuna's thigh was large, and during the previous night, he had died from lack of blood. Pakalai Jawichi sat naked near him. His foot was tightly wrapped in his bloody loincloth, and he sat with swollen eyes and sang mournfully, a boy experiencing the death of his adopted father.

*   *   *

Dari Jowa, Yolaina, and Pakalai Jawichi sat facing the pyre. They ate some recently smoked salmon that Dari Jowa had brought along, and drank some freshly prepared, smashed berries and water from the basket Dari Jowa had used to carry the salmon.

"The saltu just rode up and chased you until they lassoed Pahnino and Kadila, and when Topuna protested, they shot him in the leg?" asked Yolaina incredulously.

"Yes," replied Pakalai Jawichi. "When I helped Topuna, they shot me in the foot, but we managed to crawl into the brush."

"We did not find your bows or baskets," said Yolaina.

"They probably took them," said Dari Jowa. "Poor Pahnino and Kadila."

"Maybe we should track them," said Yolaina. "Maybe we could rescue them."

"No," replied Dari Jowa. "They are already at a white man's home. Surely many would die. We have not been cautious enough on our journey to Tcapalauna. We could be tracked from Black Oak Mountain. Over these many years of hiding, I have wondered when the white would accidentally find us. We have been hiding for seven years and have not killed them or taken from their storage houses for seven years, yet when first we come into contact with them, they kidnap two women, kill one hunter, and maim one boy. The evilness in white men astounds me."

Yolaina stood and began throwing the second round of gathered wood onto the dwindling flames of the pyre. Soon the flames roared high, and the wood was in place. In the morning they would bury Topuna and sing for him before taking Pakalai Jawichi back to Tcapalauna. Pakalai Jawichi had wrapped his nasty wound well, and only at a later day would he know the extent to which his foot would be useful. Nothing else could be done. Pakalai Jawichi could burn his hair and put pitch on his head at Tcapalauna, where he could be taken care of properly. After Yolaina finished, he sat next to his bow and arrows and tinder pouch, and drank from the reddish, cold liquid.

"Telling Demauna his wife has been kidnapped will be very painful," said Dari Jowa. He then changed his voice slightly. "For gathering acorns your wife is now a white man's slave, an object of rape and scorn and servitude."

Tears rolled down Pakalai Jawichi's cheeks once more on their silent journey to the leaves, and wind blew the clouds over the moon. The night would be long and chilled, and the next day would bring little relief.

       *   *   *

Yolaina cleaned his basket in the stream, rinsed his mouth, and walked toward Hitchinna's family home where Dari Jowa was still eating and explaining about the events of the tragedy. Halai Auna and Hitchinna sat in their spots. Lawalila was in the men's house preparing a sweatbath. All the men except Demauna and Pakalai Jawichi would become very hot, rub thickened ointment from boiled bay leaves on their bodies, and slip in an euphoric slumber.

"Why can't they leave us alone?" asked Halai Auna, now a fine young woman with full breasts. "We will miss Pahnino and Kadila. How could they steal them?" Halai Auna fumbled with some dyed redbud bark, but she could not force herself to work on a basket.

"They will never leave us alone," replied Hitchinna.

Dari Jowa just stared Hitchinna, for how could one reply to such a sad truth?

"I have a hard time understanding, or, I guess, accepting that we should mourn and not do something, anything in retribution. I have heard the logic of how more harm than good comes from such practices, and I have seen camps destroyed because white men have followed hunters who exacted retribution. I do not enjoy, however, this sickening feeling of allowing their evilness to eat at my heart. I think I would feel better if we killed them," said Yolaina.

"Would you then feel good if they killed Halai Auna or Hitchinna or everyone else in camp, also?" asked Dari Jowa.

"They probably will, anyhow," said Yolaina.

"So you believe we should fight now and die, rather than later?" asked Dari Jowa.

"Maybe we could stay on the move and post scouts, like in the old days, and kill those who enter the foothills one at a time," continued Yolaina.

"Before you were born, that is exactly what I would have done, along with most of our hunters. Our women and children would be left alone to feed themselves without a proper meat supply, and we would kill white men or women for killing us. We would think, 'Now the white man will leave us alone, just as the Wintuns did before the white men came.' White men seemed to appear in ever-larger numbers, though, and we never forced them to leave. Instead, over the years they somehow tracked us down and killed us in great numbers."

Yolaina stared and felt no need to reply. "Let us take a sweatbath, Dari Jowa," he said finally and left for the men's sweathouse.

Hitchinna looked at Dari Jowa and the wrinkles beginning to form in the corners of his eyes and at his sad reflective demeanor. "Yolaina does not mean to challenge your word," she said. "He wants to strike out against the saltu because of our diminished status, but when he thinks of a way to strike, he can find no purpose. He has his youth and pride to deal with. His blood is hot. He is too young."

"I will sweat with Yolaina," said Dari Jowa as he stood to leave. "His words do not make me sad. I get great joy from our new man. He will not exact revenge. He will do all I ask, and time will change his heart. He perhaps he will become even a better hunter than he is now. He will not want to make more mistakes in judgment. When he sees the order of life change, he will stand in the way, as does a leaf in the wind. We will continue to hide. I go. You stay."

In the sweathouse Dari Jowa removed his loincloth and sat with the other naked men: Hwipajusi, Chunoyahi, Lawalila, and Yolaina. He spread the pungent bay leaf oil on his skin and lay down. No one said anything for a very long time. All waited for Dari Jowa to speak, for he was chief. "I am very tired," he said and lay down to sleep.

       *   *   *

With the morning's sun to his back, Yolaina sat naked and alone on the cliff near Ocholoko overlooking Salmon Creek Canyon. He gazed happily at the fall colors, a myriad of yellows and browns among the evergreens, and he beat his wet, black, long hair with a smooth stick to help it dry. He remembered the long summer in the green meadows around Wahkanopa and the view from its pinnacle, the white man's towns and belching demon running along Daha, the great water of the valley. He remembered the freedom Tcapalauna felt as they hunted and dried venison and gathered leopard lily roots for the moons of winter, soon to come. The long canyon faded away to lower elevations beyond Black Rock where the vegetation turned to grass and jagged rocks and the valley. He realized that the Yahi were few, that the white men were many, and that the course of events that shaped their future was a mystical uncertainty. He thought of Topuna lying dead at the edge of the brush and of Pakalai Jawichi crying so pathetically over his protector, but Topuna's limp, breathless body with hanging jaw and colorless expression was a sight hard not to think about. *The Yahi must be like a ring-tail cat in the dark of a moonless night, sneaking quietly about in search of small bits of dropped acorn cakes, never seen or felt or heard, never coming face to face with white men,* thought Yolaina. The sounds of Salmon Creek and birds filled his ears, and then Yolaina heard others walking through the pines to where he sat.

"I knew Yolaina would be here," said Hwipajusi between heavy breathing. On his back was Pakalai Jawichi, his foot newly wrapped in clean white man's material from old seed bags. "I thought we would dry our hair with you on this fine autumn morning, Yolaina, and talk about the ten most fun ways to kill white men," continued Hwipajusi as Pakalai Jawichi slid off his back and seated himself next to Yolaina. Hwipajusi also sat down.

Yolaina glanced at his good friend, Whistling Swan Man, the oldest Yahi, and noticed the gray hair and broadened stomach.

"We could feed you so much that you fill up the great valley and smash all their towns," said Yolaina.

"Sounds delicious," said Hwipajusi, "but my wife and daughters would have to work too hard, and then when my daughters became women, they would be too skinny. I would not be able to get you young men to kill enough deer for me."

"What is number two, then?" asked Pakalai Jawichi.

"We could snare a couple of cow chasers, hang them upside down from a sturdy oak branch, swing them back and forth, and shoot their eyes out from forty paces. Then we could watch the coyotes eat them. You two could use the target practice, that is, since my daughters are so very beautiful."

"You are even a better shot than Chunoyahi, though," said Pakalai Jawichi, "and you would shoot out their eyes first. Then your daughters would be too ashamed to marry anyone not as good as their father. You would get no deer in your old age."

"That is true," said Hwipajusi thoughtfully. "Well, we could stake them to the ground directly below the spires of Kashmauna there, and drop huge boulders on them. I have never heard such a sound. The white men would have to watch the rocks fall, as if they were stupid cows. I hit a cow in the head with a rock yesterday, and the cow just stood like an oak tree until the rock bounced off its horn and struck it above the eyes. Only then did it consider moving."

"You are the biggest, though," said Yolaina, "and you would throw the largest boulder. Your daughter would think we were not worthy of them."

"We could poison them and watch them die in their vomit," said Hwipajusi, still with a large smile on his face.

"That is too easy," said Pakalai Jawichi.

"We could give them soaring lessons off the flat mountain," continued Hwipajusi.

"That is your best idea so far," said Yolaina, "but a woman could do such an act. Your daughters would not be impressed."

"We could burn them in a large fire," said Hwipajusi, "and listen to them beg and scream."

"Your daughters would feel sorry for them and think we were cruel," said Yolaina.

"My daughters know we cannot be cruel to a white man. They know white men are without spirits and decency. They would not care."

"Women are too soft hearted. They would cry and say a man must kill the saltu in a noble way."

"We could lie in wait, show our faces, wait until they reached for their lightning sticks, and then fill them with arrows."

"That is the old way, Hwipajusi," said Pakalai Jawichi. "Your daughters would think we were stupid and not sporting enough."

"We could boil them in a large basket."

"No good. That would be same as burning them," said Yolaina.

"We could flay a few," continued Hwipajusi.

"No style," said Pakalai Jawichi.

"We could shoot them to the sky from a bent over pine tree," he said.

"The sky is too far away," said Yolaina. "They would fall back to Salmon Creek, probably in Salmon Creek. That is not a way to kill white men."

"Okay then. How is this? We give each one of them a bow and arrows and a spear and all the tools he needs to live. We let them free at the top of Wahkanopa and dress them as we dress, without moccasins or skins. We give them one day to journey home or to prepare to hunt us, and then we hunt them."

"The white men would probably freeze to death or roll off the mountain, but I admit fully that treating them so fairly would at least add pleasure to killing them. Your daughters would even think we were brave hunters, even though killing the white men would be easier than killing cows," said Yolaina.

"Your daughters would bring us all your baskets, Hwipajusi. They would not ask us to give you any food in your old age if we killed white men in such a way. They would think we were too brave, and they would no longer listen to you," said Pakalai Jawichi.

"No wonder Dari Jowa sits so thoughtfully by the feeder stream and watches water skippers. He cannot think of a good way to kill white men," said Hwipajusi.

CHAPTER 8

Returning a Favor

As Halai Auna, Pakalai Jawichi, Hwipajusi, and Yolaina walked toward the storage cabin on Dry Creek north of Salmon Creek Canyon, they chatted about the prospects of who would marry whom, since one of Hwipajusi's daughters had become a woman recently and since the other two were ready at any time to become women. The spring's sun was high in the morning's sky, and the new heat of summer had begun to turn some patches of green grass to brown. Their skins and bows and arrows and dried cow meat were cached not far from Bay Tree Village, where they hoped to spend the night with their new supply of seeds and other wonderful white man's food: salted meat; sweet, white crunchy powder; and a type of ground seeds, white and perfect for making cakes. The white men were very friendly to store continually food of all types in such remote cabins so that Hwipajusi and his young cohorts could steal it. Only in the middle of the winter when all their acorns and meat had depleted to the point that the people of Tcapalauna would starve did Dari Jowa allow the stealing of food from cabins, and all those who stole had to be very cautious to step on rocks, to walk in stream beds, to spend extra nights away from Tcapalauna, and to check thoroughly for those who might track them. Stealing from the cabins began to make a lot of sense, however, since the gathering of acorns and even the killing of deer had become increasingly difficult. Too many white men hunted the deer with lightning sticks, for instance, and the deer were hard to interest in decoys and would often bolt away. White men seemed to love the peaceful acorn groves and the cows that ate the grass beneath their boughs; consequently, gathering acorns was about as dangerous as stealing from the cabins. With such alternatives and with the adults ready to try any effective method of survival, the results of the thievery were a welcome relief from the many hours of toil and of fear they had to face when gathering food. The black oaks were brilliantly yellow-green when compared to the foothill pines, as were the buckeye and laurel, and at their feet shooting stars, owl clover, tidy tips, brodiaea, and lupines were in full bloom.

"Your oldest girl might get too fat from the seeds and sweet, white powder we will get. Then not even Demauna will want her," said Yolaina. "She will think life is too easy and will forget how to cook properly, also."

"That is not true," replied Hwipajusi. "Tsanunewa, Wren Woman, is very well trained and never eats too much. She is perfect in all respects, more beautiful than seashells and manzanita flowers, thriftier than a squirrel, more polite than a ringtail cat. No. I know you and Lawalila and Pakalai Jawichi, here, want to marry her, and you are deciding how to give me the smallest gift for such a fine woman. She is worth many fine pelts and mountain goat meat and antelope meat and elk meat and bear meat and deer meat."

"She is a very fine woman," added Halai Auna. "I know Yolaina stares at her too often. He is sneaky, but he likes her. The other men like her too. Even Dari Jowa has commented on how well mannered Tsanunewa is."

"See," said Hwipajusi, "Halai Auna knows the truth. I figure you young braves are trying to demoralize me to the point I let my daughters marry you for nothing."

"We just do not want you to get any fatter than you are Hwipajusi. You are old and gray and wrinkled, and if you get too much for your daughters, life will become too easy for you. You will not hunt anymore. You will only want to stay home to eat Periwiri Yupa's cooking, but you are still too young to receive very much for your daughters," said Pakalai Jawichi.

"These two tease you too much, Hwipajusi. I know they sneak small, beautiful gifts to your daughters when you are not looking. Periwiri Yupa must keep a close watch on them. Yolaina gave Tsanunewa some white woman's powder, very sweet smelling. It is hidden in her personal basket," said Halai Auna.

"Oh, Halai Auna," sighed Yolaina. "You should not have told Hwipajusi I gave the powder to Tsanunewa. Hwipajusi will get the wrong impression. I was just repaying her and the others for the wonderful meals they had prepared for our sings."

"How long have you been sneaking gifts to my daughter?" asked Hwipajusi. "I should have known you would try to steal her."

"See the trouble you have caused, Halai Auna?" commented Yolaina. He sighed again.

"Now, Yolaina, you cannot even approach my house unless you bring me a black bearskin to prove you are worthy of sneaking gifts to my daughter."

"If I kill a black bear and give you the skin, your daughter will get the wrong impression, Hwipajusi. She will think my heart is just for her, and she will take her baskets from your home and ask me to marry her. Then we will live happily together, and she will expect me to bring all of my venison to her. You better be careful. You better find a way for your daughter to marry someone pretty soon, or she will fall in love with me. She will become unreasonable and fussy. Her acorn mush will be full of leaves, and her baskets will leak. She will think only of me then, but I am not sure which of your daughters I wish to marry."

"Well, you are probably too late anyhow. I think that Lawalila has been collecting beautiful pelts away from Tcapalauna and that he hopes to marry Tsanunewa. He has stopped making jokes about her, and if his eyes could sing and fly, they would arch and coo across the evening's sky as wood doves in the spring," said Halai Auna.

"You think so?" asked Hwipajusi in a high-pitched voice.

"Yes," replied Halai Auna. "I think Lawalila has been gathering otter skins, for he goes fishing often and brings home few fish. Demauna trained him too well for him to be just fishing. Even Periwiri Yupa thinks Lawalila will give you anything you wish for Tsanunewa's heart in marriage."

"That is very good news," said Hwipajusi with a big smile on his face. "Yolaina, you better state your true intentions quickly, and you should bring two bearskins, twenty beautiful pelts, a freshly killed buck, two sacks of white man's seeds, and a solemn promise to provide me with all the meat I need for the rest of my life."

"See what you have done, Halai Auna?" asked Yolaina. "You have filled poor Hwipajusi with the wild rumors that you women like to spread when you gossip at night. Pretty soon Hwipajusi will want twenty grizzly bearskins a moon for the rest of his life. Hwipajusi will not be able to control his greed, and his daughters will never be able to get married."

"Well, I think Hwipajusi should accept the otter pelts for Tsanunewa's heart, and I am sure Lawalila will not mind bringing home an extra deer every moon for his in-laws. He loves Tsanunewa."

"Do you really think so?" asked Hwipajusi incredulously.

"Yes," replied Halai Auna.

"I knew you should have stayed home," said Yolaina to Halai Auna. "You always say the wrong words to Hwipajusi."

"We are getting close to the cabin," said Pakalai Jawichi.

"You stay. I will see if anyone is about," said Yolaina. "I will make the call of the flicker if it is safe for you to come." Yolaina continued on his hands and knees through the brush until he reached the meadow above the creek where he could clearly see the cabin. Yolaina scurried to his feet and ran to the back of the building where a clear glass window could be opened. He looked inside and felt secure that nobody was about, and he began to make the call of the flicker when an actual flicker made the call for him. Soon Hwipajusi, Halai Auna, and Pakalai Jawichi arrived, and he opened the window. They climbed in one at a time, and only Hwipajusi had trouble.

"These are beautiful clothes," whispered Halai Auna as she slipped her arms through the straps of some pants, the front of which almost covered her breasts.

"Look," whispered Hwipajusi. He wore a thick, long, gray coat with many buttons and pockets. "This could keep a man warm many seasons." His eyes bulged with delight as he searched the pockets and looked about the dark, one-room storage house.

"The saltu have not brought new seeds to this house, however, since we took from it two moons ago," said Yolaina as he folded the clothes neatly for carrying home. Stacked on the floor were pants, socks, shirts, and a coat. "We will have to visit the other cabin before we go back to Bay Tree Village. We need some seeds."

"Part of a lightning stick," whispered Hwipajusi. "Maybe I can use this for something." He held the heavy, hollow end of the lightning stick in his hands. "Perhaps I could shape arrows with it. This will really impress Periwiri Yupa. She will think I am a young brave if I bring home part of a lightning stick."

"I will climb out. What are you doing, Halai Auna?" whispered Yolaina as he watched her.

"They are easier to wear than to carry," she whispered as she stuffed her legs and pants into the legs of the third pair.

"Hand me the clothes once I am outside," whispered Yolaina to Pakalai Jawichi, and he climbed out the window into the face of a white man and his pointed lightning stick. Yolaina stood for a long moment and then backed into the wall.

"Yolaina," whispered Pakalai Jawichi as he stuck his head out the opening and saw the white man. The man motioned with his lightning stick for Pakalai Jawichi to come out.

"Get the clothes," whispered Halai Auna to Pakalai Jawichi as she fumbled with hooking the last strap before she looked out the window at the motioning lightning stick. She also obeyed silently.

"I could make fine points with this," whispered Hwipajusi as he stared intently at the clear blue obsidian container used to make light in the white man's storage house. "I should take it. Hey. Get the clothes. You all left the clothes." He set down the container on a wooden shelf near the opening, moved the clothes to the shelf, picked up his piece of lightning stick, and stuck his head out the window and toward the waving lightning stick.

"We are doomed," whispered Hwipajusi as he crawled awkwardly out the window. He then backed into the wall with the others. He still held the heavy piece of lightning stick.

Yolaina looked carefully at the whiskered man, his black hat and fine clothes, his tall shoes and long knife, the hand lightning stick on his side. The man pointed the lightning stick at Pakalai Jawichi's crippled foot, spoke a few strange words, and looked carefully at Halai Auna's breasts, partially hidden beneath the straps. He shook his head back and forth, and his facial expression became less taut and more relaxed.

"*Dos chiquitos papooses,*" said Halai Auna as she pointed toward Salmon Creek Canyon. She had learned the words from Periwiri Yupa, Black Oak Acorn Woman. They were white man's words that Yolaina did not understand. He could not tell if the white man knew the words or not. He spat on the ground, put his lightning stick in his left hand, walked to the window, grabbed a large amount of stacked clothes, stood back, and tossed them to Pakalai Jawichi. Then he reached in again and threw the remainder of the stack to Yolaina. He stood back some more, stopped pointing his lightning stick at them, moved some part on the top of it with his thumb, and placed it on his shoulder. He made movements with his left hand for them to go away, and he said a few more strange words. When at first they did not move, he raised his voice a bit and continued to motion for them to leave.

Yolaina, Pakalai Jawichi, Halai Auna, and Hwipajusi decided that the time was correct for fleeing into the brush, and they scattered like a startled flock of ducks. Halai Auna and Hwipajusi faired the best since they both had on clothing, and Yolaina and Pakalai Jawichi scratched themselves too much in their retreat toward Salmon Creek. When finally they stopped scurrying, they had traveled a long distance and had reached a feeder stream in Salmon Creek Canyon. There they drank water and talked.

"What did you say to the white man, Halai Auna?" asked Hwipajusi.

"I used the words which say I have two children," she replied.

"Do you think that is why he let us go?" asked Pakalai Jawichi.

"I do not know," replied Halai Auna.

"Normally a saltu would have at least killed the three men and kidnapped the woman," said Yolaina. "This white man is moved by a different spirit than their First Person's."

"White men are not all the same," said Hwipajusi. "I have heard stories from women who lived with white people and then escaped. The women are dead now, all shot, but white men can be friendly. For some reason, I do not know exactly why, they like to kill and steal us, however, as a general rule."

"These clothes are very good," said Halai Auna, who was staring at all the different colors of buttons and hooks.

"I know," added Hwipajusi. "This coat only has holes in the pockets."

"Too bad we did not have these last winter," said Pakalai Jawichi. He was trying on a type of clothing which fit closely to his body from his ankles to his neck.

"Maybe the white man was afraid I would hit him with my piece of lightning stick," said Hwipajusi.

"I cannot wait to get back to the men's house," said Yolaina. "I know Hwipajusi will tell the men a very funny story about capturing a white man and stealing his lightning stick."

*   *   *

"Returning to the cabin scares me," said Halai Auna.

"Your idea is still good, however," said Yolaina. "We should give the man a present. He showed us an act of good will."

The day was bright and cool, and fall leaves chattered in the wind. The manzanita berries were sticky and reddish-brown, and the grass was tall in places and tan. The moss was dry and brown, and lichens lay in patches of bluish-gray and dull yellow-green on the craggy surfaces of the strewn about boulders. Both Halai Auna and Yolaina carried a basket, decorated with gyrating, black squares, and each wore a white man's shirt to take the chill off the air.

"I want to talk to you about Tsanunewa," said Halai Auna.

"I do not wish to talk to you about Tsanunewa," replied Yolaina.

"Why not?"

"Tsanunewa married Lawalila. She belongs to him, and I should not think about her. No good could come from such a conversation," said Yolaina as they continued to edge closer to the cabin on Dry Creek.

"But you have bad feelings inside. Yolaina, you sit around by yourself too much. You hunt too much. You do not act normally, and you must somehow get rid of your bad feelings."

"This conversation does not help me, Halai Auna. You speak too much of people's feelings; you are like a fly at the village toilet."

"Do not speak that way. See. You are too touchy. You can marry either of Hwipajusi's other daughters. You just have to wait. Some women just take a while to mature, and others are just too young. You must wait."

"Your advice is so helpful. I was seriously contemplating not waiting for a while. I was going to become invisible like North Wind Man."

"You know what I mean," she replied. "You do not gather any gifts for Hwipajusi. He is not as greedy as he sounds. He just jokes way too much, and none of you will stop teasing him."

"Hwipajusi is my good friend, and I do not mind giving gifts. You do not know if I gather gifts or not."

"The other girls know you are upset about Tsanunewa's marriage, and that does not make them feel good."

"They do not know how I feel. I have not spoken about my feelings to them."

"Everyone knows."

"Have I said or done anything which is improper in regard to Tsanunewa?" asked Yolaina.

"No and Yes."

"Your answer is nonsensical; I have done nothing improper," said Yolaina.

"Having a sick heart for too long is improper, even if you speak no bad words."

"A heart is like a grizzly bear, Halai Auna; a grizzly bear can be destroyed, but it cannot be told what to do."

The strong image surprised Halai Auna, and she was not sure how to respond.

"See yourself in still water, Halai Auna. Your position is the same as mine. You can marry Demauna or Pakalai Jawichi. One is too old, and one is too young. What will you do? Does your heart cry like a wounded rabbit? I know you want children. Who will be their father? You speak much of my feelings, and your quickness with advice is exceptional.

Whom will you marry? Do you collect gifts? Tell me all your secrets so that I can tell the men all that you think."

"Even though my position is not good, I do not get so downhearted," she replied.

"I am happy for you," said Yolaina.

"No. You are caught up in bad feelings."

"Enough. You sound like the croaking Ichpul Sisters, Frog Women, all stinky and ugly, singing different songs at the same time. Nothing good can come from your choice of conversation."

"If you say so," said Halai Auna. They continued walking in silence until they came upon the brush near Dry Creek. They made their way silently to the opening in back of the cabin on their hands and knees. The cabin looked as peaceful as it did in the spring when they were caught, but both had decided that giving the gifts of baskets was appropriate. Everyone in Tcapalauna thought so, also. Halai Auna and Yolaina ran to the window, and Yolaina pushed it up and climbed in. Halai Auna gave him the baskets, which he placed on a table. The room was filled with new provisions: sacks of seeds and flour, salted meat, and brown crunchy, bitter material. Yolaina stared at it for too long.

"You cannot take this white man's food. Let us go. We must get acorns today," whispered Halai Auna.

"I know," whispered Yolaina as he crawled out the opening. They both ran to the brush and crawled until they could find room to walk again.

"Do you think the white man will understand we gave him gifts?" asked Halai Auna.

"Of course," replied Yolaina. "Our actions do not need words. Because he gave us the clothes, we gave him the baskets. Surely he will understand."

"Do you think the white man was handsome?" asked Halai Auna.

"Not really," replied Yolaina.

"Why?" asked Halai Auna.

"He was all hairy, for one, and his face was sort of skinny. Why do you ask? Are you in love with the white man?"

"I have never seen one so close before. That is all."

"Do you think he was handsome?" asked Yolaina.

Halai Auna paused before speaking. "Well, he was sort of hand-some, in a way I find hard to describe, because you are correct—he was too hairy."

"He was a sneaky white man. I have often wondered how he was hidden or if he just accidentally walked up and heard us."

"I do not know," replied Halai Auna, "but I hope he likes the baskets."

*   *   *

Just as the birds began chirping in the first gray of the morning, Yolaina lay awake under a rabbit-skin blanket on his spot in the men's house. Yolaina thought about three white women he had seen on lower Deer Creek not far from Acorn Hollow. The people of Tcapalauna had been about to travel to Wahkanopa the previous summer, and Yolaina had hunted a sheep. He was skinning the sheep behind the brush near Deer Creek when three, young women arrived and took off most of their clothing. They spoke their strange language and laughed and splashed each other. They swam in the cold water but quickly got out and lay in the sun. One had black hair like a Yahi, but she did not look like a Yahi. One's hair was light brown, and she had blue eyes and sparkling earrings of fine crystal. One had yellow hair and matching eyes. Yolaina sat quietly on the opposite bank from them, and he watched them until they left. He quite clearly heard them sing a song and saw them eat some food, a type which Yolaina had never seen before and which was wrapped in something they discarded. After they left and Yolaina could safely move about, he finished skinning the sheep. The thought of the women came to him often, though, and in the early morning, uneasy sexual thoughts filled his mind. He looked forward to Hwipajusi cracking his first joke of the day.

That cold, fall morning, however, Yolaina arose first in the darkened, earth-covered, cedar structure and walked to the feeder stream some distance from Tcapalauna. He watched the sky move in shades of gray. Yolaina dipped into the snow-fed stream where a section was dug out in a natural pool so that the Yahi could bathe, and he submerged fully and rubbed his hands over his body to remove his dirt and body odor. When his head became full of pain from the cold water, he drank deeply, and then he climbed onto the bank. At least the cold relieved his thoughts.

In camp Hitchinna had already begun rebuilding a morning fire for the baking she had planned, and Yolaina helped her add tiny sticks and pine needles to the small flames. When the fire was snapping with wrist-sized branches, Yolaina was relieved from the overpowering cold of his wet body, and his mother then went to bathe. She preferred to have a guaranteed source of warmth, however, before she chilled herself so thoroughly. Yolaina kept the fire going and watched the camp come to life. He warmed one side of his body, and then turned to warm the other. The sun would not hit camp for most of the morning.

For a while, when Yolaina recovered some of his warmth and became dry enough to wrap himself in a blanket, and before the other men got up from the sweatbath of the night before, Yolaina thought again about marriage. He decided he must get many gifts for Hwipajusi so that he could marry his youngest daughter, Weanmauna, Hidden One, but he had decided long before that he would try to marry Weanmauna because he thought she was the prettiest and most quiet of Hwipajusi's daughters. She gossiped less than Halai Auna, for instance, but everyone in camp gossiped less than Halai Auna.

Halai Auna arose in their family house, emerged into the daylight, and walked toward the fire. Yolaina noticed her but did not stare. She was bundled in a rabbit-skin blanket around her shoulders.

"You are up early," commented Halai Auna sleepily. "Has mother gone to bathe?"

"She is bathing," said Yolaina. "What will she cook this morning? I wish to know what I will miss."

"She will bake venison, and you do not need to hunt again today. You should remain in camp to visit or to work on hides or to make tools."

"You will not think so when winter is about to end and our baskets are empty and snow falls deeply on the ground," said Yolaina. "You will think, 'I am glad my brother hunts during the gray days of late fall.'"

"Is anyone at the village toilet?" asked Halai Auna.

"No. Go ahead," replied Yolaina as Halai Auna scurried out of the circle of homes and south up the hillside.

Hwipajusi walked out of the men's home and to the fire. He wore a rabbit-skin blanket and was slightly stiff in his morning movements. "At least you are not snooping near my home as I dreamed you would be," said Hwipajusi.

"Hwipajusi, you are a man of honor, and you deserve ten mountain-lion skins to give a man permission to snoop about your home."

"I know all about your type. You are Metsi, Coyote Man; and Ututni, Wood Duck Man, sings a song in your blood."

"I am too generous with you, Hwipajusi. You do not appreciate my gifts. You should let me take a walk in the woods with your daughter. I need to know how she feels about me. I need to know if I should wait for her heart in marriage, but you will not let me talk with her."

"You are trying to trick me. I can tell," replied Hwipajusi.

"I bring you meat, and you accuse me falsely," replied Yolaina.

"Well, when we have celebrated her womanhood and you wish to ask for her heart in marriage and you bring us gifts, you will have time to talk."

"I guess you have a deal, Hwipajusi, but I do not know how I will kill two thousand grizzly bears, five hundred mountain lions, and four hundred otters before she becomes a woman."

"I only said one thousand grizzly bears," laughed Hwipajusi.

CHAPTER 9

Protector of the Camp

The morning was hot for late spring, a summery type of day, and per-fect for packing sheep meat back to Salmon Creek Canyon. Hwipajusi and Yolaina were at the bottom of Antelope Creek Canyon and were cutting up two, freshly killed sheep. Hwipajusi hunted very little by now and never for game harder to kill than a sheep, for sheep were easy to kill. Hwipajusi was not sure how Yolaina had talked him into hunting, but he dutifully skinned his sheep. Yolaina had promised to carry six quarters, and Hwipajusi had agreed to carry two front quarters and his skin. Yolaina left the hide on four quarters for the trip home, one night's journey. Yolaina removed the liver and heart from the sheep for their dinner that evening, and he set them on a round, flat river boulder. He then picked up the carcass and tossed it into Antelope Creek. He rinsed the liver and heart in the stream, and splashed water where he had been cutting. He then washed the blood off himself and walked to Hwipajusi. Hwipajusi handed the hindquarters to him, and Yolaina walked to where the other four quarters lay. He twice bound two hindquarters and a front quarter together so that he could carry one in each hand for the hike out of the canyon. Hwipajusi tied his front quarters together with a wide piece of skin from the pelt Yolaina had thrown away, and he threw his carcass in the river. Hwipajusi wrapped his pelt around Yolaina's liver and heart, splashed water to hide their butchering area, cleaned up, put the front quarters around his neck so that they hung on his chest, tucked the pelt under his left arm, and carried both of their quivers and his hunting pouch. Yolaina and Hwipajusi then began the long trek home.

"Periwiri Yupa probably believes I have another Yahi woman stashed secretly in a cave on Deer Creek. I should not be gone away from home for so long again," said Hwipajusi. "I would not want Periwiri Yupa to sulk and to stop cooking."

"I would not want Periwiri Yupa to stop cooking either," said Yolaina, "especially fat sheep legs, because then I would not be able to tease you about being more round than acorns. Then again, maybe hiking around these canyons once in a while is what you need."

"I know what I need. I need a large basket of blackberries to eat. I need the hard green berries to turn instantly black and to jump off their thorny stems into my basket," commented Hwipajusi.

"You give in too easily to your passions and fantasies, Hwipajusi."

"Too bad I cannot jump these canyons like Pul Miauna, Colored Bow Man, or wish myself from rim to rim, like Igupa Topa, son of Tuina, Sun Man. I need magical powers," said Hwipajusi. "I am too old not to have magical powers. I should be able to decide my age, also," said Hwipajusi.

"And how old would you be? Would you be almost twenty-seven, like me? I would remain the age I am now."

"Well, I would choose to be older than I am so that young braves like you would show me more respect."

"You mean so that you would not have to hunt any more. How old are you, Hwipajusi? You do not look a day over thirty-seven."

"See. You do not show me respect enough. I admit to looking very young, not more than one day older than thirty-seven, but I must confess I do not know my age. Somewhere many years ago after so many people were killed, I lost track. I forgot to count a couple of winters, and then I forgot," said Hwipajusi breathing heavily. "I wish we had fresh salmon already baked," said Hwipajusi.

"You see what I mean about your uncontrollable fantasies. You should not talk so much about food when you are fasting. We will eat soon," replied Yolaina. He looked about the dry gully they had been climbing and decided he should get a clear view of their surroundings since little vegetation grew at such a low altitude. They were using the only natural covering available to them, the gully. "Let us stop," said Yolaina, "and I will look around." He set down his sheep legs and climbed the boulders to the rim of the gully, and there, to his annoyance and fear, he saw a white man carrying a lightning stick. A dog was with him. Yolaina watched closely. The man, actually more of a boy, meandered slowly, not on their tracks but toward the gully. Yolaina looked at the top of the gully where a clump of buckeye grew under the high cliff of the canyon. They had to reach the buckeye before the man, or boy, reached the gully. They should not have a problem climbing the distance in time, but the dog would cause them problems if the boy walked as far as the gully. Yolaina scampered down the embankment to where Hwipajusi had implanted himself on a boulder and was enjoying the sun like a lizard after a frosty morning.

"A white boy is coming. He has a lightning stick and dog," said Yolaina as he picked up his six legs of sheep and began walking up the steep gully.

"You are trying to trick me. I am an old man, and I need rest."

Yolaina stopped and looked at Hwipajusi. "You should hurry with me or string your bow and remove your arrows."

Hwipajusi jumped off the boulder, put the legs once more around his neck, picked up his skin, quivers, and pouch, and began a steady, fast pace up the hill and toward the only real cover available, the buckeye clump at the base of the cliff above them. "If this is a trick, I will have to string my bow and shoot you many times, Yolaina. My legs were already sore before I began this hunt."

Yolaina said nothing in reply but kept a steady pace that would probably cause Hwipajusi pain but which would ensure reaching the desired cover. Yolaina kept his pace the full length of the gully and into the buckeye, and Hwipajusi arrived shortly after. Yolaina's hands had sweat to the point his imprints were on the fur of each bundle, and he was wet from head to toe. Hwipajusi looked nauseated and was not in the mood to talk when he reached the buckeye. He set down his skin and the quivers and pouch, and then he sat down himself.

"Wait," said Yolaina, and he crawled out of the buckeye to the edge of the gully. He gazed down on the white boy steadily making his way to the rim of the canyon and to the buckeye patch. He could not understand the reasoning behind the boy's movements, but the boy none the less made his way directly toward Yolaina and Hwipajusi. Yolaina went back to the buckeye where Hwipajusi sat with meat still over his shoulders.

"The boy comes toward us," said Yolaina. "We will have to be very quiet and hope his dog has a stuffed nose."

"Here is your quiver," said Hwipajusi. He took out his bow and strung it.

Yolaina wiped the sweat from his forehead, removed his bow from his otterskin quiver, and did the same. They each slipped an arrow into position and waited in place where they had a limited view of the gully but where they could quickly move to another spot for full covering. The moments became long, and Yolaina considered making another check. The boy, however, moved into the gully. When Yolaina and Hwipajusi ducked into the covering next to their belongings, Hwipajusi touched a limb and shook some leaves. Moments later, of course, the dog came in directly to where Yolaina and Hwipajusi had drawn arrows.

Yolaina showed his teeth and motioned menacingly with his bow. For some reason the dog did not bark, but it left quickly and was obviously taken aback. Without forethought, as a gesture which would explain the dog's behavior and perhaps scare the boy away, Yolaina screamed loudly like a cornered wildcat, and Hwipajusi jumped like a man sitting next to a screaming wildcat. The boy, whom Yolaina could barely see, was not unnerved and did not raise his gun; he instead picked up a rock about half the size of his palm and threw it into the buckeye. The rock hit Hwipajusi in the neck and caused him to grunt. The boy still had no fear of whatever was in the brush, and with his gun ready but not pointed, he walked into the buckeye directly toward Yolaina and Hwipajusi. Yolaina picked up his quiver, and being sure not to catch his bow on a buckeye limb, he made his way out of the gully and east along the edge of the cliff. Hwipajusi was not far behind, except Hwipajusi had his quiver, bow, and arrow in one hand, his liver and heart in the other, and his two legs still around his neck. When they reached the first, semi-available covering, a large boulder, they stopped to look back. The white boy was visible, and Hwipajusi set the heart and liver on a rock and sat blankly just a moment.

"He insults us," said Hwipajusi. "How could a young, white boy throw a rock and chase two Yahi hunters away from their food and pelt and arrow making pouch? He did not even raise his gun. I will shoot his eyes out."

Hwipajusi stood, took a hunter's instantaneous aim, loosed his arrow, and watched it glance off the boy's hat and into the buckeye. "I missed," he whispered incredulously, and he crouched down, "but the boy moved just in time to save his life when he looked at our belongings."

Hwipajusi took another arrow from his quiver, stood, aimed, listened to Yolaina say, "Hwipajusi, stop. No. Do not shoot the white man," and loosed his arrow just as the boy stood up from examining their meat, skin, and pouch. The arrow shattered with great force into a rock which just a moment before had been hidden with the boy's bent over position. The boy looked about as if something very strange might be happening, and Hwipajusi removed several arrows from his quiver.

"Maybe he is an evil spirit," said Hwipajusi as he strung another arrow, peeked around the boulder, and stood to shoot again.

Yolaina quickly climbed a little closer to Hwipajusi and used his bow to whack Hwipajusi on the back of his knees as he shot. Hwipajusi's arrow fell short and into the leaves at the boy's feet. Hwipajusi instantly ducked and tried to peek at what the boy was doing.

"How come you hit me?" asked Hwipajusi as he saw the boy and dog rushing down the gully. He had his lightning stick, the sheepskin, and Hwipajusi's arrow and arrow-making pouch. "Look. He runs away with my skin and my pouch and my arrow. All he had to do was walk up, throw a rock, hit me in the neck as if I were a stupid cow, let me run off, stand there, let me shoot arrows at him while he examined my belongings, and then run away unharmed. We should hunt him, Yolaina, so that he will not laugh at us when he gets home. He will tell all the white people we are cowards. Let us kill him before he gets away."

"We should not try to kill white men, Hwipajusi, especially one as stupid as that poor boy. Killing him would do no good and would be like shooting a tree stump."

"This is not the time for talking, Yolaina. We should kill the boy before he spreads shameful words about Yahi men."

"He is scared almost to death already, Hwipajusi. You have done plenty. You stood and faced a lightning stick, Hwipajusi, and the boy must have the Lizard Man's spirit in him. He should not have been able to dodge your arrows the way he did and just stand there at the same time. I saw your arrows. They were truly shot, and the boy dodged them."

A calm expression came over Hwipajusi's face, and his deeply brown eyes widened against his wrinkles and long white hair. "Do you really think Lizard Man was part of his spirit?" asked Hwipajusi.

"Well, he just stood there, and your arrows could not hit him," said Yolaina, very relieved that Hwipajusi was not trying to kill the white boy.

"He hit me with a rock, though, and when a man misses such an easy target, he must feel ashamed," replied Hwipajusi.

"He was Kalchauna, Lizard Man, a saltu Lizard Man. No one could have shot him, Hwipajusi. Your arrows went true. He just moved at the last instant both times," said Yolaina, who stood to watch the boy run down the side of the canyon toward the valley. "I will get the legs," said Yolaina, "and then we better get out of here before that white boy reaches the valley." Yolaina walked back to his six legs in the buckeye trees, and soon they were hiking around the cliff and to the rim of the canyon where open ground had to be covered quickly. They breathed heavily and stepped on rocks when possible.

"What will I tell the men in the sweathouse? This could be a very bad story. They could make fun of me for many moons, and I know they will not believe me if I tell them the white boy was Lizard Man. They will all laugh at me and say I am a coward. In the old days we would have shot the boy about seventeen times just for fun. Little white boys did not walk around so brazenly throwing rocks at Yahi men."

"Do you think I am a coward, Hwipajusi?" asked Yolaina.

"I did not accuse you of being a coward, Yolaina."

"I stopped you from killing that white boy, Hwipajusi. Surely your last arrow would have punctured his heart. I do not understand how the boy is alive, but you must know that the boy will never make fun of you. Never. You scared him so badly that he will remember you the rest of his life. He actually lived when you shot at him twice, and he has one of your arrows to prove it. Has any other white man been so lucky?"

"No. I have never missed a white man before."

"See. He might not be Lizard Man, but he acted just like him," continued Yolaina. "You saved our meat, and the white boy has a good story. You faced a lightning stick, and Periwiri Yupa will think you are a young brave. You must remember, also, that the boy is alive, so white men will not march in great numbers through our canyons."

"I try to make sense of the events, and all our actions seem out of place. Not much of what happened should have happened. He should not have found us. He should have shot us. I should have shot him. In the old days we would have just added some new clothes, even though a bit filled with bloody holes, to our collection of white men's belongings. We would have felt good in our hearts that we had carried out justice. Now, all I feel is confused."

"I understand your feelings. I am confused also, but, accidentally perhaps, our incident has turned okay. We are lucky. Everyone will love the sheep legs."

"I lost one of Periwiri Yupa's deerskin pouches, though."

"No, Hwipajusi, you have gained magical powers. You scared off Lizard Man with your swift arrows and lived to tell about it."

*   *   *

The men, Dari Jowa, Demauna, Chunoyahi, Yolaina, and Pakalai Jawichi, sat in the hot sweathouse and rubbed oil from the boiled leaves of a bay tree on their skin. They had brought in many hot rocks from a fire outside their entrance, and a small fire was burning in the men's house. Outside the air was still warm from the hot day.

"I wish to tell the story about Lizard Man," said Dari Jowa with too much humor in his eyes.

Hwipajusi looked up but did not say anything.

"Lizard Man, as you all know, was a great chief with many hunters and with many women and children to serve them. One day when he was making arrows, he put aside his work, and he decided to explore to the west across Daha, the great water of the valley, where the wicked Wintuns lived. Lizard Man traveled two nights and crossed to where pine trees grew in the western hills. There he set down his quiver of two, leather-bound deer antlers on the ground, and he shook all of the pine cones from the trees. While he was heating the pitch from the cones, beating pine nuts from the cones, and storing the nuts in his storage baskets, the wicked Wintuns let out a war whoop. They shot arrows at Lizard Man from many directions, but Kalchauna, Lizard Man, continued gathering the Wintuns' pine nuts. After he filled his storage baskets, he put his deer-antler quiver on his back, removed his bow, and said 'The wind rushes about me as if I were in a great storm.' Then Lizard Man shot off all of his arrows and hit the Wintuns in their faces. He shot to the east, to the west, to the south, and to the north, and everywhere he shot, he hit a Wintun's face. When Kalchauna finally gathered up his baskets, all the Wintuns had scattered from sight, and Kalchauna made his way back across Daha with all of his baskets. When finally he reached his village, the night had fallen, and he put away his baskets. In the morning all of his people came to him, for they were hungry. Lizard Man presented them with many filled baskets of pine nuts, and said, 'We do not have very many pine nuts to eat.' All of his people ate until they were full, and then they filled their storage baskets, however. Lizard Man was very pleased, and he sent Long-tailed Lizard Man to get him foreshafts for the new arrows that he was making before he gathered pine nuts west of Daha." Dari Jowa paused a long while before he spoke again.

"Hwipajusi, I have listened to your story, and I have thought about it enough. Is it really true that you shot three times at a white boy who stood no farther away than the cedar tree by your home?"

"Yes."

"Did you honestly try to kill him?"

"Yes."

"Did one arrow bounce off his hat?"

"Yes."

"Hwipajusi, you make me very proud to be a Yahi. I wish I could have seen you try to kill him; however, I am happy you did not. A Yahi hunter has not tried to kill a white person in twenty-four years, and you could not have known he had their First Person, their Kalchauna, in his spirit. Consequently, I am making you protector of our camp, especially when the other men are hunting. I want you to sit often on the cliff in the sunshine, to work on hunting gear when you wish, to make sure all the food is cooked well, and to shoot any white man who threatens us in camp. For this, since you are a man of great honor, you get one-fifth of all the meat every man kills. Also, at his very instant, should you accept my offer to be the constant protector of Tcapalauna, I will give you my mountain lion's tail quiver, and you can have a skin of your choice from every man as a gift for Periwiri Yupa so that she will never stop cooking."

"Do you really wish for me to be the protector of the camp and to watch from the cliff for white men?"

"I do."

"I accept," said Hwipajusi. "I am pleased to be so honored, and I promise to kill any white man who gets near our camp."

"Very close to or in camp, Hwipajusi," added Dari Jowa.

"I still accept."

Dari Jowa removed his arrows from the mountain lion's tail quiver, and handed it to Hwipajusi. "Take the fur you like the most, Hwipajusi, from each man's place." Hwipajusi took Demauna's black bearskin, wildcat skins from Yolaina, Dari Jowa, and Chunoyahi, and otter pelts from Lawalila and Pakalai Jawichi. He set them on his spot, and then climbed to where he had been sitting. Pakalai Jawichi added small branches to fire.

"We would offer you more, Hwipajusi, but you would become too brave and would begin to hunt white men," said Demauna.

"I cannot figure out how I missed Kalchauna," said Hwipajusi thoughtfully as he rubbed sweat from his forehead. "No man can dodge unseen arrows at such a range."

CHAPTER 10

Five Mourners

Yolaina was walking quickly in an easterly direction on the southern, upper slope of Salmon Creek Canyon below Black Rock; on the other side of the canyon lay the green meadows and destroyed Yahi villages, replaced with cows and more than its share of white men occasionally riding horses. The clouds were set solidly in blue, like that of Crater Lake in the *Mapchemaina Stories*; they were black and gray and rimmed with the lightest of whites, sometimes gleaming with red, orange, yellow, green, and blue of the colored bow. Within each was Ilhataina, Lightning Man, ready to throw his light upon the ground and to roar mightily a resounding echo through the canyon. All the types of black oaks were filled with yellow-green leaves, and the soil was still moist from a previous rain. Yolaina thought of the young yellow pine he had seen in that morning's light. When upon its long green and brown needles the frost melted from the previous day's rain and freezing night, the yellow pine danced with light of the colored bow and gleamed everywhere a bright yellow. Yolaina thought about all the stored provisions in the cabin he had just observed and was delighted that they would soon have enough food to allow them to live somewhat easily until they could again visit the high country and Wahkanopa.

Yolaina worried a bit, however, about Hwipajusi, who barely made it back to Tcapalauna from the last raid on the cabin on the north side of Deer Creek, not far from their camp. Hwipajusi at least took great pride in being protector of Tcapalauna, though, and he was always happy to take one-fifth of all the men's meat for his family, still including his daughter, Weanmauna, Hidden One, too quiet and unmarried. Yolaina had spent many years putting her out of his mind, and his age, thirty-one, helped a little.

Yolaina noticed he sometimes left a foot print of his cracked cal-luses in the moist soil of the deer trail he was on, but felt he was not in danger of being discovered. He had not been in contact with any white man since he and Hwipajusi had been caught in the buckeye patch four years earlier, and all Tcapalauna had been in total avoid-ance also, except for the robbing of cabins, a necessity if they were to live easily. At least most members of Tcapalauna were in agreement on wanting the white man's seeds, food of many varieties, and other odd items. They had been able to live stealthily for ten years, and life had become acceptable, even if somewhat remote and hard. As the sun shone brilliantly, a large cloud passed lazily overhead in a south wind, Yolaina gazed closely at a redbud bush in bright bloom and at a gray-blue butterfly. He strode higher into the canyon above a small cliff and below breast-like mountains and cliffs which he did not need to climb to reach Tcapalauna. He thought of the feast all the women were preparing for the dance and sing that coming evening. Then they would go respectively to the men's and women's sweathouses to sweat and to rub bay leaf oil on their skin and to tell stories about the Mapchemaina, the First People. He thought maybe he would tell the story of Kalchauna, Lizard Man, and Ilhataina, Lightning Man, since the story seemed appropriate for the day and since Hwipajusi had a great interest in all stories about Kalchauna. Then Yolaina heard a cracking noise behind him. He turned instantly and stopped.

Two white men with lightning sticks had walked onto the trail and were looking at his footprint. Yolaina hid behind a large manzanita bush and stared through its pink and white flowers at them a moment to determine their movements, and as the men looked up to see in his direction, the direction of the footprint, Yolaina recognized the white man who acted like the Yahi Lizard Man, Kalchauna. The once scrawny boy was fully-grown and thick. His eyes were still blue; he still wore a black hat; he had the same type of lightning stick as before. The other man with him was young, also, and eager to follow Yolaina's trail. They spoke quietly and then walked the deer trail, no longer available to Yolaina.

Yolaina turned and bolted down the hill, for at that point he had but one real choice, to run more quickly than the white men until he could lose them in the water and on the rocky shoreline of Salmon Creek, where he would scurry up a feeder stream, toward Antelope Creek, and to the other side of Wahkanopa if necessary. The men, of course, heard the rustling leaves and brush, and began to run along the trail to the point where they could follow Yolaina. They stood on the trail and looked down the hill toward the moving brush; then down the hill they ran in full pursuit. Yolaina became aware of their pursuit when he paused to look at the lay of the land and to check his trail. The men were pounding through the brush, so Yolaina bolted downhill again just in time to check his speed before running off the point of a small cliff. He could jump or run backwards around brush and into the charging white men. Yolaina saw the white men, glanced at a fluffy, soft-looking bay tree below him, and jumped fully into the air, his legs and arms spread apart, his bow outstretched in his right arm, toward the highest part of the bay tree. The men almost charged off the cliff and stood breathing heavily, barely able to hear the crashing sound of semi-moist leaves over the wind gusting in the canyon.

Yolaina had not expected the results of flying to be so devastating; he never expected, for instance, that he would move through the wind like an arrow or that the willowy, soft-looking limbs would feel like great boulders. He bounced off the ground and could not see for a moment. When he realized his situation again, he noticed blood coming from his nose, and then he ran, his bow still in his right hand, his arrows still in the quiver on his back.

A long while later when stopping on the upstream, southern side of Black Rock, Yolaina paused and drank and noticed that the men did not follow him, and he did not blame them. As he drank, he noticed a black eye in the undulating water, and his arm was badly bruised. He laughed out loud for joy because he could hardly believe that he had jumped off the cliff like a soaring eagle, as if he had no brains in his head, and had actually lived. He could now pretend that he had more magic than Hwipajusi.

The white men absorbed Yolaina's thinking as he stood in the shallow water, picked up his bow, and began making his way upstream. The white man was just the same as before, all full of curiosity and just as willing to chase a Yahi hunter as he had been four years earlier. Yolaina wondered if the other man with him was his brother, and if either of the men had any kind of spirituality in him, or whether he was a being without a spirit. Most of the people of Tcapalauna believed white men to be incapable of spirituality, and simply thought of them as others, capable of making interesting contrivances but not capable of decent behavior based on moralistic principles which humans adhere to. They lived with the belching demon, and they stunk like Skunk Woman and like Wintuns. "At least," observed Yolaina quietly to himself, "white men are fun to joke about."

*   *   *

Yolaina sat on a log near the cooking fire where Hitchinna removed the last of her cooking rocks to add to the basket of bubbling broth containing finely cut pieces of venison. Many types of greens floated on top, and Hitchinna used white man's salt and dry black and white flakes that tasted like uncooked watercress. She had used the last of the acorns with the remainder of what would have been their last bag of ground white man's seeds to make her cakes. The day before, Hwipajusi and all the women except Periwiri Yupa had raided the cabin on Deer Creek to get more seeds. Wirula and Periwiri Yupa used the new provisions. As Hitchinna placed the new batch of hot stones into the basket, Yolaina watched his mother with a great love. Her temples had gray hair, and her skin had begun to sag about her neck. He wondered how his beautiful mother had gotten so old, and he thought about Dari Jowa, no longer young, with new wrinkles, but still with black hair. He thought of Wihlaina, very pregnant and in her home, waiting for dinner and taking a nap. As Yolaina gazed about, he almost forgot about his very black eye and swollen nose, but when Dari Jowa returned from washing his hands and face in the stream, he was full of questions, as all the others had been. Dari Jowa sat on the log with Yolaina.

"So, you thought you would turn into White-headed Eagle Man or Condor Man and soar into the sky, and further, you say that one of the white men was the one Hwipajusi had tried to kill?" asked Dari Jowa.

"Yes," said Yolaina. "Except I did not think; I jumped instead."

"Every year my hunters get more and more irrational," said Dari Jowa. "When you have the right to stand and kill white men, you fly like boulders off cliffs; when you should run and count your blessings, you try to kill a white boy. With each passing year, you make me progressively happier, especially since I have forgotten my age."

"I have not forgotten your age," said Hitchinna, who set a basket of cakes near their feet. "I will get the bowls."

"You will forget, though, probably within a year. I think maybe that then I will age many years very quickly and help Hwipajusi guard the camp. That way I will only hunt once a moon, and you young braves," he continued talking, but to Yolaina as Hitchinna entered her home, "will have to show your chief respect and bring home even more meat than you do now." Dari Jowa glanced at Hwipajusi as he sat on a log near Periwiri Yupa's fire.

"All of the men cannot act like Hwipajusi, or all the white men east of Daha, the great water, would be dead," said Yolaina.

"You should not make fun of old men," said Hwipajusi. "I do a very good job of keeping white men out of the sunshine on the cliff."

"Lizard Man, Kalchauna, the new First Person of the white people, is still on the loose, though, Hwipajusi," said Dari Jowa. "Yolaina soared like an eagle instead of killing him. He might come into camp. Are you ready? Is your new bow ready to be strung?"

"I will not use three arrows next time," replied Hwipajusi. "One will be enough. My magic has grown with my age. For instance, I have become patient and can wait forever in the sunshine on the cliff for a white man. My bow is always near. I always sniff the wind like Ututni, Wood Duck Man, always aware of those who approach, especially women with platters of baked sheep legs and warm cakes."

Periwiri Yupa and Weanmauna set down platters of food in front of where her family would eat, and so did Hitchinna and Halai Auna at their fire, and Tsanunewa and Wirula at their fire. When the food was all ready to eat, Wirula took a platter to Wihlaina resting because of heavy pregnancy in her and Dari Jowa's home. Ketipku, Periwiri Yupa, and Hwipajusi sat at one fire; and Demauna, Chunoyahi, and Tsanunewa sat at the third fire. Lawalila decided to sit with Hitchinna because she was his adopted mother and because the greens floating all over her salted venison soup were more delicious looking than a baked sheep's leg. Tsanunewa, however, still wished to eat the sheep's leg.

When Dari Jowa stood to speak before they ate, everyone listened carefully, for they were all very hungry. "I dedicate this meal to Yolaina, a man of magical talents. Too bad we do not have enough good food." He sat down and laughed, and everyone began eating.

"Yolaina," said Dari Jowa after he had sipped the broth from his small bowl and had eaten a piece of venison. "Maybe you should give Hwipajusi soaring lessons, for Kalchauna might sneak up behind Hwipajusi as he dries his hair in the morning's sun on the cliff. Hwipajusi's arrow will not be ready, and he will need knowledge of soaring."

"I hear you, Dari Jowa, and my bow is strung this very instant and is by my side, just in case I should need to stop eating my cake long enough to kill a saltu."

"That might be too great of a sacrifice," said Periwiri Yupa while pinching his fat.

"Stop that," squealed Hwipajusi.

"You should finish your cake first," said Periwiri Yupa. "A white man would not be able to shoot a man of your magical abilities."

"All of you should stop teasing Hwipajusi," said Halai Auna. "I feel much better knowing he remains in camp with his bow by his side, and sometimes he shoots deer and other game."

"Halai Auna speaks the truth; neither white men nor grizzly bears dare enter our camp," said Hwipajusi, already eating his second cake and chewing on some sheep meat.

"I miss you on our hunts, Hwipajusi," said Chunoyahi. "Now I am afraid that a bear will attack me and that you will not be able to save me."

"I miss you, too, Hwipajusi, but I am afraid of ringtail cats and mice and grasshoppers when you are not there to protect me. Even a blossoming lupine bush will make me jump. I also miss your stories," said Demauna.

Yolaina glanced at Demauna's gray hair, and then at Hwipajusi, from whom he was waiting to hear, for Hwipajusi could sometimes make him laugh for days. Hwipajusi sat blankly, and his hands, filled with meat and a cake, rested on his knees. He did not respond, and he panted like a dog.

"I am sick," he said. "My…" Hwipajusi threw up violently, dropped his food, and dropped to his hands and knees, where he lay supine and looked as if he were choking. Yolaina set down his bowl and rushed to Hwipajusi, but others began acting just as Hwipajusi. Dari Jowa, Yolaina, Halai Auna, Lawalila, and Hitchinna rushed from person to person as each of them vomited, fell to the ground, stopped breathing, and quivered. Dari Jowa ran to his home where his wife, Wihlaina, Chipmunk Woman, lay motionless in her own vomit, and Wirula was motionless on the floor. Lawalila shook Tsanunewa and cried; Dari Jowa held Wihlaina, his dead, pregnant wife, in his arms and cried as he had never done before. Yolaina walked hopelessly in a circle, checking each corpse for a sign of life. Hitchinna and Halai Auna retreated to their home and closed their hide and wailed and sobbed and put curses on white men. Yolaina dragged each person by the armpits into his or her respective home. He covered their faces, and when Dari Jowa emerged from his house, he carried Wirula to Chunoyahi lying dead on the floor of their home. Dari Jowa placed a rabbit-skin blanket over her face. He then went to Lawalila, singing over Tsanunewa to Sukonia, Pine Martin Man, to strike his wife with his bowstring to bring her back to life. Dari Jowa placed his hand on Lawalila's shoulder and then squatted beside him.

"I will place Tsanunewa in your home. You help keep the fire in Hitchinna's home. Go. It is dark, and a cold, north wind blows. A storm is coming. Take the wood from your home to Hitchinna's. We will burn our hair there. Come," said Dari Jowa.

Lawalila stood and walked to his home. He gathered a large armload of small branches. Dari Jowa waited with Tsanunewa in his arms for Lawalila to emerge and then set her down on the tule mats. Yolaina placed away all the materials of their feast, for even in tragedy, they could not leave food out to attract beasts or spirits, even poisoned food. Yolaina made sure to place all belongings where they had been stored before the poisoning. Night had thoroughly fallen by then, and Yolaina met the others in his family's house. He had the last of their small baskets and another armload of wood. The others had prepared to burn their hair, and Lawalila was on his knees and slightly bent over. Hitchinna and Halai Auna were burning his hair and splashing water on his scalp to stop him from burning. The family stunk of the charred wet hair, and they chanted many different dirges. One by one they burned their hair, and then they covered their stubble with pitch from Hitchinna's basket. Late into the night they sang, until complete exhaustion took away their anguish.

*   *   *

The morning greeted the five mourners with ankle deep snow. From Hitchinna's entrance the snow could be seen falling in large clumps from the windswept and heavily laden cedars and pines, and individual flakes raced so quickly across the view that they looked like disappearing white lines. Only directly under one live oak was the snow not covering the ground, and the north sides of the tree trunks were damp and dark and encrusted with snow.

Yolaina kept the entrance open long enough to rekindle the fire, and the others lay under their rabbit-skin blankets and skins. He closed the black bearskin and added wood to the fire, and when the fire snapped loudly and new wood was added to it, Yolaina wrapped a piece of canvas around his white man's shirt, and left for the village toilet. He was in pain because of waiting so long, and he did not notice the blowing wind and snow between his toes. He ran down the trail from the village and then to the bathing hole in the feeder stream. He removed his clothes quickly and walked into the pool. After rubbing his hands over his entire body, except for his swollen eye and pitch-covered head, and rinsing thoroughly, he immediately collected his clothes and ran through the blizzard and clumps of falling snow to his family's house. He stood on his spot and dried off with a white man's seed sack, and he thoroughly appreciated that Dari Jowa had tended the fire well while he had been bathing.

As people moved about and discussed the events, Yolaina sat and listened and occasionally responded, but mostly he thought and tended the fire. The inevitable annihilation of all humans on the earth would happen when they died, probably tragically, and only others without spirits would walk the earth, beings incapable of acting with human decency. Many problems had to be resolved, also. The dead were frozen, but soon the spring's sun would appear. They would have to gather huge stacks of wood for the pyres, and the wood would have to dry. They would have to cover the bodies with snow, and Yolaina hoped that the wood would be dry enough to burn when the snow melted from the bodies. Hitchinna confirmed she believed only the newly stolen sacks of the white man's finely ground seeds could have poisoned the people. All the other food had been shared; for instance, Hitchinna had eaten a piece of sheep from a leg the others had cooked and eaten, and all of the cooks had shared the same salt. Only the flour was different, the flour from the cabin on the north side of Deer Creek. They decided that after the funeral they would destroy Tcapalauna and move to a lower elevation on Deer Creek, where they would be constantly hidden in the brush and where they could easily fish for salmon, a luxury they had long denied themselves at Tcapalauna on upper Salmon Creek. They obviously never wished to use again any food touched by the saltus, and they would have to gather food as best they could, when and wherever they could, from the canyons of the Yahi.

The snowstorm let up at the end of day, dissipated to rain, and then stopped as night fell. A deep chill froze the heavy, wet snow. They all wished sunshine would appear the next day, but the clouds were still thick above them. Yolaina rubbed bay leaf oil on his moccasins, for if the following day were pleasant, he would have much to do in freezing, wet snow. When he checked again to look for stars, hail began to pound from the clouds. A bit later, Ilhataina, Lightning Man, struck with great force up and down Salmon Creek Canyon, and the inside of their family home lit up through the smoke hole. The earth almost shook in the resounding echoes of the canyon. Storms, of course, were a fact of life, but certain storms seemed to be the thoughts of angry spirits.

The following day after Lawalila, Dari Jowa, Yolaina, Hitchinna, and Halai Auna had washed and eaten and cleaned up, they took baskets about the village and gathered snow, heaped it on the bodies, and looked for signs of sunshine. The sun, however, remained hidden, and periodically a wet snow fell heavily throughout the day. The snow drove them back inside their earthen home. They watched the fire and tried to forget the dead bodies they had covered. The delay in burying the corpses weighed heavily on their minds, but they turned in upon themselves, as does a black oak in winter, with only a few, brown pinnately lobed leaves dangling from its snow-laden, crooked branches. Life for it is hidden and waiting for a favorable season to grow. They gathered all the dry wood from every house and the remnants of food they knew was good, primarily the food from their surroundings, and they prepared themselves mentally to wait out the last large storm intruding so rudely on the spring. When night began to fall and cold descended again up Tcapalauna, a light snow covered the encrusted layer already on the ground.

"One of us must hunt," said Dari Jowa, "as soon as the sun shines. One of us must always hunt, no matter what our circumstances. I do not know how we became so small. Once I was a boy, and no white men came near us. Our neighbors either respected us or ran like Wintuns clacking like dry leaves. We were brave, and for twelve years we killed those who killed us, yet we were destroyed as the white men grew in numbers and in hatred." He paused and thought a moment. "I guess we will have to live honorably until we die, and the last person to die will have to let his spirit roam, lost in these canyons, wondering where all the people are and why only beasts roam the earth."

Dari Jowa had not said too much during day, and no one wanted to say the names of the dead. When he spoke, consequently, his words seemed to carry extra weight, and everyone sat for a long time until Hitchinna spoke.

"I would like one of our camps to be where we hid when Yolaina was born and Halai Auna was still in the womb, Grizzly Bear's Hiding Place, near the cliffs, in the laurel, above the thick brush, and where the fishing is good and sun sets late every day. I would like to live in as much of the late sun as possible. You know the spot, Dari Jowa. You killed many rabbits there."

Dari Jowa placed a small piece of cedar through the septum of his nose. "That is a good spot. A white man's home is not far from there, but it is totally out of view. The white man will never use that part of the canyon."

"How come life is so beautiful and fun one moment, and the next, a completely hollow existence, as if one were a rotten log?" asked Halai Auna, who desperately wanted to hold tightly to an idea that was as real as life, that gave a human a reason to live, but she could not find such a solution or answer. The sky gave her snow, and her heart gave her grief.

"Maybe we should kill the man who owns the cabin," said Lawalila. "He does not deserve to live, and we have so little to lose. We will just die, and no Yahi will replace us. Being peaceful does not help us. We still die. We should kill him."

"Then we would not be able to sit in the late afternoon sun and eat rabbits at Grizzly Bear's Hiding Place," replied Hitchinna. "The whites are great in number, and we are not. They would search the canyons until they found us."

"They do not need to find us," said Lawalila. "All they have to do is poison us."

"We can live without their food, Lawalila," said Halai Auna. "We are five, and they are many."

"What do you say, Yolaina? Do you think we should kill the man?" asked Dari Jowa.

"Whatever we do should be based on what helps us to live the longest," he said almost automatically and without forethought, for he was reared with only the thought of survival and the essence, philosophically speaking, of what survival required.

"When the sun shines," said Dari Jowa, "I will hunt and think. I will probably return without an answer and with only a desire to live where the salmon run thickly up Deer Creek every spring and fall. I wish to watch the seasons change and to kill large bucks. Perhaps now would be a good time to pretend all of us had been poisoned. Perhaps we could live happily a long time."

Halai Auna touched her pitch-covered head and tried not to think about her dead friends, but they would not leave her mind. Yolaina could see her anguish and felt the same, for evil images of a once happy people dying filled his thoughts: faces covered with snow, quiet houses without laughter or anger, unborn children in cold bodies, the gagging horror of prostrate people. The thoughts would not go away.

*   *   *

Yolaina, Lawalila, and Halai Auna walked the entire day in and out of Tcapalauna to gather wet wood to add to their already immense piles. They stacked in ten different places and dug holes near each stack, and the sun was helpful. They gathered large stacks of pine needles and very small twigs to place neatly in large bases for their fires. Then they placed slightly larger sticks above those until solid bases had been built to hold bodies. They then gathered another immense amount of pine needles and small twigs to place over the bodies and to keep in reserve to help the fires remain lit after they added coals to the pyres. They wished to avoid removing a charred corpse from a smoldering pile of blackened, wet wood. They hurried with their work, though, for they raced with and against the heat. They had not looked upon the bodies for two days, and they hoped to light the fires on the following day. After the burial of the bones and the singing was completed, they would move all of their personal belongings, except their caches, to Deer Creek Canyon.

Hitchinna gathered greens, clover, watercress, and leopard lily roots, and she cooked the remainder of a sheep and tended their fire and ground dried acorns for mush and generally kept their home in order. Hitchinna always worked very hard, and she did not get real rest then because she had lost her blood time. She had reached the beginning of old age, just as Yolaina had reached the beginning of middle age. She was stiff in the mornings, but always kept a bright outlook, even in such a tragedy. Her eyes were lively like a water ouzel scampering under the water crashing over a river boulder. She seemed very much alive and full of happiness in her despair. Perhaps she had come to accept despair as the inevitable, and thought that worrying about the inevitable was not worthwhile. Yolaina admired his mother very much, and with great love and respect he knew he would always take very good care of her until her death. He knew he would bury her with dignity.

Dari Jowa hunted in the first decent day of good weather since the storm, and as they all knew, he would bring home any type of game. They hoped, however, for a deer. Dari Jowa had become very philosophical as he became old. He was full of humor but not of quick decisions. He, in essence, was more than Yolaina's uncle, however; he was his adopted father. Yolaina could not understand how Dari Jowa showed such strength when his wife and baby were poisoned, but Dari Jowa had experienced grief many times before Yolaina was born.

Lawalila gathered wood, but at times he cried silently. He could not really accept the death of Tsanunewa, for he loved her beyond the strength of imagination. Lawalila was emotional in a strong way, and he wanted desperately to strike, even in futility, at something unknown that could bring his wife back to life. He could not think of any thing or action that would help. Revenge, the normal course of action for a Yahi, would not help him with his need. He was doomed to live alone and without a wife for the rest of his life, and no outlook of inner strength was on his face. As Yolaina watched Lawalila, Yolaina was almost happy he had not married, for the grief Lawalila felt was deeper than his. Yolaina had grieved sorely in a festering way about not being married to any of Hwipajusi's daughters, but the look on Lawalila's face was swollen and filled with a wrathful hate he might not lose. Even stacking wood was almost more than he could bear.

All of the death had shaken Halai Auna terribly, but with her immediate family all intact, she bounced back practically. She needed to feel centered. Hitchinna was like a fire in a distant cave, and Halai Auna saw the greatness in Hitchinna. Halai Auna was almost whole in a necessary way, and sometimes during the day she spoke of how much she looked forward to moving to Grizzly Bear's Hiding Place. She said a new place would bring back their joy. Yolaina respected Halai Auna for her calm temperament and good cheer in the face of such evilness.

Yolaina was extremely sad, of course, but he also looked forward to moving. The dead bodies lying around Tcapalauna had sneaked into his dreams, and horrible images of those dying moments would not leave his mind. When he walked to camp with wood, he envisioned Hwipajusi and then Demauna and then Weanmauna, Hidden One, whom he had still loved enough to marry. He thought about how much grief Weanmauna must have felt as a child to be so withdrawn as an adult. Yolaina tried not to think about the dead, and he cursed the storm for keeping them in camp. When they had at last gathered enough wood for the pyres, Yolaina was relieved. He washed his hands and face in the stream, and rinsed his mouth and rubbed his teeth. He would be glad when Dari Jowa arrived in camp, and he would be glad when he would not have to think so much about dead bodies, especially ones he had to carry, to burn, to bury, and to forget. He did not know if he could forget.

*   *   *

"I do not know if this will serve us well enough in the winter," said Halai Auna as she dug into the soil. "This does not seem to be a warm enough shelter. Perhaps we will need to make a real winter's shelter."

Yolaina was with her, and Dari Jowa and Hitchinna worked on a new village storage house. Lawalila was down the hill hunting rabbits.

"Perhaps," replied Yolaina pleasantly.

"How come you have been so considerate lately?" asked Halai Auna as she stopped to stare at Yolaina.

"I thought I was always considerate," replied Yolaina.

"Well, you seem to have grown up. You even look like a man instead of a brother."

"I am glad you think I have finally become a man," said Yolaina, "but I think I have acted like a man for many years."

"You were a man, but you acted like a boy. The way your passion bubbled in you made you too unpleasant."

"My passion still bubbles, but even passion fades away. Passion does not make a young man into a boy, however; you are wrong. Being a man of compassion and youth is not easy. You have never understood how hard being a man is. You seem to be every bit a woman with too much advice for men."

"There you go again," she said.

"You bait me too much, Halai Auna," Yolaina said and smiled. He scraped some dirt onto a flat platter, picked it up, and walked to the dirt mound where he dumped the dirt and set down the platter. He then walked past Dari Jowa and Hitchinna. He climbed onto a pile of loose rocks not far from the cover of the laurel where Dari Jowa stood and watched him. "Dari Jowa, would you care for some soaring lessons now?"

"Yes. Tell me the proper way to soar," replied Dari Jowa.

"The most important quality one must have is the proper attitude. One must have an absolute desire to jump into the air without thinking. One must then spread one's arms and legs far apart to catch the wind and to feel which way the wind blows. Now that I have told you the magical lessons of soaring, will you climb onto these rocks and jump into the canyon?"

"I do not have the proper attitude," said Dari Jowa. "For instance, I cannot muster the absolute desire to jump without thinking. I doubt my ability, and when I see your face, I think even more that soaring might not work."

"Soaring feels good, though, Dari Jowa," said Yolaina. "You will travel quickly; you will feel wind in your hair; you will feel alive; you will be able to look all about from the air."

"I admit to dreaming about soaring. I have often watched eagles and hawks and condors and buzzards and birds of all types fly. My name, White-headed Eagle Man, suggests I should fly instead of dream. However, I see your eye, still yellow and black and red, and I lose my absolute desire to jump without thinking. I would like to see you jump without thinking. You make me very proud that you soared and lived, and I think you should try to soar again so that we could watch."

"I lost my concentration, though, Dari Jowa. As soon as I reached the air, and spread my arms and legs, and felt the wind rush across my face, and tested the wind with my arms, and looked about at the bay leaves in my face, I lost concentration, bounced off a limb, and hit the ground."

"Tell me," continued Dari Jowa, "was soaring worthwhile? Do you remember anything pleasant about the experience of being free in the air?"

"I have never traveled that fast before," replied Yolaina, "and I have never been out of contact with earth for so long, even though it was a brief period of time."

"Under the situation, would you jump again, or would you remove arrows from your quiver?"

"I would remove arrows from my quiver, for I have developed a very poor attitude about white men, even Lizard Man, and I think shooting two men with arrows would be easier than jumping off a cliff, even a small cliff with a soft looking bay tree below it."

"Maybe you better stay away from cliffs. Maybe you better climb off those rocks before you stop thinking."

"I think we should all bathe and gather wood and cook the three rabbits Lawalila is bringing into camp."

Dari Jowa looked at Lawalila, his pitch covered head and red eyes, and remembered their tragedy, but he did not feel any worse. In fact, Lawalila's success was good news, and the rabbits were skinned and cleaned and plump.

"Rabbits here have never been hunted," said Lawalila. "They are not very smart, and when a hunter dozes, they jump on his arrows."

"Yolaina is correct," said Hitchinna. "We should prepare dinner, or we will not have enough time gather wood for tonight."

"Good idea," said Dari Jowa. "I never wish to argue with the cook. Let us walk through and around the brush to bathe and to gather water for our meal."

"We are too far from the water," said Lawalila, who was negative about much of their decisions.

"Perhaps," said Dari Jowa thoughtfully, "but we are safe. No one will penetrate the brush or climb the hill or lower himself from the canyon's rim into the brush. No one can see us from above. The salmon will soon run, and we can watch the sun set in real peace, something I have not felt in many years."

CHAPTER 11

A New Chief

Yolaina sat thinking by the side of Deer Creek below Grizzly Bear's Hiding Place. He was happy his hair had reached the middle of his back, and that he no longer thought about Lawalila dying of a rattlesnake bite or of the past in general. In the midday's sun heat waves rose off the black river boulders, and the high, golden grass waved in the light breeze from the stream. From where he sat in the shade of a live oak near the brush, he did not have a clear view of the canyon's rim. He was happy to have killed a sheep since the salmon run had not been good the previous spring, and since he felt they needed another warm skin.

The story of Ututni, Wood Duck Man, ran through his mind, and of how Dari Jowa told the story after the sun set the previous night until the moon raced one-fifth of the sky. Ututni was a fine hunter and had a lot of wealth, many fine skins of all kinds: otter, bear, rabbit, mountain lion, and pine martin. His storehouse was filled with baskets of roots, acorns, dried salmon, dried venison, dehydrated berries, and pine nuts. He had red beads of baked magnesite and bright abalone buttons. His two sisters served him well and obeyed his every wish, but Ututni had no wife.

He lay on his bed of rabbit-skin blankets one day. He sniffed the air in all directions, to the east and south and west and north, to see if any woman were approaching, and he said to his sisters, "I believe young women are talking about me and that they will visit me. See that you give each one a filled basket with dried salmon and venison, for I would like to get married." He sang a love song, "Wino-tay," over and over, which Dari Jowa sang at great length before each woman arrived to visit Wood Duck Man, Ututni; Dari Jowa loved to hear himself sing. The first woman to visit was Kitipku, Little Striped Skunk Woman, but Ututni thought she smelled and sent her away with a filled basket. Tsulwalkai, Red Obsidian Woman, came next, only after Dari Jowa sang a great while, however, "Wino-tay." Ututni had to send her away because she had no eyes. One after another the women came. Brown Bear Woman brought sweet smelling herbs and roots, and was sent away. Abalone Woman, Waterbug Woman, Chipmunk Woman, Fishhook Woman, Shikepoke Woman, and Bat Woman were sent away, and Dari Jowa kept singing between each one "Wino-tay." Magnesite Woman was given beads but sent away. One woman, Dentelium Woman, spent the night and made his house shake and ring. Girigiri, Blue Crane Woman, was sent away, but only after she had spent the night. Finally, number twenty, Morning Star Woman, Halai Auna, captures his heart. She is a beautiful young girl with many skills.

Kalchauna, Lizard Man, however, saw Halai Auna and fell in love with her. He shot Ututni with arrows, and he married Halai Auna. He gave her many gifts and promised always to be gentle.

Ututni's sisters put his eyebrows in a basket of water and brought him back to life, but Ututni was not able to marry Halai Auna, Morning Star Woman. He was left alone.

Yolaina had to laugh when he thought of the way Dari Jowa told his long story. Dari Jowa was very happy that Ututni did not marry Beaver

Woman, for instance, because she spoke Wintun. Beavers lived mostly in Daha, the great water of the valley, where the Wintuns once lived. The Yahi had always despised them and had occasionally killed a few when robbing from them after long winters. The Wintuns had been afraid to enter the mountains, for in the mountains they had been unfamiliar, easily hunted, and weak of body. Yahis had not liked Wintuns because Wintuns had been barbaric and without spirits, saltu, and so they had always been, that is, until the white men came.

In front of Yolaina, the pool was calm, and water swirled lazily at its edges. Debris from trees and bushes floated there, and trout fed on the bugs. The sound of white water from upstream was the loudest noise about him, and it was a gentle whisper, like a chant from the Seven Stars. Tall river grass grew in the moist, green clumps on the banks, but other colors faded to the dull greens of summer. The buckeyes had already lost their leaves to the heat, but on one lightly moist section of the bank, leopard lilies bloomed in the tall ferns. Yolaina watched a kingfisher fly rapidly in front of him. Grasshoppers snapped their wings in flight, and swallowtail butterflies warmed their wings on the moist sand. Yellow jackets and dragonflies also landed on the moist sand. Dragonflies were always brightly colored, always different, each one, and they commanded the sky very well. Yolaina heard the oak leaves behind him and turned.

Halai Auna hurried past him and into the cold water, but she filled a water basket and immediately walked to Yolaina. "Hurry with me," she said. "Hitchinna fell to the ground and has no consciousness. She lies on a skin in the shade. Dari Jowa looks over her."

"Does she breathe?" asked Yolaina.

"Yes," replied Halai Auna as she scurried back up the steep canyon and around the brush, "but she is very ill."

"What caused her to fall?" asked Yolaina while following his sister back to camp.

"She grabbed her left shoulder. I think that maybe her heart quit for a while. She is so old. She was taking coals off the buried leg of sheep," said Halai Auna carrying the large water basket.

"Will she live?" asked Yolaina.

"I do not know," replied Halai Auna beginning to cry.

They hurried up the trail as quickly as possible, always a tedious task, but never had the hike seemed to take as long. The manzanita berries were ripe, and the buck brush was thorny. Back in Grizzly Bear's Hiding Place, Yolaina saw Hitchinna lying in the shade of a laurel. Dari Jowa cooled her with water that he applied with the remnants of a twelve-year-old seed sack.

Yolaina stood helplessly and hopefully and fearfully over his dear mother, Hitchinna, Wildcat Woman, frail and motionless. She was always slim, but never was she so withered, so like a crumbled brown leaf in the soil. She seemed to choke and moved her lips quietly. Then she whispered with great effort, "Water." Dari Jowa lifted her head and gave her a drink from the basket he had ready. Dari Jowa seemed as helpless as Hitchinna. Yolaina stared at the scene, especially his white-headed, old uncle, Dari Jowa, bent and frail, trying desperately to give life to his failing sister-in-law, whom he had always loved and respected as a true Yahi should, for whom he had provided with all of his tremendous knowledge for his entire manhood. Tears filled Yolaina's eyes, and he quietly watched the scene and paced back and forth and watched some more. He noticed the leg of sheep still needed to be uncovered and moved onto a basket.

"Halai Auna," said Yolaina, "you must finish removing the leg. Maybe Hitchinna will eat later. I will gather more manzanita berries and prepare a cold, sweet drink. Surely Hitchinna will have smashed manzanita berries in water."

"Yes," she whispered as Dari Jowa continued to keep her cool in the sweltering heat.

Halai Auna moved slowly at first and then concentrated on her new task. Yolaina went to their family home over the grizzly bear's den to remove two baskets, one for washing, smashing, and straining the pulp from the seeds, and one to hold the reddish liquid. The drink was sweet and refreshing on hot summer days. Yolaina hurried down the trail and looked at the shelves of the great stone cliff, the northern wall of the canyon. A wood dove flew by, and grasshoppers jumped at his feet. He thought of his mother, who had finally arrived at the time when her body would no longer function. He remembered her as she climbed out of their swimming hole that morning after her bath. The sky was turning from gray to pink and blue, and her mind was filled with wit and charm. She wanted to know about the new settlers in Salmon Creek Canyon near where Black Rock Village used to be. The settlers looked like Yahi, but they wore white man's clothes and had lightning sticks. They lived in a white man's house and chased cows on horses. They had little children and many loud, large dogs. Hitchinna was curious about all of their manners and clothing. Yolaina could not satisfy all her curiosity because he only observed them from a distance. They were perhaps some form of Yahi but still saltu, others without spirits. How had so much time slipped by that Hitchinna could have turned from a beautiful young woman into a dying, old, wrinkled, white, immovable woman? Yolaina gathered many berries and continued to mull over the horrible image of his mother. When his straining basket was full enough to make manzanita berry water, he walked to the stream. First, he bathed, swam, and drank from the stream, for the heat would not go away. Then he washed and smashed and strained the pulp from the four, hard, black seeds in each of the berries. When his basket was filled with the drink, he hurried back to camp, to Hitchinna still lying comfortably, at times with her eyes opened, but very ill.

*   *   *

Hitchinna lay sleeping on a bearskin in the warm air of the evening. A half moon lit up the sky; and stars, although very evident, were pale compared to Wakara, Moon Man, as he grew in strength. The fire was small as always, but not really needed. Dari Jowa wanted one to make their talk formal, and the fire was peaceful. He smoked a bowl of tobacco. He was crippled in his movements and wrinkled and gray, but was extremely spirited about life in general. He still hunted small game near camp and collected water and brodiaea bulbs and seeds and manzanita berries, and he smoked skins and set snares. He was old, however. Halai Auna was still able bodied, but she was as old Yolaina, late middle age. No one knew their ages, for somewhere, Hitchinna stopped counting or lost some magnesite beads she was using to keep track.

"We are faced with many new problems," said Dari Jowa. "We must do all the work we have been doing plus take care of Hitchinna and do the work she had done. I do not see how we can manage to live. Hitchinna had always allowed Halai Auna to gather many kinds of food, and now one of us, primarily Halai Auna, because I am becoming too old to do much carrying, will have to take care of her. I wonder how we will eat."

"We should take the seeds from the white men again," said Halai Auna. "Yolaina says he has watched them use the bags they have stored over and over. Never have the bags been poisoned."

"Then they will know we are alive," said Dari Jowa. "They might poison us," he said calmly.

"We could make a cake from each sack we take, and we could feed the cake to my friend, the fat chipmunk. If he lives, then we will eat the ground seeds. We will test all the food," replied Halai Auna.

"Then we could live here and eat and survive," said Yolaina. "I do not know a way to live if we do not take seeds from them. We have too many responsibilities and too few people."

"Your point is well taken, Yolaina," said Dari Jowa, and then he smiled and replied, "but can you still escape? Are your legs fast enough?"

"Every time I see a white man, my legs are very fast and strong. I can jump large manzanita bushes in a single bound and carry large seed sacks at the same time. I am harder to catch than the wind."

"How about you, Halai Auna? Are you fast enough?"

"I am a sneaky old woman now, and you know a sneaky old woman can never be caught at anything." She laughed. "I am brown like a tree trunk, and at night I am gray like the distant shade from an oak branch in the moonlight. White men never see me."

"I was sad that we had to stop eating the flour and seeds," said Dari Jowa. "We sometimes have been too hungry. I notice, for instance, that my arms and chest are no longer large and strong."

"I am no longer a little girl, also," said Halai Auna.

Yolaina smiled and spoke. "Hitchinna is doing much better than a couple of days ago," said Yolaina. "I think she will live."

"She can talk and sit up and eat, but will she be able to use her arm and leg again?" asked Halai Auna.

"I do not think she will get too much better," said Dari Jowa quietly.

Yolaina stared at the fire, the blues, oranges, and yellows. He placed several sturdy looking sticks on the small flame. He squatted down and looked at Halai Auna's hat, a white man's hat; its rim was sewn with deer sinew and its top was replaced with deer hide sewn on with sinew. Halai Auna wore a string of magnesite beads interlaced with small snail shells, and she wore a deerskin shirt with tassels cut in the bottom. She was also squatting by the fire. She was obviously no longer young. She was practical and sincere and loving; she was the last able-bodied Yahi woman. She still remembered how to speak some white man's words, and Wintun and Maidu and Paiute, also. Halai Auna always knew too much about what people were thinking.

"We should take seeds from the new house near Smoky Creek where the men dig in the earth on Deer Creek," said Yolaina. "Those men do not chase cows and are easy to avoid. We should take from them at night, and that way they will not sneak up on us like Lizard Man. The moon is getting full, and tomorrow would be good time to travel. Tomorrow night we will walk down Smoky Creek to Deer Creek and borrow all the food they have and anything else that might be useful: bottles for points, clothes, axes, lightning sticks!" He laughed.

*   *   *

The rabbits were boiled in a thin broth covered with watercress, and cakes of flour were made. The chipmunk had not returned from the previous day, however, which made everyone perplexed, distressed, and hungry. He was a greedy fellow and should have returned for more of a cake.

"Let us just eat rabbits and set out a crumb. He will return to join us, and then we can also eat the cakes," said Yolaina settling for a meal of rabbits.

Hitchinna sat in the shade and on bearskin. She was leaning against a rock covered with the skin, and she was happy to be out of the family house. Her left arm and leg were paralyzed, and she did not have too much to say. She seemed mostly alert and was hungry, and Yolaina noticed she always responded to their conversations. She would move her head toward the person speaking or nod her head gently or say a few words. Her speech, at first, had not been as clear as it was now. Yolaina could see that Hitchinna would always be paralyzed, but he was happy Hitchinna was alive. Yolaina knew his mother had to die, of course, as all humans did, even the last four.

Halai Auna removed a rabbit's leg from the broth and set it on a flat, clean rock sitting next to Hitchinna on the bearskin. Hitchinna picked it up and began eating, slowly, with small weak bites. Halai Auna also served Dari Jowa, Yolaina, and herself with parts of the rabbits.

Yolaina eyed the cakes, the bulk of the prepared meal, but he was afraid to eat them, afraid, somehow, that after twelve years of not taking a seed sack from a white man, that the first one they took would be poisoned, but as he stared at the cakes and chewed from his rabbit's leg, the fat chipmunk scurried from the brush, picked up the crumb of cake, sat back on his legs, took a bite, and then ran back into the brush, only stopping once to nibble on his new crumb.

"Our fat friend likes to play jokes," said Dari Jowa while reaching for a cake.

The others also ate from the flat basket of cakes. They ate greedily, for food had been in short supply since Hitchinna had become sick. The large reserve of food would allow Halai Auna time to cook and to take care of Hitchinna. She had to be carried to the toilet or supplied with a flat pitch-lined basket, but she could converse and notice life and enjoy her food. Yolaina became free to hunt. He could spend less time digging for roots and gathering firewood. He could work on much-needed arrows and a new bow. One had broken, and he could not afford to put off starting a new one. Dari Jowa was not really able to make quality weapons now. His eyes were weak, and his hands were shaky. He shot a light bow, however, and brought home birds and rabbits from the brush.

Yolaina looked into the blue sky, and Wakara, Moon Man, was rising almost unnoticeably but three-fourths full. "We should immediately get more food from the cabin at the mouth of Sulfur Creek," said Yolaina. "Then I could hunt deer and sheep until the salmon run. We need the food."

"Good idea," said Dari Jowa. "Then you could raid them again in the fall, and we could make our chipmunk into one of the fattest creatures in the forest."

"You must be careful," said Hitchinna very quietly.

"I will be," said Yolaina. "The white men will be far away sleeping, dreaming of being brave hunters of cows and sheep, and I will be nothing but footprints on water."

"Do not forget, Hitchinna," said Halai Auna, "that Yolaina can soar home, if he so chooses."

Hitchinna smiled a bit and nodded her head. She set down her cake and swallowed her small bite. "You, my son, have had to carry many burdens," she said very slowly and paused, "and you have always acted honorably, have always been Yolaina, Bravest Man. You fill me with great pride." Her eyes watered.

"In fact," said Dari Jowa, "I think you should be chief, now, since I think I should become protector of the camp."

"Is your bow still strong enough to kill a white man?" asked Yolaina with merriment in his voice.

"My bow is still strong enough, but I do not need a bow now that I am so old. All I need to do is stand before them and show them my wrinkles. My wrinkles would scare white men to death."

"Would you still hunt in the brush if you were protector of the camp?" continued Yolaina.

"I always hunt," said Dari Jowa, "and waiting for white men has been my specialty now for twelve years. I have been waiting a long time, but they are afraid to find me where I sit in the sun on this beautiful ledge behind a long walk through dense brush in front of a great cliff but under a tree. I must have strong magic like Kalchauna, Lizard Man. I have become more invisible than a trout at the bottom of a deep pool."

"I do not know if I could handle the responsibility of being chief," said Yolaina. "Think of the great decisions that would have to weigh on my mind. Now I do not have to make decisions, and you must hunt all the time to remain chief. If I were to be chief and you were to be protector of the camp, I would have to hunt all the time, and you would sit in camp and drink manzanita-berry water. You would sing in the sunshine too much, and you would not hunt enough. I am very used to following orders now, and I do not know if I could make decisions. No, I think maybe you should be chief. You have always been chief, and I have gotten too used to sitting on the banks of feeder streams and waiting to kill deer. If I were chief, I would forget to concentrate on hunting. I would probably start talking to myself about the orders I would have to give, and then I would frighten the deer. You better remain chief, Dari Jowa; you have always been a good chief."

"If you were protector of the camp," added Halai Auna after swallowing some rabbit, "all you would do is sit in camp and sing, 'Wino-tay,' and you would feed the squirrel too many pine nuts. I think you go swimming when you say you are hunting, anyhow."

Dari Jowa was a bit shocked, for he had never considered that Yolaina might not want to be chief. He had looked forward to being protector of the camp and to honoring Yolaina with the respect and dignity of being chief. "You do not want to be chief?"

"No," said Yolaina, "but if I happen to find another band of Yahi women, say on upper Antelope Creek, I would accept the honor. You would have to promise to keep hunting, however. I would have to have a new big house and plenty of free time to be with the women."

"My mind is very tired, though. I have made too many decisions in my life, and I need less responsibility. I can no longer make good decisions because I can no longer scout. You must be chief now."

"I will be happy to scout for you, just as I always have."

"A good chief needs to check up on his brave, though. He needs to know if his brave is hunting or walking around upper Antelope Creek looking for a lost band of Yahi women. I have been singing to them a lot, lately, and I think maybe you wish to visit them. They probably think you are Wood Duck Man."

"I have searched upper Antelope Creek many times, and never did I find a lost band of Yahi women. Maybe you should stop singing, 'Wino-tay,'" said Yolaina. "Maybe you should sing 'The Old Witch Doctor's Song', instead."

"This was a good piece of rabbit, Halai Auna," said Dari Jowa, "and my stomach has been begging for such delicious cakes many moons. In many ways we are very fortunate, especially when we can visit like this, rich people with food for many days, and talk." He swatted a fly from his white hair, and he dipped a bowl into the broth.

Yolaina looked closely at his mother, and he could not tell what she was thinking. One side of her face was slightly drooping, and she looked forlorn. He was not sure she really appreciated living any more. Her paralysis seemed to be an overburdening part of what she thought about. She lived, but had no real sparkle like sunlight on white water, no real reason for continuing with her life. Perhaps she was just too sick to show much good cheer.

*   *   *

"This window is too high," replied Yolaina, "and it is hard to open."

"You must hurry," said Halai Auna.

Wakara, Moon Man, was shining on them, and they were in the meadow near Sulfur Creek. Halai Auna was holding Yolaina's foot so that he could get better leverage to open the window. When the window yielded, Yolaina climbed halfway in, but the window fell down on him. When he could find no real place to set either his feet or hands and when Halai Auna was not helping in the least, she opened the front door and walked in. Moonlight flooded through the doorway, and Halai Auna stood in full silhouette.

"Look," said Halai Auna as she began filling the seed sack she had brought for the occasion with salted meat and a sweet smelling, smooth, hand-sized object. "You must hurry, Yolaina."

"Help me, Halai Auna," he finally said. "This is very awkward. I am too old to be stuck in a wall."

"Well, you have not said enough good words about my cooking lately. Look. A sack of flour and a sack of seeds. You really should hurry."

"You are the best Yahi cook. You must help me."

"That is not good enough, for I am the only Yahi cook," she replied.

"You have been the best Yahi cook for several days," Yolaina replied. "You must help me."

"That does not sound like a compliment to me," she said.

"You have been the second best Yahi cook for many years," said Yolaina. "How is that? Now help me."

"That is not a very good reply," she said. "I guess I will take the flour. Do not forget the seeds before you leave the cabin." Halai Auna stooped over to pick up the large seed sack. "See you at Grizzly Bear's Hiding Place."

"Wait. You are the best cook to have ever lived. Even your boiled water that is all full of ashes tastes better than venison broth."

"See. You make fun of me," she said.

"No. Really. You are a good cook. I very much enjoy all of your cooking. Help me."

"Do you really believe I am a good cook?"

"Sincerely. Believe me. You are a very good cook, as good as Hitchinna was."

"Okay. I guess I will help you then." She walked to the window, shoved up on it, and let Yolaina brace himself on her shoulder.

When he was finally unstuck and on the floor of the cabin, he was in no mood to understand Halai Auna's behavior.

"How could you leave me in the window? I needed your help," he said.

"I helped you. Are you going to fill your seed sack or not?"

"You play a child's game," said Yolaina. "Ouch!" he yelped as a small mousetrap snapped shut on his big toe. He hopped around.

"You should be more pleasant to me. I am your sister," she said, "and besides I always wanted to see you stuck some place and needing my help. You have always been too independent." She put the bag of flour on her back, and out the door she walked.

"I should have known better than to raid cabins with you. What if a white man would have come?" whispered Yolaina from the door of the cabin where he examined the small trap.

"You should hurry," she replied while walking toward Deer Creek. "The white men might come."

"You always play games with my mind," said Yolaina as he placed the trap in his bag. "A sister is supposed to be more respectful than you are."

Halai Auna was out of safe hearing distance, however, so Yolaina cleared a couple shelves, and took a large sack of seeds. He followed Halai Auna to the edge of the shore and walked briskly downstream. He had a clear view of Halai Auna in the moonlight. She was traveling quickly for carrying such a heavy load, but she had always been a hard worker. Deer Creek was difficult to walk down, and the weight made each step a meaningful movement. The slippery boulders of varying sizes sometimes covered the bottom, and the stream had to be crossed several times in rapid water. Pools of water among the rapids would be on one side of the creek and then the other. Yolaina and Halai Auna had to be careful not to drop their seeds and flour into the water, or their trip would become a waste. Far downstream, they stopped where a large, flat boulder lay exposed near the shore, and their aching arms and backs were greatly relieved.

"I will probably start my blood time," said Halai Auna. "When you gather blackberries, bring me branches of redbud for my baskets. Also, do not get too many ashes in the broth of my meat or in the seeds. I prefer cakes made of the seeds, however; you might wish to spend time gathering seeds of clarkia. You should make your meals very big so that you will not have to cook more than once a day. Do not forget to hunt, to make your bow, to finish the foreshafts on your new arrows, and to weave some string for new salmon toggles. You really should get ready for the salmon run, and you could use some more sinew for new bowstrings. I would like to eat venison. Are you rested yet?"

"Maybe Dari Jowa should make you chief," said Yolaina. "You seem to have no trouble making decisions, and you are skilled in giving orders. Your command of all the work that needs to be done is astounding, and I am sure you would not mind giving minute instructions about how to accomplish every task. You are always ready to spend time thinking about all the work I need to do, for example."

"That sounds like a good idea, but Dari Jowa would then have to stop singing, 'Wino-tay,' in the shade of the bay tree so much. He would have to sit in the brush, kissing his fingers to make the sound of a wounded rabbit. He would have to make more arrow points."

"He can no longer make points, Halai Auna. He is too unsteady. In a way he is as crippled as Hitchinna, except he can still hunt. I do not know if his hunting is all that profitable, though, for he has lost or broken too many arrows."

"I know," said Halai Auna, "but we must still let him hunt. He feels very good about the occasional game he brings in. I would like to be chief, though. You would not have so much fun making jokes about me. You would hunt and cook and weave baskets and work all the time so that I could make decisions."

"Some day I will get you stuck in window," replied Yolaina, "and you will admit that you get too many ashes in your cooking and that your meat is tough."

"I cannot wait until dinner tomorrow. I will be having my blood time and visiting with Hitchinna and listening to Dari Jowa sing, 'Wino-tay,' and smelling the venison broth boil. If you wish for any instructions, do not be afraid to ask, Yolaina, for I will practice becoming chief when I weave my basket and chat with Hitchinna. I do not know if I will be able to say anything good about the cooking, though, for you are the second best Yahi cook."

Yolaina watched the moonlight bounce off the noisy, black water and shook his head. He could understand clearly that getting along with Halai Auna was at its usual pace. She was always spunky and filled with plenty of advice, but if she became chief and Dari Jowa became protector of the camp, he would not have time to take baths in the mornings. He laughed and was amazed at their jokes. In the distance he could see a raccoon at the water's edge.

"I do not think Dari Jowa will want you to be chief once he knows you get stuck in windows and step in traps," said Halai Auna. "I will probably become chief."

CHAPTER 12

The Best Cook

As Yolaina made his way up the north side of Salmon Creek Canyon, he stopped several times to rest. He was half a morning's walk upstream from Black Rock. His otter-skin quiver was filled with arrows, lumps of pitch and paint, part of an old lightning stick, chips from bottles and white plates, a pitching stick, an awl of a nail and black oak, a shaped piece of obsidian for cutting, and skin pads. He also carried a meal of dried salmon and cakes wrapped in part of an old seed sack and a hand spear. Each time the muscles of his legs burned and his breathing became very heavy, he stopped to notice Salmon Creek Canyon. Yolaina was about three-fourths the way up the canyon and above a knoll covered with white-blossomed buck brush. From there he had a clear view of two feeder streams, one to the west among the old yellow pines and tall ferns, and one to the east with crumbling rocks on its side and brush and pines above them. A knoll was on both his east and west, and he had a clear view of the major rock monuments of the canyon to the south: Dewihaumauna, Kashmauna, and Ocholoko. Above the cliffs and crags where the southern slope ascended into the pines lay many good and horrible memories, but Yolaina kept them from his mind.

As Yolaina continued again, he noticed how he intruded so rudely upon the forest. A deer lying peacefully in its soft bed of pine needles and hidden behind a manzanita bush and a black, rough rock formation bolted away across the steam. A flicker flew to a scrub oak, not yet budding, and called loudly, a colorful silhouette against a blue sky, and a stellar jay called loudly many times as it arched from pine to pine. They called to many creatures that a man approached. After Yolaina entered the pines from the open knoll, he noisily stepped on leaf-covered boulders and grass, and the canyon steepened considerably. At times the brush became thick, and he had to maneuver as best he could to avoid being scratched. Above him an occasional deer bolted either east or west along the canyon, and he could not see Daskema, the major rock formation above him, his destination. He had to stop frequently to check his footing and route and to let the pain ebb from his legs. He found an eaten coyote; little was left but its skin. At times water flowed beneath the rocks at his feet, and waist high ferns surrounded him. Where the sunlight shown through, blue lupines and red paintbrush waved in the wind. Mostly, however, he was heading as closely as he could into the fall line and stumbling at times from the rolling talus and sliding pine needles. As he came close to the bottom of the cliffs, the brush became thick and most of the ground water disappeared. Oaks became interspersed with brush and pine.

He walked into the wind and searched for signs of a black bear, for one probably lived among the many shallow caves directly below Daskema. As he caught sight of some rock formations above an oak tree, he spotted a wide trail heading into the brush and toward the rocks. On the trail he found black bear droppings, some fresh, some old. He noticed what the bear had eaten, including whole acorns. Only the thick, wooden, dark brown shells of the acorns were not digested.

Yolaina climbed higher up the slope and followed the bear's trail to its den, a comfortable looking dirt spot in back of some brush and under a great overhang of rock. Several very fresh droppings lay on the dirt of his den.

Yolaina retraced his steps to where he first discovered the trail, and from there he climbed to a flat spot above a boulder. He could see clearly the relatively long stretch of open trail where the bear would travel when it finally decided to return. Above him was water dripping rapidly from the cliff and into an overhang. He could get water there after he waited a long while for the bear, after he became silent like the rock he hid behind, and after the birds quieted and only the wind and falling pine cones interrupted the forest. The bear would crash noisily up the trail before it discovered his scent, and Yolaina would have plenty of time to shoot it from close range.

Yolaina took his quiver from his back and removed three arrows fletched with owl feathers and tipped with clear, green points chipped from a bottle. He placed one upon his bow, and noticed the feel of the deer-hide grip resting comfortably in his left hand. His spear, meal, and quiver were within easy reach. He decided he would kill a deer or a mountain lion or wildcat if any came along, but he was there primarily to get a new bearskin and a large supply of meat. The previous winter was not as warm as it should have been at Grizzly Bear's Hiding Place, and they needed the skin. Yolaina also needed to try to stop Halai Auna from accusing him of being able to kill nothing but rabbits and sheep when she gave orders. He had visions of eventually double packing the entire bear, except for its large bones and entrails, back to their camp. He wanted to see Halai Auna's face when he brought home a bear about three times his size. He wondered how she would react, but he realized she would somehow make light of his kill. Yolaina watched a bright, white, and orange-tipped butterfly, and saw a hawk in an overhead updraft.

He thought about how the canyon had changed so much. No more grizzly bears were alive, and condors had long since disappeared. The elk and antelope were gone, and he had seen no mountain sheep for a long time, either. The lightning sticks and over abundance of cows and white men destroyed them all. Even the gray wolves had disappeared. He thought about the new loud demon that a white man rode on when encroaching between the canyons. A few flies sometimes buzzed around him, but Yolaina sat patiently and waited.

When he finally had to urinate, he stood, untied the leather thong holding up his deerskin loincloth, took two steps away from where he stood, and totally lost his footing. He was sliding and catching his balance and grabbing for his loincloth when the loud pounding through the leaves was fully evident. When he climbed to his feet and reached for his bow, the reddish-colored black bear was charging him from the opening in the brush where its trail led.

The bear was in no mood to do anything but eat him, and Yolaina did not have a clear shot at its heart. He had hoped to shoot it in the side after it entered the clearing, but the bear had other plans. Yolaina drew upon him before it reared to strike with its right paw. Yolaina finally shot and stumbled toward his spear and away from the bear. The bear let out a loud bawling sound and faltered upon the steep slope. Yolaina plunged the spear deep into the side of the bear's throat and watched the bear tear at its chest as it fell completely to the leaf-covered talus and dirt. Yolaina would have stabbed the bear again but it had few breaths left. The arrow was almost hidden from view within its heart region. Yolaina sat naked above the rock, for in the process of falling and shooting the charging bear, he had lost his loincloth. Only then did he realize how close he had come to dying. His heart pounded, and great relief came over him. The bear bawled once more but did not move more than its head. After a few moments, he calmed down and wondered what story he would have to make up about killing the bear, for if he told them the bear charged and almost killed him, they would laugh.

Long ago memories about Dari Jowa and the others killing the large grizzly flooded over him.

When the bear showed no signs of life, Yolaina began the long process of skinning the thick hide from the bear and cutting the meat from its heavy bones. He used a very sharp piece of obsidian from his pouch to cut the hide, and all the while he cut, he was almost shaking with fear and pride that he was lucky in being able to make the proper shot to kill the bear quickly. Generally, a black bear did not charge, and escaping a charging bear's fury was rare. The bear was two-thirds of Yolaina's height at the shoulders and about as long as he was tall. It probably weighed two and one-half times as much as Yolaina, and the creature had used great speed and force when charging. Yolaina noticed the sun in the sky and thought about the work that lay before him. He would have to walk up and down many sections of the talus-ridden, steep slopes to remove the skin and meat, and he knew he would probably fall several times, an unavoidable occurrence. He then would be faced with crossing Salmon Creek, climbing the canyon in a southwesterly direction, descending into Deer Creek Canyon, crossing Deer Creek, and climbing the steep, long grade into Grizzly Bear's Hiding Place. He would not reach home until the following night, but so far the trip had been extremely quick. He was tired from the previous day's journey, and his bones seemed to tell him he was too old to work so hard. He felt his tendons as they stretched in his movements, and he noticed the pain never really left him. Yolaina also felt lonely, for he had no one with whom to talk or to joke. His life had been too solitary to suit his heart. He paused and swatted at the flies, always a burden when one dealt with food in any form, especially butchering. He was very proud, though, just to be alive, and Dari Jowa and Hitchinna would love his story, even if Halai Auna would continue to tease him.

*   *   *

196   The Last Yahi

"This is very good bear meat," said Yolaina to Halai Auna, "even if you were the second best Yahi cook for many years."

"You should not tease your sister about her cooking," said Hitchinna as she ate a cake. "She works too hard already."

"Insulting me is just a natural outcome of being a great hunter of charging bears," said Halai Auna, "but Yolaina was just lucky as usual. He actually was caught away from his bow and lost his pants when the bear charged. How did you lose your pants? I am not fully clear about that point. I wonder, for instance, if you jumped out of them when you saw the bear."

"I had untied the knot so that I could urinate when the talus gave way. I fell and then the bear charged and somewhere in there I lost my loincloth. These are very good cakes, too, Halai Auna, especially after I remove the little specks of dirt."

Dari Jowa drank some water and said, "He was a very large black bear." He looked admiringly at the staked out skin. "Did you wait until the last moment to shoot?"

"Due to the circumstances, I waited until the last half moment," replied Yolaina. He looked at Hitchinna's burned hair and weak movements. She had lived sadly for nearly two years, but she lived and functioned mentally well. She told stories at night to amuse herself and others, and she sang and conversed often. She had become noticeably weakened, however, and Yolaina did not know how long she could continue to sit by herself. Her prolonged illness made Yolaina wish for his death to be quick, a harsh blow to the heart or a quiet sleep that becomes endless. A swallowtail butterfly, brilliantly yellow and black, erratically flew by, and Yolaina continued to eat. "Are you ready to raid the cabin below where Sulfur Creek runs into Deer Creek again, Halai Auna?"

"Will you try the door before you climb through the window?" she asked.

"If we have to use the window, you have to climb through first," said Yolaina. "I am older than you, and you are the youngest and most agile. I think you should have to be the one to climb through first."

"I liked the way you kicked and squirmed, though, and I especially liked the very kind words you said about my cooking. I think maybe you should climb through the window without checking to see if the door will open first."

"A black bear almost kills me, and you can only remember that I was stuck in a window almost two years ago."

"I do have an awfully good memory," she replied and laughed.

"You do, Halai Auna, you do," said Yolaina. He took a long and exaggerated look at his cake, and then said, "I am not sure whether these are of flour or of bugs, pine needles, and dirt. Which of these ingredients did you use the most?"

"As I recall, you said that I was a very good cook and that you enjoyed my cooking very much."

"Maybe you just dropped my cakes in the dirt on purpose because I am just your brother, not worthy of appreciating, even when I risk my life killing a black bear."

"Well, I do appreciate you giving me such a fine skin to lie on in the winter, and this roast is very delicious. I wonder, however, if the bear slipped on the talus and fell on your arrow when you were trying to find your loincloth."

Dari Jowa examined his cake carefully. "Did you drop these in the dirt?" he asked seriously as he squinted.

"No. They are perfectly good cakes, Dari Jowa. You know that. Yolaina has too much fun sitting around the woods when he hunts. He sits and thinks of bad things to say about my cooking."

"I did not get such sore tendons and a bruised body from thinking about bad words to say about your cooking. I got them from carrying meat to my sister."

"That hide reminds me of hunting bears," said Dari Jowa. "A bear can fill a hunter with a full lifetime of thought in just a few moments. I have killed several bears in my life, and never was I charged. You are lucky, Yolaina, very lucky. Now you will not have to remind the cook about what a wonderful hunter you are, and you can say good things about her cooking. Then she will not cook with so many pine needles."

"You should not join in their silly conversation, Dari Jowa," said Hitchinna.

"But I have a pine needle in my mouth," he said and removed the needle. "See."

"That was supposed to be Yolaina's cake," said Halai Auna.

"I thought you two were teasing," said Hitchinna with a large smile. "Well, Halai Auna, they will be able to mention your ability to prepare pine needles and dirt for some time."

"Next time, Dari Jowa, you will not grab the large, delicious looking cake closest to Yolaina," said Halai Auna.

"Seriously, though, Halai Auna, once I spit out the bugs, dirt, pine needles, leaves, grass, bark, twigs, and small bits of pine cones, I enjoy the taste of your cakes, and if you try very hard, maybe you will again become best Yahi cook. Until then, however, I will have to be the best cook," said Yolaina.

"I am starting to agree with Yolaina," said Dari Jowa, "and since I am chief, I must pronounce that Yolaina's cakes are now much superior to yours. Not only does he slay charging black bears, but he also cooks cakes with much less dirt in them than you do."

"I am sad I do not have any more blood time," said Halai Auna, "because if I did, I could exchange dinners with you Dari Jowa. Then you would not be so tempted to declare me to be the second best Yahi cook. After all, a man like Yolaina, Bravest Man, slayer of a charging bear, was often too busy thinking of his next kill to worry very much about the cakes he always accidentally dropped in the dirt on his way to the bear's den. Some of his cakes were so hard I had to hide them and to eat strips of a rabbit skin to stay alive."

"Those events only occurred a few times," replied Yolaina. "After you stopped giving me so many orders and after I could think clearly, I learned to cook delicious meals."

"Too bad you did not serve them to me," replied Halai Auna. "I often noticed that Hitchinna's cakes, for instance, were not coated with powdery dirt."

"I blew your cakes off as best I could," replied Yolaina, "and I only dropped them once."

"That is true," replied Halai Auna. "Each time you made a batch you only dropped some of them once, and I, for some reason, always got those cakes."

"Those were just occasional accidents," said Yolaina, "and besides, you needed to experience eating the second best Yahi cook's food for a while. Now, however, I am clearly the best cook."

*   *   *

Yolaina and Halai Auna sat very still in the shade of a black oak tree and behind a clump of white-blossomed buck brush. They could barely see south across Deer Creek where the cabin sat at the edge of the small meadow and at the base of where the canyon rose steeply into the bluffs. They had been there, whispering occasionally, for some time, and they expected the white men camped in the meadow to leave food for them to steal, as the saltu did on a semi-regular basis. Their quiet conversations could not be heard above the white water of Deer Creek. They did not wish to alarm the abundant amount of nesting birds in the forest, however, because they wished to make a daylight raid as soon as the white men had been gone for a safe amount of time. Halai Auna sat on a grassy spot with yellow, purple, and white flowers among the grass, and she wore her tasseled buckskin skirt and her patched white-man's hat. Yolaina wore his loincloth and did not have his bow or arrows. They carried seed sacks to store eatables smaller than the sacks of seeds and flour. The men slowly loaded their horses, urinated a couple of times, drank a brown liquid from an awful tasting substance sometimes left in the cabins, and eventually rode out of camp with their unloaded donkey in tow. In the cabin were sundry items: flour, seeds, salted meats, salt, and maybe something sweet smelling or tasting. The cabins were often filled with surprises, but mostly they were filled with food. The food stored in metal containers was wet, heavy, and like mucous, and no Yahi liked it. The dried foods, however, were always light, easily stolen, well packaged in fine cloth, and easily stored at Grizzly Bear's Hiding Place. After the men had been gone a safe amount of time, Yolaina and Halai Auna waded across the swift, swollen creek, drank from the stream, and marched across the meadow and to the cabin.

"Would you care to try the window before we walk in the door?" asked Yolaina.

"No, but you go ahead. I like to see you climb in windows," said Halai Auna as she opened the door. Before her were two good loads of food. She instantly began filling her sack with dried meat and seasonings, and when finished collecting about half of the goods, she lifted the heavy seed sack onto her back.

Yolaina examined some bottles and had not filled his sack.

"You better hurry before those sneaky white men catch us," she said and tried to open the door. She turned the knob and pulled on the door, but the knob came loose from the door. "They play tricks on us," she said as she set down her bag and knocked off her hat.

"I must take all of the bottles," said Yolaina. "My trip will be heavy." He loaded in his half of the meat.

"I cannot open the door," said Halai Auna as she tried to attach the knob and stared at its complex parts. "You better help me, and you should hurry, also. You can stare at your thievery later."

Yolaina set down his sack, and looked at the various angles of the knob's mechanisms, but he could not determine in which way it could attach to the door, since the door had only a hole in it, and since the knob had only a hole in it, and since the cabin was relatively dark compared to the bright sunshine. He placed the handle over the hole to no avail and said, "Something is missing. We cannot fix this."

"We better try the window," said Halai Auna. "I will go first, and you can hand me the food. Then you can follow."

"You are trying to trick me," said Yolaina.

"No. You must hurry and open the window," she replied. "We cannot stay in here and be idle. We must go quickly, and you must not get stuck this time, either."

Yolaina pushed with difficulty on the window, and it opened haltingly. However, he was sure Halai Auna was playing a trick. "I will go first, and you can go second," he replied.

"Okay. You go first, but go now, before we are caught," she replied.

Yolaina thought about what she said, and then replied, "No. You better go first, Halai Auna. That will be safest for you."

"Thanks," she replied and began climbing out the window.

"Wait," said Yolaina as he grabbed her skirt and held her from jumping farther in the window. "If you get outside with all the food, you will leave me stuck in the window or will make me tell lies about the taste of your pine needles."

"Okay then, you go," she said and stood back.

Yolaina hesitated but finally decided he would go first, and just as he got ready to jump fully into the window, he saw a white man run the short distance of an opening under the bluffs above the cabin. The man, of course, had a lightning stick, and he was certainly trying to catch them. "A white man," he said and removed his hands from the window's opening as it slammed loudly shut. He ran to the door and struck it with his palm; the door slammed against its jamb and lazily opened. Yolaina picked up his two sacks and ran out the door, across the meadow, and into the cold, murky-green, spring run off. He looked back, and Halai Auna's hat flew from her head as she adjusted the seed sack on her shoulder and ran at the same time from the meadow and onto the boulders at the river's edge. They waded as well as they could in the waist-deep water, and the weight of the sacks helped to steady them in the current. Once they reached the other side, they scurried out of view as far as they could downstream in the shallow shoreline.

At that point Yolaina felt a little assured of safety. White men did not cross swollen streams because they were afraid the water might clean them, and further, they only liked to track Yahi with dogs. He also felt the white man was too entrenched in the brush and trees of the descent to have seen them leave. Yolaina knew, however, that their escape had been narrow, and that in the future, they would have be even more observant than they had been that day. The white men would be sure to think of some maneuver or trick to try to kill Yolaina and Halai Auna.

"I see you lost your hat," said Yolaina after he caught his breath. Halai Auna was sitting next to him.

"I know," said Halai Auna.

"Now they have proof we are alive," he said.

"They did not need proof. They have known for some time," she replied.

"White men are not quite clever enough to catch us," he said. "They try to be sneaky, and I enjoy watching them, the way they ride their horses to their cabins and leave their food for us. When they ride away and think we would rather starve to death than to eat their food, I am amazed, however. They must not be too smart. Maybe that is why they ride horses after cows. Perhaps white men think cows are smart and worthwhile as company. Perhaps they have conversations about the stars at the sky and the colored bows in the clouds."

"We were just lucky not to have been caught," said Halai Auna. "He would have killed us." She paused. "I miss my hat. I had it for a long time, and I had sewn the deerskin to it so beautifully. Even you liked my hat," she said. "The sun could not reach my eyes when I wore it."

"Maybe we will be able to steal another one some day," Yolaina replied.

"I hope we do not get caught again," said Halai Auna. "I think facing a lightning stick once is plenty in a lifetime," she said. "We should go so that I can make you a new batch of cakes. I want to prove I am the second best Yahi cook." She stood and gathered her sacks from the river boulder.

"Maybe you should try to be the best Yahi cook once more," replied Yolaina. "I liked your cooking better when you were the best cook."

"Then you think I was the best cook for a while?"

"Yes," he said. "For a while when I accidentally dropped my cakes in the dirt, you were the best cook. Now, however, all you cook and set before me seems to have something wrong with it. I might even snare you a nice wildcat skin if you were the best cook again, though."

"Okay," she replied, "but when you no longer find pine needles in your cakes, you better remind me what a good cook I am."

CHAPTER 13

Alone

Yolaina stood quietly on a large boulder of basalt at the edge of Deer Creek below Grizzly Bear's Hiding Place, and comfortably in his hands was his long salmon spear, its toggles poised for jabbing a large salmon. The days were becoming short, and the black oaks had lost their leaves. The evening was still and warm, and even though naked, he was not cold. Autumn was a good time for their tiny band, for they then had plenty of dried salmon and acorns. They did not have to make the increasingly risky raids for food. Yolaina did not have long to fish as the sky turned into pink, orange, and lavender, but he was quite content as he thought and watched for a fish. He had enjoyed Halai Auna's cooking that evening: acorn mush and fresh salmon. He was happy they no longer raided very much because he knew that the white men could only be pushed so far before they tried to kill the Yahi. The water was clear, and colors rippled off the surface of the current that ran through the pool. He thought about Hitchinna, how her leg was covered with sores. The deerskin wrappings seemed to do no good for her. She had gained about half of the use of her paralyzed limbs, but she had trouble sitting. Dari Jowa was so crippled that he could not hunt. Still, however, they lived pretty well. Their filled baskets made their immediate future secure. The saltu's tools he had stolen from the cabins were very useful and saved him much time. The metal tools made working with wood, always difficult, a bit easier. He, for instance, had three bows and many arrows, and the saws, files, knives, axes, and other curious objects made his bows jump into their forms. He missed their annual trip to the high country around Wahkanopa, for there they had always enjoyed the vibrantly green meadows and cool air. There the venison was almost dried and in baskets when they arrived. He thought about the seven white men he had seen camped near the mouth of Sulfur Creek, and wondered about their presence. They had tools they looked through, and were a mixed bunch in that some did not ride behind cows and were unknown to him. Halai Auna had watched them more recently than Yolaina had, and she said they were camped farther downstream and on the northern side of Deer Creek. Yolaina began thinking of hunting a deer in the near future when from downstream, two white men appeared from around a bush near the water.

Yolaina's heart pounded, and he was instantly angry. They stood a bit shocked and had gaping mouths, and Yolaina snarled loudly at them. He brandished his fishing spear at them, a motion to give them clear directions. They did not wear lightning sticks, and, of course, they were completely clothed. Yolaina felt insulted in their presence, for he wore only the leather thongs in his septum and ears and tied abound his long, black hair in the back. The men darted into the waist-deep end of the pool where Yolaina fished, and he kept motioning for them to leave with his spear. He repeatedly and angrily said, "Go away," and they left hurriedly, especially when they reached the old Yahi trail on the other side of the stream.

Yolaina stood in amazement on the rock as he watched them run. His heart filled with a sickening fear, for now the saltu knew his favorite fishing hole and the exact spot which led to Grizzly Bear's Hiding Place. They did not know exactly where the Yahi lived, but they might, or probably would, try to find the shelters soon. Yolaina jumped off the boulder and into the water of the shoreline. He examined the shore closely for tracks, saw none, and walked a little further to be sure he would not leave any tracks. He climbed on rocks until the brush thickened, and then he crawled with his spear back to the main trail leading to their camp. When he finally reached the ledge, he walked by their reservoir used to hold snow in the winter, and he placed his spear next to their storage house. He then walked back by the large foothill pine and bay tree, between the smokehouse and cookhouse, and to the front of their family house over the grizzly bear's den. There sat Halai Auna sewing an old moccasin for the rapidly approaching winter, Dari Jowa chanting, "Wino-tay," and Hitchinna watching the evening star. Yolaina sat and paused. He looked at his mother, almost immobile, and Dari Jowa, who walked with a limp, and realized how tragic their situation would truly become if the white men discovered their camp. Hitchinna still wore her hair burned from her head, and some of the sores on her leg were open and an obvious discomfort.

"I see you did not spear a fish and that you have come home early," said Halai Auna. "Do you think the fish will grow legs and walk up the trail?"

"I have very bad news," said Yolaina.

Dari Jowa stopped singing "Wino-tay" and asked, "What news?"

"Two white men from the encampment upstream discovered me as I fished from the rock. I snarled at them and told them to go away. I brandished my fishing spear, and they crossed the creek and ran toward their camp on the old trail."

"How come they did not shoot you?" asked Hitchinna.

"They did not have lightning sticks. They were not the ones who chase cows and supply the cabins."

"Could you smell them?" asked Dari Jowa.

"The wind was not right," said Yolaina.

"What were they doing?" asked Halai Auna.

"They were just walking," said Yolaina. "They looked as if they were very frightened or startled, just as I was. I, however, did not try to escape toward our camp, and I gave them no clue about where we live. I fear they will search for us, though. On the way up the trail, I realized how desperate our situation could become. We cannot move. You, Hitchinna, are in no condition to travel and to suffer the burdens of winter and making a new home. Neither are you, Dari Jowa. We would have to travel to upper Deer Creek, and we would need a real winter's shelter. The caves would not be good enough. The weather could catch us totally unprepared and destroy our belongings and cause us too much grief. We will probably have to wait quietly and hope the white men will not search in the brush this far up the canyon's incline above the stream."

"We are in a good spot, Yolaina," said Dari Jowa. "As I listen to you, I think we are still safe. The white men do not know exactly where we are, and they have no dogs. You said that they had no dogs, at least."

"They would have to walk directly into camp to see us," said Halai Auna.

"I will rise early tomorrow morning and cover any possible footprints we might have left on our trail."

"We should bathe, though," said Dari Jowa. "We must not let them smell us, and we will need to get water for the entire day."

"What will we do if they catch us?" asked Hitchinna. "I do not wish to move anymore. White men frighten me very much, but I can no longer travel. I wish only to remain quietly in camp, where they would have to walk directly to find me. They could come very close and still not see that we live here, and we could sit as does a spotted fawn among the tall pines or as does a lizard in the shade of boulders. My only hope is that they do not discover our camp."

No one replied, and after a while Halai Auna spoke.

"How old were they?"

"They were much younger than I am, but they did not look any younger than I do," said Yolaina.

"I forgot that since you have become the hunter of a charging black bear, your wrinkles went away," said Halai Auna.

"Your eyes have just become crossed from weaving too many beautiful baskets, and you no longer see that I still look handsome and young. Only Dari Jowa is beginning to show his age, but not a day over thirty-seven."

"I wish I still had my beads," said Hitchinna, "but I think Dari Jowa threw them away when I told him he was over sixty and that was long ago before...well...long ago."

"I think you like looking at men too much, Halai Auna. You worry too much about how they look, and not enough about what those two young men will say in their camp to the men who often chase cows. I think maybe we are in serious trouble, and all we can do is wait patiently like a still night."

Yolaina stood, walked to the family house, crouched down, entered, and took his wildcat and raccoon-skin cape from his place next to Dari Jowa's spot. He placed the cape over his shoulders and followed the trail by the brush between the cookhouse and smokehouse, and from the bay tree he walked through the brush to the loose rock pile. He stood and watched the stars beginning to take charge of the blackening sky. Faint remnants of rose-colored clouds still hung over the cliffs on the canyon's north slope. Many times he wondered why he was so helplessly stuck in such a futile effort to be last of the human race. All humans wanted to live and regretted perhaps that they aged and died, but to die and have all the humans die also seemed the cruelest of realities. He wished to be able to throw stones at white men until they were crushed and all their buildings were destroyed forever, but when he had those feelings, he relaxed and tried not to let evil consume him. Sometimes the thought of never having a loved one still cursed him, even though his youth had long since vanished, but he enjoyed the jokes Dari Jowa told of Ututni, Wood Duck Man, lover of many women, even if they lived near the land of smoking demons and horseless wagons and long lines hanging from denuded tree trunks. The stories were still very good, and often they laughed together before sleeping. The wind blew his long hair over his left shoulder, and he calmly watched the forest of brush darken. He wondered what life would have been like if he could have had children able to live freely in the mounds of Tcapalauna, able to laugh and grow and think their father was worthy of great respect. Large tears filled his eyes. He did not know why, but sometimes he sat quietly and let his eyes fill. In the distance Dari Jowa began singing, "Wino-tay," but still no one answered.

*　　　　　*　　　　　*

With the first gray light of dawn, Yolaina, Dari Jowa, and Halai Auna hurried to Deer Creek. They bathed, filled water baskets and a canteen, and scrambled back to their village. They ate acorn cakes made the previous day and some dried salmon. Halai Auna used a folded seed sack to bathe Hitchinna, and Yolaina carried his mother to the village toilet where with his aid she could still function properly. After Yolaina placed Hitchinna back on her spot in the family house, he rinsed his mouth and rubbed his teeth with his finger. He then removed his best bow of mountain juniper and his most well-equipped otter-skin quiver, which included a fire drill and board, an arrow making pouch, and ten arrows. He wore an old, brown, white man's shirt for warmth, and he walked back into the brush to wave a branch over their trail and to scout for lurking white men.

After Yolaina thoroughly brushed signs of their existence from their trail, he walked and crawled as best he could in a descending, easterly direction and finally chose a spot where he had a very limited view of a potential path in the brush that a white man might use and where he

could see much of the other side of the bank and canyon, in case the
white men would try to go west before sneaking across the stream to the
southern slope. He hoped they would not come, but he feared their
actions would be for the worst. He sat quietly and wondered exactly
what he should do if the white men did come. Maybe he should actually
shoot them since they obviously would try to kill him, Halai Auna,
Hitchinna, and Dari Jowa. If the saltu carried lightning sticks and were
determined to keep snooping in the brush, however, no good would
come from shooting them, only evil. *Perhaps*, Yolaina continued thinking, *I will shoot an arrow past them, and they will scurry away like their
Lizard Man.* He knew, though, at that point the white men would keep
coming, and Grizzly Bear's Hiding Place would no longer be safe. They
would have to move if they could then escape the men. He thought
about where they would move, but the alternatives were bleak. They
would need a shelter first, for Hitchinna could not be exposed to the
elements anymore than she was. When the furious wind had blown
their shelters and lightning had lit up the sky, Yolaina had been amazed
his frail mother had kept existing. She was just too weakened, and she
needed the warmth of a fire and skins and the dryness of the den.

The morning was beautifully blue, and birds chirped wildly. Ducks
and geese flew overhead, and a small spotted hawk soared in the
updrafts. Yolaina knew he should be hunting for their evening meal or
trying to spear a salmon, but the ever present fear of white men meant a
depletion in their food reserves that they could little afford. Very smelly
ants occasionally crawled on Yolaina, and he picked them off and
flicked them away. They stunk worse than a skunk, and Yolaina was glad
they were no bigger than they were. When Yolaina began to become
hopeful that the white men would not seek them in the brush, he spotted two of them in the early morning's sun crossing the stream. Both of
them were men who chased cows and kept food in the cabins. They
were camped with the others who looked through funny metal instruments and hung weights from lines. Yolaina knew the men by sight

quite well. One of them gesticulated wildly like a wounded bird all the time, and one looked carefully about the stream's bank before they headed up the hill and toward the most likely path in front of Yolaina. Yolaina removed an arrow of buzzard feathers and witch hazel and green glass and pitch and sinew and salmon-skin glue from his otter-skin quiver. He held his bow in his left hand and placed his arrow into position. He was almost stupefied that his alternatives were so limited that the most intelligent action he could take would be to shoot an arrow past two white men who carried lightning sticks on their sides. He could not think of another course of action, however. The men would keep coming, and he would have to watch them or kill them. No matter what he did, however, they would probably discover Grizzly Bear's Hiding Place.

When Yolaina heard one man talking above the noise of the wind and water, and when the brush moved near the small opening in the brush, Yolaina crouched to his right knee and balanced with his left foot. The big finger of his right hand was in place over the sinew string, and two fingers held the notch of the arrow in place as it rested in the fingers of his left hand holding the bow. As he had predicted, the white men appeared on the path. Yolaina lifted his bow, drew the string, aimed, and loosed the arrow. He watched it carefully and held his position, letting the string quiver and bow fall forward gently in his grip. His arrow missed the head of the white man who did the least talking and the most snooping by less than an hand's length, and man jumped back into his companion still talking in the brush. Both of them tumbled; at least they appeared to have fallen. Yolaina listened to their loud noise and wondered why white men were always so obvious and noisy. If it were not for pure chance, they would not have discovered him fishing. Yolaina strung another arrow, for he remembered how slowly Lizard Man had reacted to arrows flying by his body. The men began scraping back through the brush in a while, however, and Yolaina sat very still and watched. After the white men left, he searched for his arrow, but then decided to find it at a later date when or if the white men left his section of the brushy canyon.

Yolaina crawled and walked as best he could back to Grizzly Bear's Hiding Place. He had become used to crawling in the brush, but still the thorny buck brush was annoying when it scraped his skin and tore at his shirt. In camp Hitchinna was still inside their home, and Dari Jowa and Halai Auna sat in the cool air and were wrapped in rabbit-skin blankets.

"What is the news?" asked Dari Jowa. "Did you frighten the white men so badly with your fishing spear last night that they have hopped away like squirrels to nest in the valley?"

"No," replied Yolaina. "Two of the men who chase cows were trying to find our tracks in the brush and were climbing the slope toward us. I shot an arrow by one of them, and they left, a bit as a cow would, very noisily."

"Do you think they will come back?" asked Hitchinna from her furs and white man's sacks.

"I do not know," said Yolaina, "but now they know a Yahi was in the brush above where they saw me fishing. I can only imagine they will return."

"I will not move unless I have to," said Hitchinna. "I am too old."

"We will wait," said Dari Jowa. "Perhaps they have had enough. Maybe they understand that you could easily kill them, and they will not take the chance."

"I did not kill them, though, and they do not seem to fear us enough," replied Yolaina.

Dari Jowa stared at him. "We will wait patiently. They do not know we live here. They only have proof that one Yahi was nearby, and he was hunting and fishing."

"Yolaina was fishing late at night and without skins in the autumn," replied Halai Auna. "That means he was close to camp. The arrow only confirmed that we live nearby."

"Well," said Hitchinna from the den, "I am still not moving, for I am too old. I like the idea of hiding. Those white men might not search all of this brushy hillside, and our brush-covered shelters look just like manzanita and buck brush and toyon. Maybe we can hide and still live here. Hiding is still my only hope."

"If they get close to camp and wear lightning sticks," replied Yolaina, "I do not think I will be able to do anything except wait in the brush with a poised arrow. I would be foolish to kill a couple of them, for certainly they would exact a horrible, quick revenge."

"I can hide as well here as in the brush," said Hitchinna. "The brush is not better than this den."

"Unless they walk into camp," said Halai Auna, "I have no intention of moving either. We have no place to move. The nearest good camp on upper Deer Creek, which already sounds cold, is a three-day journey for us and our belongings. Poor Hitchinna would have to be carried the entire way."

"Do you have any manzanita berry water made?" asked Yolaina.

"Yes. In the basket by the door," replied Halai Auna.

Yolaina stood, drank from the tightly woven basket with the gyrating squares around its circumference, and set the basket down. "I will climb onto the rock pile and observe from there," said Yolaina. "We will wait to see what future this morning brings us." He picked up his bow and quiver, and walked through the village and brush to the rock pile. There he found a comfortable looking stone among the jagged shapes and watched for white men. When he was seated, however, he saw the seven white men wading across Deer Creek toward the southern slope and Grizzly Bear's Hiding Place. They carried their strange instruments and metal axes and lightning sticks on their sides. He set down his bow and quiver and hurried back to camp.

"They cross Deer Creek in strength," he told the others as they watched him.

"Too bad we are not all young braves," said Dari Jowa. "We could shoot them, steal their lightning sticks, burn their homes, kill their women, poison their dogs, and eat their food."

"In the meantime, we will have to wait," said Yolaina as he left for the rocks again. "Be prepared to run." The words hurt Yolaina after he said them, for his poor mother lay in such a pitiful state.

*   *   *

Crouching below the rock pile and by the brush, Yolaina could readily hear the white men talking and cutting the brush with axes in the morning's sun. Their actions made no sense, but such logic often applied to white men. Halai Auna and Dari Jowa sat quietly in front of the den, and Hitchinna had readied skins and seed sacks to put over her in case the white men entered camp. The white men were obviously not searching for them as a hunter would, or they were the most stupid of men. Even Yolaina did not believe the men were so stupid. They were heading toward the west, and if they reached the trail, Yolaina was not sure if they would spot Grizzly Bear's Hiding Place. He would not bet any beads on the outcome of the Yahi's immediate future, and as they neared the trail, Yolaina backed into the brush below the rock pile and took with him his bow and quiver. He could no longer see, but what he heard made him sick. The white men were obviously walking around Grizzly Bear's Hiding Place, for they had entirely stopped chopping. Their voices came from the flat by the den. Halai Auna and Dari Jowa made the rocks slide above where Yolaina had been sitting.

Hitchinna covered herself in back of the den with many skins and seed sacks, and lay as quietly as she could. The thought of being left alone among the white men filled her with tremendous fear and grief, and when she was fully covered, she shook, listened to footsteps and white men talking, and thought of how Halai Auna had helped Dari Jowa escape toward the cliffs in the east. When at last the men entered the family house, they began hauling all of their belongings outside: skins, blankets, bows, arrows, quivers, toggles, jute, rope, a deer snare, a deer-head's decoy stuffed with dried grass, moccasins, white man's clothes, and seed sacks. When two men uncovered Hitchinna, she shook uncontrollably, and seemed unable to move at all. They picked her up by the arms as she cringed, and they set her outside in front of the family house. The seven of them wore lightning sticks and leather over their fine pants to protect them from the brush. Hitchinna lay shaking, naked except for the strips of deer hide wrapped around her paralyzed, sore-ridden leg. The men stood about her talking. They scratched their heads and wiped their brows and talked some more. When a man who rode behind cows bent down near her, Hitchinna spoke the white man's for wanting water, and she pointed at the nearby canteen Yolaina had stolen from a white man's cabin. He understood, opened the canteen, propped her up, and helped her drink, even though Hitchinna still trembled tremendously. The man looked at her leg, pointed, and said some white man's words that Hitchinna had learned from Periwiri Yupa, "*Mui Malo?*" Hitchinna was shocked at his comprehension, but she repeated what he said while nodding her head, "*Malo. Malo.*" The men continued searching the entire village until they removed the cooking stones, baskets, fire drill and hearth, paddles, stirrers, and pounding rocks from the cookhouse, and all the acorns and dried salmon from the storage house, and Yolaina's fishing spear and saws and files and knives and tools from the various houses. They looked at the village toilet and examined where Yolaina had sat in the brush to chip glass points. Some began to leave with the Yahi's belongings, and then a discussion began about Hitchinna. As she continued to tremble below them in the dirt, they pointed at her and talked some. Then the man who had given her water searched his pockets and looked almost sympathetically at Hitchinna. After the discussion one urinated on their storage house, and they all left, most with full arms of everything Hitchinna, Yolaina, Dari Jowa, and Halai Auna owned.

When the men were out of hearing and the canyon again became quiet, Yolaina heard Hitchinna call him as he crawled from the brush with his bow and quiver. When he reached base of the rocks, he stood and hurried to where Hitchinna lay trying to prop herself up.

"I have urinated where I lie," she said. "Help me to the shade."

"Oh, mother, what have they done?" Yolaina placed Hitchinna in the shade and held her hand as they talked.

"They have taken all of our belongings, Yolaina, everything, including the seed sacks. You said they discarded their seed sacks."

"They do," he said. "Did they take all of our food?"

"Yes," she replied.

"No," Yolaina said while standing. He walked to the storage house and saw only the earth beneath the branches and canvas. He looked in the family house and saw only dirt where skins had lain. All of his tools and bows and arrows and quivers were gone. He did not even have a fishing spear. The horror of facing the coming night without skins and shelter was too real for his imagination.

"Did Dari Jowa and Halai Auna leave toward the cliffs above the rocks?"

"I think so," said Hitchinna. "I saw them leave in that direction."

"Good," said Yolaina. "We are in very bad trouble. I do not know if we can survive with so few possessions. I have only one bow, nine arrows, an arrow making pouch, and a fire drill and hearth. We will have to go toward upper Deer Creek. Halai Auna and Dari Jowa will probably try to reach the cave from where I hunt. I have a bearskin there. Did they take anything with them?"

"I think they just sat quietly on a skin until they could only run. They were mostly naked and with no possessions," replied Hitchinna.

"We must try to find them. Our night will be cold, and it will take two nights to reach the cave. The journey takes most of a day when I have no weight or responsibilities."

"I will not be able to live long, Yolaina. Maybe you should just leave me here."

"Do not talk that way," said Yolaina, almost shocked.

"I am too old for such a journey," she replied.

"If you can sit in the shade and talk about your age, you can rest on my back and tell me to walk carefully and to stop scratching your legs on the brush." He propped his quiver and bow against the pepperwood tree, picked up his mother, and carried her out of camp and over the jagged rock piles toward the direction of the cliffs. When he reached the brush where they would have to battle their way to Sulfur Creek, he set Hitchinna in the shade. "Remain here awhile. I will brush our tracks and get my bow and quiver. I do not wish to be tracked or found again."

"You are not strong enough to carry me such a distance. You are too old, also," said Hitchinna.

Yolaina knew his mother was speaking the truth, for already he was breathing with difficulty. His arms ached, and they had barely begun. "Ah…," he said, "you should not speak that way to a hunter of a charging black bear. You do not want me to lose confidence and to cower just because I have a little weight to carry and have no food or skins, do you?"

"No, but I am just old Wildcat Woman, and you are only Bravest Man. You do not understand how hard your task will be," Hitchinna replied. "You walked like Dari Jowa for two days after you returned from killing that black bear."

"My heart is so young, though, and I am so handsome that I feel I can do anything. You stay. I will be right back." He gathered from the ground a dry branch with leaves still attached to it. He walked back to camp, removed the canvas from their home, folded it, unstrung his bow and placed it in his quiver, held the canvas and quiver in his left arm, and brushed lightly using mostly air to destroy all of their tracks as he backed out of camp and to the rocks. From there he tossed the branch into the brush, and walked to Hitchinna. He placed the canvas and quiver on a high rock, and lifted Hitchinna to her feet where he supported her until she crawled onto his back when he kneeled. Yolaina

stood, picked up the canvas and quiver, and began the arduous task of
carrying Hitchinna all day through the brush. He hoped to reach Sulfur
Creek by sundown, or perhaps earlier, and he hoped Dari Jowa and
Halai Auna would wait for him there. They could have decided, however, to travel to Deer Creek first and to ascend into upper Deer Creek
on the northern slope of the canyon. He did not know, but he did know
that Dari Jowa and Halai Auna would be in serious trouble if he were
not there to build a fire and to hunt. They had no weapons or tools; they
had no food or clothing.

"I should not feel so downhearted," said Hitchinna. "After all, I carried you through this brush before."

"Well, we are poorer than I ever thought we would be," said Yolaina
between breaths, "but I always hoped to have a big house with many
magical baskets that never emptied and to have at least twenty or thirty
wives in my life." He breathed heavily and stumbled with difficulty over
the rocks and through brush. He knew the scraping brush must be
causing Hitchinna a lot of pain, but she did not complain. He almost
began to cry, and then remembered he should save his energy for the
heavy haul to Sulfur Creek.

       *   *   *

Yolaina laid his mother propped against a boulder in the deep shade
of the setting sun. Sulfur Creek bubbled just above him where the water
cascaded into the pool. He took off his shirt, laid it next to his quiver
and canvas on the trail, waded into the pool, and drank deeply. Then he
cupped his hands together, collected water for his mother, and walked
to her side. Most of the water was wasted, and he made twelve trips
transporting water into his mother's cupped hands. Her leg was bleeding in several places, but then again, so was he. During the day's toil
through the brush, Yolaina had shoved against thousands of thorns and
still, jagged branches. Yolaina dried his hands on the front of his shirt,

and went to gather pine needles, pitch, and small branches for their fire, and after several trips he had enough. After clearing the dead debris from the area of his proposed fire, he placed his hearth, tinder, and drilling stick in place to begin the required, steady, hard work, and Yolaina wondered if he had the strength. Yolaina pressed his palms tightly on his smooth, dry stick, and twirled it back and forth until his hands reached its bottom. He repeated the process until he obviously was taking too long and did not have enough strength without resting. He stopped.

"I must stop thinking of lost Yahi women so much," he said to Hitchinna. "I cannot concentrate on my fire."

"You are very tired, Yolaina," replied Hitchinna. "I did not think we could make it to Sulfur Creek, but here we are. All of you Yahi men have always been too strong for your own good."

"Once more," replied Yolaina, and again he began arduously turning his drill back and forth. The fire hearth finally blackened and smoked in the notch above its hole, and the finely shredded inner bark of the willow ignited. Yolaina quickly stopped drilling, leaned over, and added a pine needle to the very tiny flame, and the needle ignited long enough to ignite others. When the fire was finally secured and coals were in place and wood was piled high enough for the entire night, Yolaina drank deeply again. He also gave Hitchinna another long drink by walking back and forth to the stream. He put his shirt on Hitchinna backwards so that the dry side would be on her back and wet side would face the flames, and he wrapped the canvas over her shoulders.

"I am tired," said Hitchinna. "I did not get my old woman's nap today. Every time I closed my eyes, my son poked me with a sharp stick."

Yolaina sat beside her, added a few small sticks to the flame, and watched his poor mother a moment. "I will gather some watercress from below. Some acorns are still good, also, and tomorow I will get us a metal container discarded at a camp below us. We can use it for water. Tonight, though, I will hike above us to hunt a raccoon. I have had good

luck here hunting a raccoon that was washing food. I will miss my raccoon and wildcat skin cape tonight. Will you be okay? Do you need
more water?"

"No, my son, I am okay. If you can do all you say, I might even have
enough strength to throw small branches on the fire until you return. You
go. Maybe Halai Auna and Dari Jowa are camped on the stream, also."

"No. This is where I stay when traveling, and Halai Auna knows this
spot. I am shocked they are not here. They must have decided it was too
far to go without water and have gone to a spot on Deer Creek first.
Surely they will come, though. Halai Auna knows I must be heading to
my bearskin and hunting cave in the great gorge. We have no other
choice, but I must get us some greens, at least, and quickly." He added a
few sticks to the fire and walked as best he could over the little flat and
down the steep, slippery embankment. He soon bent over his favorite
patch of watercress and pinched two large handfuls from the muck of
the wet soil near the stream, and then he scampered back up the hill to
Hitchinna. After washing the rocks and pine needles and leaves from
the long, stringy, white roots and leaves of the watercress, Yolaina
walked back to Hitchinna, and they ate the spicy plants together in front
of the fire.

"I can taste a raccoon," said Yolaina. "I have not hunted one here in
over a year, and I bet a big, fat raccoon is slipping about gathering his
food. They eat everything: rabbits, birds, frogs, fish, acorns, berries, and
bugs. I can see one in my mind washing his food as my arrow slides
through his heart."

"Then we would have one skin also, enough to warm one foot in a
few days," she said and laughed. "You have done a very good job taking
care of me, Yolaina. I wonder how you found the strength to carry me
so far."

"I wish I were more tired than hungry. I am very worried about Halai
Auna and Dari Jowa, for they will need a meal very soon. I do not think
Halai Auna can build a fire without a well-made drill and hearth," said

Yolaina between chewing his watercress and tending the fire. "Maybe she could, though. Without food from my hunting, they will not be able to survive long, but the weather is temporarily in our favor." He finished chewing his watercress, stood, and removed his bow from his quiver. After stringing his bow, he removed two arrows and said, "I hope I will not be gone long, but I am certain a large raccoon of at least five black rings will soon be at the water's edge."

"You go. I will watch the fire until I can no longer stay awake. I will sing very quietly to myself for an early supper; maybe I have magic because I am so old."

"I go," replied Yolaina as he walked to the edge of the water. Far up the canyon he would come to a small waterfall with boulders on both sides, and on the far shore of the pool above the fall, a pleasant, sandy shore lay at the end of a path beneath some manzanita. Not far away a large, old, partly hollow oak tree was the raccoon's den. Yolaina would cautiously walk into the wind and wait behind the boulders until the raccoon appeared from the darkness and became somewhat silhouetted in front of the lapping shoreline, and if Yolaina had to wait there a long time, the moon would help him. A big raccoon would feed them well, and allow him to travel, to hunt, and to search for Halai Auna and Dari Jowa. Yolaina felt almost guilty that he had misjudged what direction they had taken from Grizzly Bear's Hiding Place. Halai Auna and Dari Jowa could hold each other for warmth and could gather some food, however, and maybe he could find them in the morning. Maybe he could bring them raccoon legs. Yolaina paused a while to see what course he would take in the darkness, for that section of Sulfur Creek was too difficult and deep. He gazed a bit at the stars at the sky, shivered from the cool breeze, and continued as best he could up a deer trail. At last he came to the boulders by the noisy fall. He carefully peeked at the opposite shore, but a raccoon was not in sight. He sat comfortably as he could on the boulders and waited, for a hunter was a man of great patience. A hunter was always hungry. Hunger had a way of giving

Yolaina great patience and much to think about should he decide to feel sorry for himself and not to hunt. Raccoons were smart and very sneaky, and he could not afford to do anything except wait very quietly. He wondered, though, how long he could sit naked in the very chilled air. He decided he could sit there hopefully long enough to keep himself and Hitchinna and Dari Jowa and Halai Auna alive. If he could not find them in the morning, they would be in wretched condition by the following night. Yolaina's fatigue began to bother him immensely. All he could do was sit, stay awake in the cold air, and think of the awful consequences of the day's forced dispersal. All of their lives were in grave danger, actually, even his, for he had but one bow and very few arrows. With winter approaching, he could surely die if his bow broke. He needed to begin a new bow immediately, but he had no time even to gather a branch of mountain juniper. He could only wait and hunt and search. He tried not to think about Hitchinna dying, or Halai Auna and Dari Jowa dying, but the thoughts would not go away. He wondered as he peeked over the rock and through the clump of grass, whether he should have tried to shoot by or to shoot at the white men as they entered camp, but always he felt that not killing was best. One or two wayward arrows would not have scared the men with lightning sticks on their sides away. They simply would have returned in large numbers.

Yolaina became gripped with cold but still waited, and from the trail a darkened shape appeared over the shoreline. Yolaina stepped into a shooting position, drew his bow, and loosed his arrow. He followed its arch across the pool and into the raccoon. The raccoon fell onto its side at the water's edge. At first he thought he might have missed, but the shape was silent. Yolaina set down his bow and remaining arrow on a boulder, and waded across the pool. He heard the raccoon cry, and when he reached it, the raccoon appeared to be lifeless. After removing the arrow, he felt a great relief, for now they could eat. From their world they would live, but still he wondered for how long.

*   *   *

Yolaina headed down the steep canyon with two metal containers found at a camp below where they had slept the night of their dispersal. His mother, Hitchinna, lay resting in the sun near a small, grassy, almost flat area among the brush above him. The previous three days ran swiftly through his mind, and he was anxiously considering the events as they had happened. After the night at Sulfur Creek, Yolaina had searched below them and on the steep northern shoreline of Deer Creek west of Sulfur Creek. He had had no luck in even finding a trace of Halai Auna or Dari Jowa, and he had been forced to return to Hitchinna. That afternoon they had forged their way again to the east but had got only as far as Wildcat Creek. Yolaina had prepared their fire and had cooked the second half of their raccoon. The next day they had reached Smoky Creek in time for Yolaina to hunt two rabbits, and from there they had finally arrived at his bearskin and hunting cave. They had a rabbit left to eat for dinner, three small skins, two containers for water, his quiver and its contents, and the canvas. Both of the arrows he had used to kill the rabbits had broken points. That morning Yolaina had been lucky enough to kill a deer and not damage his arrow. On his mind still weighed the condition of Dari Jowa and Halai Auna. He left plenty of signs about his and Hitchinna's presence, but his lost relatives had not followed him. He hoped they were still alive, but he feared they were dead. Thoughts of them drowning in Deer Creek or dying some other tragic death and being eaten by a mountain lion or black bear disturbed him, and his responsibility to Hitchinna overrode much of what he could do to search for them. He drank from the stream, filled his metal containers, and then sat in the sun awhile. He bent over and stretched the backs of his legs and then lay back in the grass and stared at the late afternoon sun a moment. Thin high clouds blocked the sun a little, and Yolaina thought a storm would enter the canyon soon. One could never tell about the weather, for during the night a clear sky could turn into a thick snow. Yolaina could not decide if he were lucky or unlucky. He lived, and Hitchinna lived. However, Halai Auna and Dari

Jowa were in very serious trouble at best. He could keep Hitchinna dry
and fed, and search for Halai Auna and Dari Jowa little by little. He
could not leave the cave, though, without having a supply of dried food
and water for Hitchinna. He had to build a smokehouse, gather a limb
of mountain juniper from the southern slope of Deer Creek Canyon,
and make arrows. He also had to tan their deer hide and make moccasins and boil bay leaves to extract their oil for water proofing. He had
to gather wood and acorns and greens. He had to bathe his mother and
wash the remainder of the deerskin strips covering the sores on her paralyzed leg, and all he felt like doing was lying peacefully in the sun and
sleeping. He could hardly move; age had crept into his joints and tendons and made him almost immobile. Yolaina thought again of his
work. He closed his eyes a moment and thought about the closest,
straight limbs of buckeye he could use to make arrows, and his day
darkened as his mind surrendered to fatigue.

The sun was not too low in the sky when Yolaina awoke, and he was
grateful. He could not imagine how he had allowed himself to sleep,
and he considered gathering straight branches for arrows so that he
could begin peeling, straightening, drying, and shaping the shafts by
firelight. He knew he should return to Hitchinna, though, for his nap
was all the leisure he could afford. The hide still needed to be scraped,
and he had to begin drying as much of the deer meat as possible. He
took another drink of water, filled the old cans again, and then began
the steep climb up the southern slope of Upper Deer Creek. He
thought of the possible ways in which Halai Auna and Dari Jowa could
still be alive. Possibly Halai Auna had started a fire, and they had
enough acorns and greens and bugs or stolen white man's food to live
for the length of time they had been driven from Grizzly Bear's Hiding
Place. Perhaps they had traveled to an overhang near a feeder stream
on lower Salmon Creek. He stopped a couple of times in his ascent and
noticed the weather again. He felt certain a storm would arrive within
a day or two, and then the day-to-day struggle for survival would be

more difficult than he had ever experienced. A man could not walk in the freezing snow and hunt. He would have to build his and Hitchinna's wealth by very small steps, just as a hunter gradually makes his bows and arrows and decoys and nets and snares. When he remembered his need to gather milkweed in order to weave rope and string for toggles and nets, he came near where Hitchinna lay in the sun.

A coyote scurried into the brush when it heard his quiet footsteps in the leaves, and Yolaina rushed to his mother. The coyote had eaten her left shoulder and breast, and blood trickled upon the ground. Her body was cool and limp, and her life had left entirely. Yolaina dropped to his knees, set down the cans, took Hitchinna in his arms, and cried and cried and cried. He knew his mother had stretched her age until she could live no longer, but he loved her very much. Pain crashed upon heart as would well-chipped hand spears, and the pain seemed to grow as do winter storms before the longest night. Tears flowed from his eyes and onto his mother's short, white hair, and he rocked her back and forth in his arms and gasped for each breath. His nose ran onto his thin, unplucked mustache, and he gasped for air a long time.

When darkness and cold completely surrounded him and his tears ebbed and his heart felt more like a rotted log than nauseating pain, Yolaina lifted his mother in his arms, carried her up the canyon to the canvas in the cave, and laid her down. He put pine needles and small twigs on the morning's coals in the back of the cave and waited there helplessly. The pine needles smoldered and filled the cave with smoke before they ignited and cleared the air. He sat on the deerskin and placed small branches on the leaping, yellow flames. He covered his shoulders with his bearskin and sobbed until he had to step around the poles he had placed over the entrance to the cave in order to blow mucous from his nose. He knew the night would be difficult and long, and sleep would evade him. He dug deeply within his spirit to find solace, but there he found nothing but loneliness and fear and doubt that Halai Auna and Dari Jowa were alive. He thought for a while about what he would do with Hitchinna, and he decided to bury her near the head of the salmon run and by the rock monument, Kachhawi. He would take her there in the morning, burn her that day, and bury her the next morning. Then he would find Dari Jowa and Halai Auna if the storm did not break first. The problems of survival made him cry, for he had too much to do even to find his lost sister and uncle. The cold, merciless night showed few stars, and as he walked back in the cave, all the other horrible deaths he had seen consumed him. His father's death was lost to his youth, but Igupa Topa, Topuna, Hwipajusi, Pakalai Jawichi, Demauna, Chunoyahi, Weanmauna, Tsanunewa, Ketipku, Periwiri Yupa, Wirula, and Wihlaina had died horribly and senselessly. The profound question with an answer lying in the wind came to Yolaina: *Why does only one human live?*

*   *   *

Yolaina did not sleep the entire night after his mother died, and the next morning, he wrapped his deerskin around the frozen carcass of his deer and placed it in the cave. He then placed the lifeless weight of Hitchinna on his shoulders, and picked up his quiver. He carried Hitchinna in a westerly direction until he was close to Kachhawi in the very steep and rugged gorge. He gathered the wood for half the morning, and carefully built the bed of sticks, twigs, and pine needles on which to lay his mother and the large limbs of wood. He fed the fire until he was certain all the flesh had been burned from Hitchinna, and he sang and waited and cried and tried not to think. The image of his withered mother haunted him, though, and when he was sure that Hitchinna was burned, he left to spend the night in his hunting cave. The night did not give him peace for a long time, but he ate some roasted deer meat and waited and cried and thought about how he would probably have to bury Halai Auna and Dari

Jowa. Finally sleep overtook his grief as he lay bundled in the bearskin and watched the fire.

In the morning the storm did not come, and Yolaina ate some venison from the night before. He bathed in Deer Creek far below the cave, and then walked with his bow and arrow to the pile of white ashes where Hitchinna's bones were covered. He dug a hole near the hot ashes with a stick of dry yellow pine, and he used the stick to shove his mother's bones from the ashes into the hole. When he rolled his mother's skull from the ashes of the pyre, he cried bitterly, for he had never felt so alone. Her skull was an awfully hideous reminder of his tragedy. He covered the hole with dirt and boulders strewn about him. He then went into the woods and gathered pitch from dead and scarred trees, and when finished, he returned to his cave and rekindled his fire. He heated a stick until it was burning on one end, and then he held his long hair from his head and burned it off one section at a time. When his hair caught fire, he splashed water from a metal container on his scalp. He threw his long, black hair into the fire one handful at a time. After all of his hair was gone, he smashed lumps of sticky yellow pitch into his stubble. When completely finished, he just sat, for he was weak and tired. Outside the rain began to dampen the earth, and the first major storm of the season approached. He had venison for a few days, a deerskin, a bearskin, a raccoon skin, two rabbit skins, a large piece of canvas, seven good arrows, a bow, a quiver, an arrow making pouch, a fire drill and fire board, and no reason to live. As the storm continued to gain force, however, Yolaina gathered as much wood as he could from beneath the trees of the canyon. When the lightning came and the rain turned to hail, Yolaina was prepared as well as he could have been. The thoughts, though, the bitter pain, took hold of him. He thought of how Lawalila had lost his strength entirely when Tsanunewa was poisoned in front of his eyes, and Yolaina did not know if he could even be as strong as Lawalila had been. Lightning cracked the sky, and resounding echoes filled the canyon. Ilhataina, Lightning Man, spoke to Yolaina of his anger, yet nothing could be done. When darkness fell on the cave, white snow streaked by in the wind. Yolaina placed the canvas around the large poles of the entrance, and he knew he would live. When the storm broke, he would search for Halai Auna and Dari Jowa in every place in Deer Creek Canyon and Salmon Creek Canyon where they could possibly live through such a storm. Bitter tears rolled down his cheeks, however, and they would not stop. Grief was an awful feeling, and he did not know if he would ever be whole again. He could not imagine how a human could be whole in empty canyons once filled with people.

"Wino-tay," he began singing to himself in a cracked voice as tears ran down his cheeks. "Wino-tay, wino-tay, wino-tay, wino-tay," he sang over and over. He hoped somehow the words would give Dari Jowa strength to live through the storm, but he could not imagine how either his uncle or his sister could be alive. All of his thoughts melted into tears, and he sobbed loudly. He screamed to no avail. Always he tried to be a decent human being, but he could see no purpose. He could only see the snow blow by in the firelight. He was as alone as a human being could be.

CHAPTER 14

A Proper Burial

Yolaina grabbed his quiver and left the bear's den on the north slope of Salmon Creek Canyon above the three knolls, and he walked down through brush, oaks, tall pines, and ferns to where the slope became a bit gentle and eventually rolled into a knoll. From there he continued down through the sloping, green meadow strewn with budding oaks, large boulders, and flowers of every color. Butterflies, echo blues, buckeyes, black and orange chiefs, and yellow and black swallowtails, fluttered all around. The lupines took his breath away, and the purple brodiaea filled his stomach with its delicious roots. The day was hot and long, and the nuthatches and mountain chickadees sang from the flowering buck brush. He had a commanding view of a large area of the canyon as he descended, and no saltu, other beings, were to be seen. Once he came into view of the collapsed men's house, he sang, "Wino-tay, wino-tay," over and over. He sat in the green soft grass at what used to be its entrance and near Igupa Topa's grave. The floor of the house was partially filled with boulders and pine cones and sticks, but the pit was still large, round, and filled with green grass and with white and purple flowers. The breeze blew in Yolaina's face, and he stopped singing, "Wino-tay." He looked down at the swollen, green stream below him, but mostly all he could see were the trees around its banks. Ocholoko, Kashmauna, Dewihaumauna, and Black Rock stood stead-fastly as primary landmarks. The grasshoppers snapped their wings as they flew, and a fly buzzed temporarily by his ear. Yolaina listened to the chirping birds and noticed how each bird seemed to change its song just a bit. A lizard, Kalchauna, Lizard Man, jumped on a rock and stared daringly in one pose, jerked to a new pose, and shoved his body up and down, almost tauntingly saying, "Go ahead, you weak and foolish brave, try to shoot me. What is wrong? Are your arrows only like rain from the sky?" Yolaina touched his short hair and removed the leather thongs from his ears.

"Igupa Topa, I have come to speak with you again," said Yolaina. "I have no trouble taking care of myself, except that I no longer try to make baskets. The ones I made fell apart, and I lost too much time from making arrows and bows. I have two bows started, but no spare. My old one finally broke yesterday. That was my best bow, too. I have broken two boughs of mountain juniper from a tree near my overhang up the canyon, and they are scraped, shaped with proper features, and dry enough now so that I can gather the salmon skins to boil into glue for their sinew backing. I have teased the tendons from the hindquar-ters of a deer, and they are soaking, ready to be chewed. I will smear the glue thickly on the back of my bow tomorrow. When it dries, I will chew the sinew and place it carefully in straight lines over the glue, just as Chunoyahi did. It will require a tremendous amount of time I can-not afford, but I must. My maple bark is ready to wind around the sinew. Then I will wait a day, remove the bark, and let the sinew dry many days before applying more glue, letting it dry again, and polish-ing the surface until it is very smooth. Then I will have to let them dry many weeks while I make new bowstrings. My life seems to be danger-ously close to disaster.

"I still believe Halai Auna and Dari Jowa are dead, but I am not sure. Perhaps a black bear or mountain lion ate them after their tragic deaths. I wish you would try to find their spirits and take them to the Mapchemaina beyond where the stars fall into the water, and beyond the sky.

"This is still the most beautiful spot in the canyons. Black Rock sits just as it did when you were young, but I do not think it is there because Salmon Woman needed a place to spawn. I think you just told an old man's story. I wish I would have asked someone else about that particular story.

"I am lonely much of the time. I cannot stop being lonely and mourning. I have too much time to hunt and not enough time to talk. Sometimes I watch saltu. Three men came last year, including the son of the man I almost shot when the saltu invaded Grizzly Bear's Hiding Place. They searched up and down both canyons, and as I watched them, they did not help my heart. They did, however, interfere with my bow making and hunting.

"I have taken up singing much more than I used to, and at night when I am in one of my overhangs, I sing and sing, often 'Wino-tay'. No maiden ever comes, however.

"I wonder about my magic now that I have become the last human to be alive and that my name is Yolaina, Bravest Man. I am chief, also, I guess. I certainly give all the orders, but I do not get to lie around with a beautiful woman. I wonder, somehow, if you spirits abandoned exis-tence or were killed evil by demons like the one that belches up and down the great valley, for you have left me to die. Do you hide from pro-tecting me because of the evil demons, much as I hide in the brush when one goes by in the distance? You have left me to die.

"I will now tell you a story: *The First Battle in the World and the Making of the Yahi*, and when I go, I wish for you to remember me when

I die. Remember that I am the spirit of your grandson, Yolaina, Bravest Man, and that I wish to live with you beyond the sky, in peace, forever. I will wish for you to find me and not let me search forever lost in our canyons, forever wondering where the other spirits are.

"After Hehku, Horned Serpent Man, had risen from the dead and gone home, Jupka, Butterfly of the Wild Silkworm Man, said to all the Mapchemaina: 'Sweat now and swim. You will go to hunt tomorrow early.'

"The Mapchemaina, First People, went to hunt on the following day, but could not kill deer. They had no good arrow points. The points that they had were made of common stone. When they went back to Jigulmatu, Round Mountain, in the evening without venison, Jupka said, 'There lives an old man in the south who kills a great many deer; his name is Kalchauna, Lizard Man. I must bring him up here to show you how he kills them. I will send someone south for him. Maibyu, Dove Man, you go for that old man; you travel very quickly.'

"'I do not know where his house is; I cannot find him,' said Maibyu. 'You better send someone else.'

"'Lawalila, Large Hawk Man, you go,' said Jupka.

"Lawalila dressed himself nicely; took his bow, quiver, and arrows, and went. He went as quickly as though it was only one long step to Kalchauna's house. Kalchauna, Lizard Man, was sitting inside the door with his legs crossed. He was making obsidian arrow points.

"Lawalila stepped in at once and surprised old Kalchauna. He had an obsidian knife at his side, and made a thrust at Lawalila as if to kill him.

"'Stop. It is I, uncle; you must not kill me.'

"'Why do you call me uncle?' asked Kalchauna, hiding his arrow points quickly.

"'I have come for you, uncle. The chief sent me here. Jupka invites you to come to Jigulmatu. He wants you to come to his house. He wants to see you because we cannot kill deer with stone arrow points. We have no other kind. The chief knows that you kill deer all the time and wants you to come to his place to show people how you kill deer.'

"Kalchauna rubbed his hands, rubbed them clean, rubbed all the obsidian dust from them, and rolled up his obsidian in a skin very carefully. Next he mixed obsidian dust, rubbed it on his face, made paint, covered his face with it, and thrust a piece of sharp obsidian through the septum of his nose. He looked very threatening and strong when he was dressed and armed for the road.

"'I am ready; you go ahead; I will come later,' said he to Lawalila.

"Kalchauna's quiver was a grizzly bearskin; his bows and arrows were made of black oak. He put his obsidian arrowheads under his left arm, and took his bow and arrows in his right hand.

"'Go on; go ahead. I will come later; I will come by myself. Go now and tell the chief to make a great fire of manzanita wood.'

"Lawalila went ahead, and gave Kalchauna's message to Jupka. The chief had the fire made, a great fire of manzanita wood. 'He is coming, he is coming,' said the First People when they saw Kalchauna in the distance. When he was near, they did not try to look at him; they hung their heads.

"'Make way for me, make way! I will strike unless you give me room!' said Kalchauna as he came near the crowd of Mapchemaina.

"'The old man always talks like that,' said Jupka; 'He is very strong. That is why he is so bold; that is why he talks so.'

"'Spread out a skin,' said Kalchauna to Jupka.

"The skin was spread, and Kalchauna emptied his robe full of arrowheads on it. He sat down and then said, 'I will divide these and put them in different places.'

"He gathered each kind of obsidian into a heap by itself, then pushed it, and said while he pushed, 'You go to this place or to that place.'

"White obsidian he pushed and said, 'Go you to Hakamatu, Buzzard's Roost.'

"The white obsidian went away; disappeared from the robe; went to Hakamatu, and there is plenty of white obsidian in that place today.

"Blue obsidian he sent east to the edge of our Yana country. Yellow obsidian he fixed at Iwiljami, a creek of the Northern Yana. To the west he sent obsidian with fine black, blue, and white stripes; he sent it to Hakachimatu, Polecat Spring. Green Obsidian he put in Jigulmatu and said, 'You will find these obsidians always in the places where I put them today, and people who come after you will find them there. There will be obsidian in the these places forever, as long as people want it.'

"Besides obsidian Kalchauna gave each of the Mapchemaina a wedge made of deer horn and a piece of stone; he showed them how to dress the obsidian and how to make arrow points. The first arrow points on earth were those that Kalchauna made.

"The next morning, after he had given the obsidian and had shown the Mapchemaina how to make arrow points, Kalchauna went home. On the second day Jupka called all the Mapchemaina together and said, 'Get your arrow points ready; sweat tonight; swim early in the morning, and go out on a great hunt tomorrow.'

"They did all that Jupka commanded, and went on the following morning toward Jidjilpa, Cedar Creek. They went west along Jidjilpa, went on both sides of it. They went west toward Tahaujwakaina, the canyon beyond Hakamatu. They went to the rock and went beyond it.

"Some distance west of the rock a grizzly bear ran out of a clump of live-oak brush. Among the people hunting was Chichepa, Spotted Hawk Man, and the bear rushed at him. Chichepa had dreamed the night before that this rock in the canyon had jumped up from the ground and frightened him. When he came near the live-oak brush, the bear growled and sprang out.

"Chichepa ran back, ran till he came to Tahaujwakaina, and the bear was close after him. The bear was so angry that he tore up big oak trees as he ran. When Chichepa ran to the rock, he noticed a hole in it and sprang in. The bear stood on his hind legs and could barely look over the top of the rock. He looked and saw nothing, dropped down, ran all around the rock, looked everywhere, and saw no sign of

Chichepa. Then the bear went into the thick clumps of brush from which he had started.

"The people went west a while, then toward the south, and began to find deer. Bohkuina, Silver-Gray Fox Man, killed the first deer, Howichinaipa, Small Bird Man, the second, Kechowala, Blue Jay Man, the third, Jihkulu, Large Owl Man, the fourth, Petaina, Skunk Man, the fifth, and so on until twenty had deer. The party divided then into two. Those who had deer turned home toward Jigulmatu, and went in the order in which they had killed them, Bohkuina first, the following each in his turn.

"The second party hunted toward the east and then toward Jigulmatu. After a while they came to Ketmatu, Poison Place, where Malewula, Wolf Man, killed a deer, and Topuna, Mountain Lion Man, killed one, and Tsanunewa, Wren Man, killed a terribly ugly big deer which seemed as though all its flesh and body were swollen. Hitchinna, Wildcat Man, Kaitsiki, Ground Squirrel Man, Wihlaina, Chipmunk Man, and others killed deer; each person killed one deer. The whole party turned toward Jigulmatu then, and there was great gladness in Jupka's sweathouse. The women prepared acorns and mice to eat.

"Jupka himself never went hunting; he stayed at Jigulmatu always, just lay in the house, told all what they were to do, and showed them how to do what was needed. When they came in from hunting, all put their venison in front of the chief, put down before him all the deer they had killed. Jupka took his obsidian knife then and cut the meat into pieces. He roasted ribs of it, roasted all they brought in. When it was cooked, the Mapchemaina sat down and ate the meat together. Jupka placed before them three very large baskets of mice in three different places, and in front of each basket sat a person to deal the mice out to each person who wished some. When they had eaten, Jupka stood up and talked to all present.

"'I wish you all to come into the sweathouse tonight,' he said. 'I wish to tell you where you are to hunt tomorrow.'

"They went into the sweathouse that evening, sat down, and smoked, and while they were smoking, Jupka rose up and spoke to them. Jupka himself never ate anything of any kind; he smoked tobacco, smoked all the time. Tobacco was the only thing that he ever took into his body. When he spoke, he said, 'I think it is better to hunt in the north tomorrow.'

"'We do not like to go north when we hunt,' said some of the people.

"'Well, let another tell where to go. Tonight I will have Howichinaipa, Small Bird Man, sing and dance for deer.'

"Then Jupka thought a while and said, 'No, I will get Ahalamila, Gray Wolf Man, to dream and to sing and to dance. Ahalamila is a good man. I will tell him to sing and to dance tonight. He will tell where you ought to go; he will say which road to take. I want you all to lie down and sleep tonight, old men and young, and all the women; let all sleep till morning, sleep till I call you to hunt.'

"When the time came that evening, Ahalamila made a fire and took his pipe. He blew smoke around in every direction. He put down his pipe then and took fir needles. He threw them on the fire, and while they were burning, he sang:

'A quartz rock, a white rock, a quartz rock, a white rock.'

He put a beautiful white quartz rock on the ground; at each side of it he thrust into the earth a small twig of fir and one of blue beech; he put these on the east, west, north, and south sides of the quartz.

"Ahalamila kept looking at the twigs, which rose quickly, grew up, and became little trees. He walked around them and sang; sang and pinched off a leaf or bud from one limb or another as he walked. Soon the stone began to move itself, and it swelled and changed shape till at last it turned into a white fawn. Just at daybreak the fawn began to walk around among the trees and sniff as though it smelled something.

"Ahalamila picked up the little fawn; he blew smoke from his mouth. He blew smoke around on all sides and then put the fawn down again. The fawn turned back into quartz.

"It was daylight then, and Ahalamila stopped singing. 'I have finished now,' said he. 'We should hunt on the south side today.'

"'I want you, my people,' called Jupka, 'to rise up, start out and hunt. Howichinaipa will go ahead and make a fire.'

"Howichinaipa went ahead to the south for some distance, and the Mapchemaina followed soon after. They went to the place where Howichinaipa had made the fire. When they came up, there was a good large fire at a place called Wewauna, Round Place, not far from Hakamatu.

"'Come to the fire, wait a while before we start, talk and get ready to hunt,' said Howichinaipa.

"Ten men went on farther south to find deer, while others waited at the fire. Those ten men went south quickly; then five turned east, and five turned west to meet again at Wewauna. They came back about the same time, but not one of them saw deer or game of any kind. Everyone wondered why no game was in any place. Ahalamila and Howichinaipa began to dispute and then to quarrel because the ten men could find no deer.

"Howichinaipa was angry; he was offended because Jupka had named him first, then changed his mind and called Ahalamila to sing for deer. He was angry, too, and jealous because he wanted one of Ahalamila's wives who was his own wife's sister. Howichinaipa's wife was Chuhna, Spider Woman, and Ahalamila's wife was her only sister. Howichinaipa wanted to have the two sisters as wives; he wanted both of them. For these reasons the Mapchemaina could find no deer that day. Howichinaipa had power over the deer, and he had sent them under ground. The ten men had looked in a great many places; they had run south, east, and west, but could find no deer. Then the whole party turned to the southeast; they went to Chupirkoto. Some said, 'What is the use in going farther? We can find no deer today. Ahalamila told us that we should find deer. Where are they? We cannot see them.'

"'I do not know,' said Ahalamila, 'why we find no deer. I sang and danced last night. I dreamed that I saw deer, that I saw them south of Jigulmatu.'

"'You will not see deer or any other game today,' said Howichinaipa. 'You cannot find deer, no matter how much you sing and dance. You are not able to find deer, but you have a nice wife. She is very pretty.'

"'The deer were coming,' said Ahalamila, 'but you stopped them. You drove them away.' He sprang at Howichinaipa to strike him. Howichinaipa dodged and went down through the ground.

"All the people took sides and began to fight; some were for Ahalamila; others were for Howichinaipa's side. Howichinaipa sprang out from under the ground, stood before Ahalamila, and shot at him. Ahalamila dodged and shot too; Howichinaipa dodged very quickly.

"They fought on in this way, fought hard, moved toward Jigulmatu, fighting all the time. At last Ahalamila was struck and fell dead; Topuna was killed too, and Hitchinna. A great many tried to kill Howichinaipa, but he dodged all the time, dodged so well, so quickly that not one of all his enemies could hit him. Jihkulu helped Howichinaipa and never stopped fighting for a moment.

"They fought all the way to Hwitalmauna, Whistling Place, just south of Jigulmatu. The battle there was very hard, and people fell on both sides. The many rocks at Hwitalmauna now are the Mapchemaina killed in that first battle.

"Ahalamila's friends fought hard against Jihkulu and spent many arrows, but could not hit him, for he had a robe of rabbit skins around his body.

"'We must hit that Jihkulu; we must kill him,' said Ahalamila's friends.

"'You need not talk like that,' said Jihkulu. 'You cannot kill me. I am the best fighter in all this world. I have been in every part of it, and no one has ever hit me or ever hurt me.'

"Jihkulu shot at Jewina, Red Hawk Man, but missed. 'You cannot hit me!' cried Jewina. Jihkulu shot off Jewina's coyote skin, and then he killed him. Jewina had dreamed a long time before that if he wore a coyote skin in battle he could not be killed, and that was why he wore it; but when Jihkulu shot off the skin, he killed him easily.

"Then Jupka was lying in the sweathouse on Jigulmatu, and he heard the noise and shouting at Hwitalmauna. 'They are fighting; I must stop the battle!' cried he. So he ran south and rushed into the middle of the fight.

"'I want both sides to stop!' shouted Jupka.

"The battle was at an end right there; all followed Jupka to Jigulmatu. That evening he said, 'You will hunt in the north tomorrow.' All were in the sweathouse then and were listening. Jupka spoke to them some time, and then they all talked at once; it seemed as though the house would burst when they were talking.

"The next day they found deer in the north, and found them in plenty. Each had one to bring back to the sweathouse. When they were coming home through thick brush, Popila, Mallard Duck Man, wished to please Ahalamila's friends, and made himself into a bear to kill Howichinaipa, who fought the day before with Ahalamila and killed him.

"The bear came out and threw his arms around a clump of brush where Howichinaipa was. Howichinaipa slipped out in time and ran. The bear rushed after him, hunted him, and almost caught him at a rock near Hakamatu. Howichinaipa sprang onto the rock and said, "I am nearly dead; I wish this rock to open; I am too tired to run; I can go no farther.'

"The rock opened, and Howichinaipa dropped in. The bear rushed up, stuck his head and forepaws after Howichinaipa, but the rock closed, and the bear was caught and killed.

"Howchinaipa came out and stood besides the bear. 'I am tired,' said he. 'I was almost dead. You tried your best to kill me, but I am hard to kill.' Then he took his obsidian knife, cut around the bear's neck and behind his two forepaws, and skinned him. He put the skin on his shoulder, and started for Jigulmatu. He came behind the others, reached home at dusk. He hung the skin near the door, and said, 'We will hear what Ahalamila's friends will say tomorrow morning.'

Popila's mother heard what her son had done, and when she saw the bearskin, she cried and rolled upon the ground. The next day, the old woman was sweeping; she swept out a little red-eared boy, Pakalai Jawichi, Water Lizard Man, and as she swept, he squealed. Mallard Duck Woman, Popila's mother, took up Pakalai Jawichi and placed him in a deerskin blanket. She boiled water with hot rocks and washed him, and every time she washed him she sprinkled obsidian dust on the little boy to make him strong. He could creep around the next morning, but she said, 'Stay in one place; you must not move. There may be poison in one place; if you touch it, you will die. Stay right where I put you.'

"The second day the boy could talk. 'You cry all the time, grandmother; why do you cry?' asked Pakalai Jawichi.

"'Do not ask that question, grandson; it makes me grieve to hear you. All my people were dead except my son; now he is killed. I have no one.'

"The fifth day the boy was walking around the house outside.

"'Grandmother,' said he, 'make a great fire.'

"She made a fire in the sweathouse. The boy stood near the central pillar and sang, 'Hala wata, hala wata.'

"He fell asleep while sweating; slept till morning. The next day when he woke, he said to his grandmother, 'What am I to do with my hands?'

"The old woman gave him an obsidian knife and said, 'I have had this a long time; take it now and fix your hands with it.'

"His fingers were joined together as far as the first joint, and she showed him how to separate them from each other. He cut the little finger first, then the third, the second, and the first. The thumb he called big finger; and when the five fingers were separated and free from each other, she told him to call the thumb big finger, and call it one, the next two, the next three, the next four, and the little finger five.

"This was the first time that counting was ever done in the world. When Jupka made the Yana, he gave them hands like Pakalai Jawichi's.

"When his left hand was finished, Pakalai Jawichi said, "I do not know how to cut with my left hand."

"The old woman helped him to free the fingers of the right. When all his fingers were free, the boy was able to shoot, and wanted a bow and arrows.

"The old woman brought all the bows of dead kindred; he broke all but one, which had a string made from the shoulder sinews of deer. He took that and went out. That day Howichinaipa hid himself in a cedar tree. He was watching a bird. Pakalai Jawichi knew that he was there, and called with the voice of the bird that Howichinaipa was watching. Howichinaipa came down on the tree lower and lower, looking to see where the call came from.

"Pakalai Jawichi was hidden in a tree opposite where Howichinaipa could not see him; Pakalai Jawichi kept calling. Howichinaipa kept coming down. Pakalai Jawichi had a good sight of him.

"'If I hit him in the body,' thought he, 'the arrow will not hurt him. I must hit him in the outside toe.'

"He did that, and Howichinaipa fell to the ground wounded. Pakalai Jawichi pinned him to the earth with one arrow, then with another; he pinned his sides to the ground with two rows of arrows. Pakalai Jawichi ran home.

"'Oh grandmother!' cried he.

"'What is the matter?' asked the old woman. 'You came near falling into the fire.'

"'There is someone out here. I want you to see him.'

"The old woman took her cane and followed Pakalai Jawichi.

"'Do you see that person lying there?'

"The old woman looked and saw the person who had killed her son. She saw him pinned to the earth. She was so glad that she cried, dropped to the ground, jumped up, and danced and danced and danced around his body until she was exhausted.

"'Hereafter,' said Pakalai Jawichi, 'everybody will call you Howichinaipa. You will be a person no longer; you will only be a little bird with arrow marks on both sides of your breast.'

"He became a little bird then and flew away, the little bird which we call Howichinaipa.

"The next morning after the second hunt, Jupka heard loud shouting in the east; a great Mapchemaina had thrust his head above the edge of the sky. This great person in the east had two dogs; they were small, but very strong. 'Which of you is coming with me?' asked he that morning. 'I want a good dog; I am always afraid when I travel in the daytime.'

"'I will give you a name now,' said Jupka to this person in the east. 'All people will call you hereafter by the name that I give now. The name that I give you is Tuina. You will be known always by this name, and your dog will be called Machperkami.'

"When Tuina was ready to start, he made his small dog still smaller, very small, and put him under the hair on the top of his head, and tied him in there.

"When all dressed and ready, with the dog fastened in his hair, Tuina became as full of light as he is in our time. Before he was dressed and armed and had his dog on his head, Tuina had no brightness, but when he started, he filled the whole world with light, as he does now in the daytime.

"Bohkuina, Silver-Gray Fox Man, had made a road for Tuina to travel on; he had made this road in the sky. Tuina went straight along to the west by it, till he reached the great water. When he was ready to plunge into the water, a grizzly bear of the water was coming out and saw him. Tuina put his hands out and motioned with his arms as if they were wings, motioned as if to jump in.

"'Tuina is coming!' said the grizzly bear of the water. 'It will be too hot here if he comes. Let us make ready and go to high mountains. We cannot stay here if Tuina comes.'

"A great crowd of water grizzlies came out of the ocean and went away to the mountains. Tuina jumped into the water, and it rose on all sides, boiled up, and rolled away over the shore. Every kind of ocean shell went to the land at the same time.

"Tuina went far into the water, way down to the bottom; he went through the bottom, deep under the water and the ground, and returned to the east.

"Long before that Jupka had made a road under the earth for Tuina to travel on, a road back to the east. Jupka turned the earth bottom upward, and made this road right through from west to east. Before Tuina started, Jupka said to him, "I have made a road, a straight road under the earth for you, a good road; no rocks are on the smooth road. Bohkuina made the road on the sky, the road from east to west for you to run on; I made the road down below, the road under the earth from west to east. When you reach the east, you will rest awhile, rise in the morning, come up and go west again on the road which Bohkuina made; you will do this every day without failing. You will do this all the time.'

"When Jupka stopped talking, Tuina went west, went back in the night on Jupka's road, and so he does always.

"The day after Jupka had talked with Tuina, given him his name and his work, he said, 'I will make Yana now, and I will give them a good country to live in.'

"He took buckeye sticks, broke off a large number, and laid them down on the top of Jigulmatu to make Yana. He put down the first stick and said, 'I will call this one Yahi, Yana of the southern place.

"When he had said these words, a man rose before him, a Yahi.

"'You will stay here in the southern country,' said Jupka. 'You will be chief.'

"Jupka put down another buckeye stick, and it became a Yana woman at Jupka's words. He put down a third stick, which became a boy.

"'This is an orphan without father or mother,' said Jupka, and he called the boy Hurskiyupa.

"Jupka put other buckeye sticks, a large number of them, around the first Yana, the chief, and made common people. They all stood around the chief, and Jupka said to them, 'This is your chief; he will tell you what to do; you must obey him and do what he commands.'

"'Now,' said Jupka, 'what will the people of the southern country eat? What will I give them?' He thought a while. 'You will eat clover and roots. I will give you sticks to dig these roots. You will eat fish, too, and venison. Eat and be strong; be good Yana people. When the chief wants a deer, he will call you together and say, *I wish to eat venison; I want you to go out, and I want you to hunt deer and bring home venison to eat.* You must obey the chief always.'"

Yolaina paused a long while and then slapped a mosquito. "Tomorrow I will spear a salmon at Black Rock. I go now. You go now, also, back to the land beyond the sky. Do not wait long, though, to search for me when I die, for I will not have a proper burial."

CHAPTER 15

Surrender

The afternoon was very hot, and Yolaina sat on the smooth stones below the dripping cliff not far from the bear's den where all of his belongings were because his cache on Deer Creek had been stolen. The canvas and barley sacks had been wrapped around tanned deerskins, a pair of moccasins, bundles of pitch and pine needles, a bar of white woman's soap, charcoal, nails and screws tied in a rag, and a sharp piece of metal with an eyehole in the end, but the bundle had not been in the live oak tree the last time he had hunted there. He let the water drip on his head and over his face, and he listened to the birds and felt somewhat successful in almost having two new bows completed. He had a new string ready, and he thought about how beautifully the new bows arched and how well the ends and nocks were covered with glued, dried, and smoothed sinew. He still had one more string to make, but he needed to kill another buck. The fresh, outer, small strips of sinew would be separated from the slender group of tendons in the deer's shank. The sinew would have to be chewed, separated into small strands, and spun into a string. He missed not having help with preparing the string, and then when he thought of Halai Auna, he became depressed and lonely. Yolaina sat up straight and rolled his head around. He let water drip into his mouth, and he drank deeply. He thought about whether he should kill another deer immediately or smoke the hide on which he had recently rubbed the deer's brains, and he decided to finish tanning the hide. He needed more hides, well tanned, and stashed a little better than his last effort. Saltu were everywhere in the canyons, however, and he could not tell when they would appear. He had to make another pair of moccasins and to waterproof them also, but he felt like doing nothing but sitting in the dripping water. He was trying desperately to decide from all of his major chores he had to do before winter which one was the most important, and tanning the hide seemed like a good choice because he could then stay home and sit in the dripping water from time to time. Yolaina glanced down through the brush at a small deer trail. A rattlesnake lay straight in the sun and sometimes tested the air with its black, forked tongue wiggling erratically. Yolaina always avoided rattlesnakes, for they had a lot of power. He tried not to think of how awful Lawalila had looked as his fist and arm swelled and as his blood stiffened.

Below in the leaves came distant, crashing footsteps, and he stood to see clearly over the brush. He saw nothing and wondered if it were a deer or perhaps a bear. He thought about scurrying to his bow, but had the advantages of silence and wind and camouflage. He sat back down and waited with only a slight view of his surroundings. When the voices of saltu came to him, Yolaina was sickened, for perhaps they had seen his smoke or were trying to search the large rock overhang of Deskema, as the saltu did out of curiosity from time to time. He could only wait, for any movement would mean certain problems. The leaves crashed toward him and then went to the west away from Yolaina and up the old bear's trail toward his only belongings. Yolaina waited, though, for the trail became brushy, and the men could easily turn back before actually reaching the overhang of the den. The footsteps and talking continued, however, and became faint. Yolaina waited nervously, and in a while the crashing came back to the trail. Yolaina saw two pairs of boots and listened to the strange, laughing voices. One man fell as they continued down the steep slope covered with talus and leaves; the man held Yolaina's only seasoned, completed bow, his quiver of arrows, and a bundle of his skins. The other man probably had Yolaina's other belongings. When the men were totally gone, Yolaina hurried through the brush and back to the small cave.

Before him behind the boulders and under the overhang, Yolaina saw only his fire pit, his shirt, and his canvas pullover: no bows, no tools, no seed sacks, no arrows, no quiver, no skins, no arrow-making pouch, no bottle, no net, no snare, no salmon toggles, no fire drill or hearth, no sinew, no hand spear, no shaping obsidian, no jerky. His mouth just hung open for the longest moment, for he knew that with salmon not running for a long time, he would probably soon starve to death. The only food readily available to him was manzanita berries and blackberries and a two day supply of fresh meat. He was in a very similar position to that of Dari Jowa and Halai Auna when they had disappeared, except they had been without clothing and food. Yolaina's only real advantage was the summer's weather. For that he would starve slowly instead of starve and freeze to death rapidly. He sat limply, pathetically, and leaned against a rock; he was a naked man with no friends or family or other humans with whom to talk; he was without any real means of survival; he knew he could not survive the length of time needed to make a bow and arrows. He needed a bow and arrow to make a bow and arrow. He had no way of killing a deer other than jumping out of a tree with a sharp stick, and the thought was absurd. Even a cow would run away. He could only remove the sinew from the meat he had, and try to live somehow. *How impossible*, he thought.

*   *   *

"I am hungry," said Yolaina as he sat at the edge of the old, men's sweathouse and talked for the last time to Igupa Topa. The hill's grass had been chewed to the ground and was brown, but the view was a valley of varied greens and a cloud-strewn sky of late summer. "I have only two shirts that I stole from the men who chase sheep, and I can no longer live here. I am dying, slowly, for I cannot hunt. I have decided to go far to the south, as far as I can. I will try to find a place to surrender, perhaps, to the saltu whom I do not know and from whom I have not taken. I do not wish to surrender to the men who follow cows. They have generally tried to kill me. I hope to find a place where not many demons smoke. I admit to you that I am frightened, and I see how much courage Bokuina, Hwipajusi, and the others had when they surrendered their bows to the saltu. I might change my mind, say if I find a lost band of beautiful Yahi women with filled baskets hidden away on the Feather River, but I do not see that happening for some reason.

"I ask again that you do not abandon me if I do not receive a proper burial, and I probably will not. Do not leave me lost forever wondering why no people and no spirits are anywhere to be seen. I cannot tell if Dari Jowa and Halai Auna are in the spirit world or are lost here, but do not let them wander anymore if they are. I built a fire for them and sang, and so you should feel that gathering them from these canyons is appropriate. I hope so, anyhow. I fear the powerful land in which you live will leave us alone. I no longer wish to be alone.

"The winter nights chilled my heart more than my toes and ears, and the pain has always remained. Sometimes I cried, and at other times, I sang. I told myself stories, and I called to the birds.

"When I had so little food, as I do now, though, I had my bow and arrows always ready to be used. My quiver gave me strength and hope, and sometimes in those hopeful moments, I was not lonely. Then, of course, a small event would make me think of someone. Even on a spring's morning, I would see a wood dove sitting on a river boulder and remember Tsunanewa. Even when I would see the yellow-green leaves sprouting from the blossom-filled branches of redbud, I would remember joyful women preparing baskets. I cannot escape my lone-liness. I almost had two new bows. I almost was able to live out my natural life until I died and was eaten. Now I will probably be hanged, shot, or poisoned." Yolaina paused a great while and looked at the canyon's steep southern slope he would soon climb.

"I was not able to spend a night in this sweathouse when it was full of men at harvest time, and when hundreds of people gathered acorns and pine nuts, and dried salmon and venison.

"I have wondered lately exactly how camping in the open on Salmon Creek would have felt like. I imagine many young women, smiling and glancing at me and pounding the shells from acorns. I imagine waiting with many hunters behind the ancient rock blinds in the forest for the deer to be driven on their well-worn trail down the brushy slope. I imagine bearskins and deerskins being smoked in many spots on the flat below. I imagine when you were a young chief. I can see you cross-ing Salmon Creek with a bag of abalone and dentalium shells, a smile on your face, and love in your heart. All the common people respected you with awe, for always you were good. I see you clearly in this house on a snowy winter's night. The flakes blow horizontally in a howling north wind, but a grizzly bearskin covers the door. A small fire keeps all the men warm and all the bows very dry. I see you tell the men a funny story about Ututni, Wood Duck Man, as he receives Salmon Woman. He gives her a gift of dried venison, tries to throw her out because she smells so badly, but cannot because she is slick with passion and deter-mined to make him her husband.

"Sometimes I lose myself in too much imagining, maybe. At those times, though, I am not lonely for a while. I am happy.

"I, Yolaina, Bravest Man, go now to the south over as many river canyons as I can until I must travel to the west toward Daha to surren-der to the saltu. Remember me old man. I do not wish to cry alone on cold winter nights forever.

"I loved you so dearly in life.
"I go."

          *   *   *

Yolaina stood among the smooth, black rocks and tall grass clumps of the Feather River. He decided to swim across even though he could clearly see a strange road made of large blocks of wood and two long lines of some material, probably that of lightning sticks. He removed his two shirts, held them in his left hand, waded into the river, and side stroked his way to the sand bar under the large boulders that seemed to support the road. In the boulders was an opening where he could hide, perhaps a small cave, and where he could live while searching for food. Not far above the road was a cabin that had not been visible to him until he crawled out of the water and looked back to the east. He was deciding what to eat, grasshoppers, gophers, or crayfish, when from the west a loud, smoking demon came toward him. Yolaina ran quickly to the opening in the rocks, climbed in, and sat in the sand. His only hope of living, he was sure, lay in hiding, for the demon was obviously very powerful. He put on his two shirts and waited, ready to run, in case the demon stopped over him. When the demon finally did run over him, the whole earth shook, but fortunately, it had not seen him when he ran for cover. The close encounter meant he could not stay at the cave on the river, however, so when the ground quit trembling, Yolaina carefully looked out and then scampered up the boulders, over the strange road with long metal lines, and up the hill toward the cabin. The cabin filled him with hope of being able to eat, for it could have been laden with seed sacks and salted meat.

Once at the cabin, however, Yolaina could find no way in. A strange metal object blocked its entrance, and its windows would not budge. He circled it many times, but he could not determine how the saltu entered the structure. The saltu were often tricky in very strange ways.

At last Yolaina quit trying and walked further up the hill, where to his luck, he found gopher mounds. He got a sharp stick from a nearby manzanita bush and jumped up and down on the mound until he was certain he had killed any gopher still in the lines of raised dirt, but when he dug out the mound with his stick, he did not find a gopher. He stumbled wearily to the shade of a nearby foothill pine and sat down. He was wearier than he had ever been.

The previous six days of travel had worn him to near starvation, and his upper body had withered from his previous strength. From upper Salmon Creek he had traveled across Deer Creek and Butte Creek, down the western branch of Concow Creek until it met the Feather River, and from there downstream until he could hardly move from exhaustion. He knew a town was not far below him on the Feather River, but he felt certain that the saltu would murder him on sight. He cursed his bad luck at not even being able to steal from the cabin or even being able to kill a defenseless gopher. He knew he could not live long sitting in the shade of the foothill pine, however.

He stood and walked almost aimlessly to the west over the rolling hills covered with oaks, foothill pines, and brush, and after a short walk, he came upon another road, several circular fences, and other saltu buildings. He walked along a fence, climbed over it, and looked inside a large building. To his great surprise, he saw large halves of cows, fully dressed and hanging from the wood of the building. The wealth of the saltu always amazed Yolaina. Yolaina walked into the building and touched the beef. He gazed about and noticed men through the windows of the building far on the other side of the circular fences. He walked from the building and into a tall, narrow structure of thick wood where cows obviously walked from the enclosed fence and into the building. He sat down and pondered what to do next, for he did not know whether he should steal some meat or wait to be caught. If he took their meat, they would track and shoot him. If he waited until they found him, perhaps the wealthy saltu would feed him. He was so tired and hungry, however, he did not seem to care if he were caught. He could not continue walking. He slumped over, closed his eyes, and faded away into a deep and restless sleep. He could not muster enough strength to care about his fate.

Sharp images from his past filled his mind. Baskets of roasted worms, women's hair belts, and smashed lice in teeth were in perfect company in his mind, as if all thoughts were like village bastards on display by the central pillars of sweathouses. Women's tassels of strung goose bones were draped over the turkeys of ancient chiefs, and the shredded bark of the broadleaf maple hung from skirts of women baking brodiaea bulbs. The gambling sticks of the straw game floated away, and men argued as to who won. A rock doctor placed a flat stone on a woman's pregnant belly, and a great chief took off the net cap of his feathered war bonnet. Damna roots and wild raspberries filled the stomach of his mind, as if they were a poultice for tooth aches and babies' skins. A water grizzly pulled a fisherman into the water of Daha, and a burned man was covered with a poultice of bracken. Broken beads covered many graves, but young women wore strips of otter skin in their hair. Salmon flies washed ashore, and children stuck deer tails in manzanita berry water and sucked the juice from the hair. Girls gathered the fungus of dead fir trees to make red paint for their dances and proposals of marriage. A man without a home dressed as a transvestite and stole venison from a village mound as women watched and wove the black strands of maidenhair ferns into their baskets. The dogs of the sun and moon ate their masters and caused a blackness in the canyons. Gambling bones, manzanita flour, roots of yellow pine, and brushes of porcupine tails lay gently without reason in his mind, and the distant sounds of saltu came to him. He could not move, though, for the inanity of a delirium possessed him.

Yolaina gasped when he realized a large saltu with a club poised for striking rolled him over. Yolaina raised his hand to protect his face, but the man did not strike him. A boy of about eight watched on, and

Yolaina said, "No, no, no, no, no, no, no." The man did not seem to understand, but he lowered the club anyhow. Yolaina sat up and looked down and away from the man who spoke the strange words of the saltu. The man tapped Yolaina on his shoulder, and Yolaina looked up at him but then away again. A hollow, disdainful feeling overtook Yolaina, and he did not feel anything but disgust for the young saltu. The saltu then grabbed Yolaina's face around his chin, squatted down, and moved his head back and forth. He seemed to be amazed. He stood up and yelled toward the other large structure on the other side of the fences. Soon another man came and a discussion followed. All the while they and the boy looked on. Then another man arrived, and he sat by Yolaina as the first man left. Soon the first man returned, lit a white man's light, and sat next to Yolaina in the wooden structure, and the third man left to talk to the others. The large man sitting across from Yolaina then rolled some saltu tobacco in a thin, white, bark-like substance often used by saltu around their fires at night, for the saltu loved to smoke. Yolaina watched him carefully, for the man avoided staring at Yolaina. When he saw that Yolaina also wished to try the saltu's smoke, he gave Yolaina the bag and the white, thin, bark-like substance. Yolaina tried to emulate the man, but he failed three times and then put the tobacco in his pocket to try another time. The man reached in Yolaina's pocket, removed the pouch, and rolled a perfectly round, long smoke. Yolaina gestured for the man to make again the magical fire from the red-tipped stick, and the man gave him the tobacco, struck the stick on a stone, and lit Yolaina's smoke. The strong smell of sulfur entered Yolaina's nostrils, but the magic of the instant fire amazed Yolaina. The man seemed to have a kindly look in his eyes as they smoked together, and maybe he understood the value of sharing smoke. Yolaina puffed, smiled at the man, and then cupped the smoke in his hands as if he were holding burning tinder to start a fire.

Not long after Yolaina finished the tobacco, two other men showed up. They wore the same type of blue clothes, but one man was extremely fat. They had metal objects on their chests and had lightning sticks on their sides. A great discussion ensued, and after a while, the slimmer of the two handed the man who shared his tobacco with Yolaina some metal object. The man looked awkward, but then motioned for Yolaina to stick out his hands. He placed the curious objects on Yolaina's wrists.

Yolaina stared at them and noticed to his delight that they had snapped shut. Yolaina smiled and offered to let the man try them also, but he declined. He helped Yolaina to his feet, held him by his arm, and walked him from the wooden structure by the fences, and toward the other building where two wagons were hitched to horses. One long, wooden wagon was laden with meat, and the other was short, black, and empty. The man led Yolaina to the black wagon and motioned for him to get in. Yolaina climbed aboard and squatted down. The two men with lightning sticks climbed aboard and sat on both sides of Yolaina. They snapped leather thongs on the horses' hindquarters, and the horses pulled the wagon in a half circle and onto the road. All the men and the boy who first found him followed in the wagon filled with meat.

So far, Yolaina thought to himself in his fear, *the saltu have been very good to me. I thought they would have killed me by now.*

Bibliography

Curtin, Jeremiah. *Creation Myths of Primitive America*. Benjamin Blom, Incorporated. 1969.

Heizer, Robert and Kroeber Theordora, eds. *Ishi the Last Yahi*. University of California Press. 1979.

Kroeber, A. L., ed. *American Archaeology and Ethnology, Volume XIII*. University of California Press. Kraus Reprint Corporation. 1965.

Kroeber, Theordora. *Ishi in Two Worlds*. University of California Press. 1961, 1976.

Sapir, Edward and Morris Swadesh. *Yana Dictionary*. University of California Press. 1960.

Smith, Richard. "An Interview with Ad Kessler." *Digging in Press*. 1984. pp. 4-21.

Printed in the United States
97763LV00003B/225/A

9 780595 127665